WAKE

OF THE

WAHOO

The Heroic Story
of America's Most
Daring WWII
Submarine,
USS Wahoo

Forest J.
Sterling

R.A. Cline Publishing
Riverside, Ca.

Published by: R.A. CLINE PUBLISHING
19971 Caraway Ln.
Riverside, Ca. 92508

Fifth Edition – December 2011

PRINTING HISTORY: Chilton Company published 1960
First printing: February 1960
Second printing: May 1960
Popular Library Edition published 1961
Third printing: March 1961
Fourth printing: October 1999

This book contains the complete text of the original edition.
Not one word has been omitted!

Copyright 1999 by **Forest J. Sterling**
All rights reserved

Includes epilogue, photographs, crew roster and glossary.

ISBN: 978-0-9663235-5-9 : $19.95

Library of Congress Catalog Card Number : 99-75046

World War II 1942-43 / Naval operations in the Pacific 1942-43
submarine *USS Wahoo* (SS-238)

Cover design: Jeff Porteous
Cover production: Triple A Graphics
Front and back cover photos: *National Archives*

Printed in the United States of America

Contents

Dedication   I

Foreword   *Vice Admiral Charles A. Lockwood*   II

Preface   *Forest J. Sterling*   IV

Chapter 1   1

Chapter 2   9

Chapter 3   14

Chapter 4   19

Chapter 5   51

Chapter 6   67

Chapter 7   85

Chapter 8   94

Chapter 9   116

Chapter 10   124

Contents

Chapter 11   155

Chapter 12   165

Chapter 13   178

Chapter 14   188

Chapter 15   204

Epilogue   Forest J. Sterling   211

Wahoo crew roster for final patrol   215

Wahoo crew roster prior to 7th patrol   216

Wahoo sinkings   217

Presidential Unit Citation   218

Glossary   219

About the author – Forest J. Sterling   221

USS Wahoo wreck site found   222

Dedication

In the Harbor of Supreme Sacrifice are 52 American submarines lost in World War II. Among them, flying a string of 21 or more Japanese miniature flags, is the *Wahoo*. Her crew is ashore in the best hotel available, and you can bet that they're having one hellu'va good time. This is the ship and the crew to whom I dedicate this book.

"Go tell the Spartans, thou that passeth by,
That here, obedient to their laws, we lie."

Foreword

Wake of the Wahoo tells the story of men who go down to the sea "in ships that have their load-lines over their hatches." From the uninhibited point of view of an enlisted man Chief Yeoman Forest J. Sterling, USNFR, who made five war patrols in the *Wahoo*, with keen observation and vivid coloring has written the story of a fabulous ship, of her skipper – who, like Gunga Din, "didn't seem to know the use of o'fear" – and of life in a World War II submarine.

Close are the relationships between submarine officers and their men – and staunch are the mutual loyalties which bind them into one splendid, fighting unit. They are all part of a team in which every player is on the line – none sitting on the benches. Even so, we who gave the commands – called the signals – never knew their full impact upon those who executed them. Nor did we know of all the thinking and planning and experimentation that went on in the clever minds of our crew members, which resulted in suggestions for better ways of doing things, better tactics, better ways of winning the war. The Wahoo was a shinning example of such teamwork – of the strength for which unity is famed. On this point, Sterling's book will be most gratifying to all wartime submariners and most illuminating to our civilian friends.

Submariners attract youngsters in whom the spirit of adventure is strong. Luckily, to such men, creature comforts, which in submarines admittedly are meager, are of little importance. These men glory in spartan living at sea. They are given responsibility early in life and develop resourcefulness, initiative, and leadership in their daily life and associations.

When a natural leader and born daredevil such as Mush Morton is given command of a submarine, the result can only be a fighting ship of the highest order, with officers and men who would follow their skipper to the Gates of Hell ..... And they did.

Morton lined up an impressive number of "firsts" during the short ten months that he commanded the *Wahoo*: first to penetrate an enemy harbor and sink a ship therein; first to use successfully a down-the-throat shot; first to wipe out an entire convoy single-handed.

There have been stories in the press and elsewhere about a submarine which penetrated Tokyo Harbor, but they are fiction. Wewak by the *Wahoo*, Wenchow by the *Barb*, Christmas Island by the *Seawolf*, and a few others are true. But no one entered Tokyo Harbor.

Morton also had another important technique in which I believe he was first: the use of his Exec to handle the periscope while he, the Captain, watched the TDC (Torpedo Data Computer) and the plot. Captain Slade Cutter of the *Seahorse* was another exponent of this technique. As he explained it to me, "In a surface night attack, if I stay up on the bridge, the target gets to look awful big and I get scared and fire – at too long a range. So, I stay down in the Conning Tower, watch the radar and the plot and fire at the proper time. I let the Exec stay on the bridge and get scared!"

Morton's reasons were probably the same except that I doubt that either of these fire-eating daredevils was ever scared ... That I cannot imagine.

Incidentally, each of them piled up a score of 19 personal kills. The only man who surpassed them in the entire Submarine Force was Captain Dick O'Kane, with his 24 kills in the *Tang* before she was sunk by one of her own torpedoes with the loss of all but nine of her crew.

Forest Sterling was aboard when *Wahoo* sank 20 of the 21 ships credited to her before her seventh and final patrol – all but the last four in the Sea of Japan. Dick O'Kane was at the periscope while Morton ran the attack. Watching two such top-notch submariners in action – one of whom was to become a legend, the other to win a Medal of Honor – was a wonderful experience for which many men would practically have sold their birthrights.

Fate decreed that Sterling was to be detached as the *Wahoo* left Midway on her last fatal patrol that he might live to paint for us a splendid word picture of this fabulous *Wahoo* and her equally fabulous Captain and crew.

For this we are thankful.

Just where in Davy Jones' Locker, the Port of Missing Ships, lie the bones of the *Wahoo* and her gallant crew, we will probably never know. Postwar examination of enemy records reveals a report that, on 11 October, 1943, in La Perouse Strait, "Our plane found a floating sub and attacked it with three depth charges."

That may be the epitaph of the *Wahoo* and 80 American fighting men.

May God rest their souls.

Charles A. Lockwood
Vice Admiral, USN, Ret.

Preface

This is the story of the *USS Wahoo*, October 1942 – September 1943, as I remember it. The patrols and the actions she went through are a matter of record, but what the crew were doing during these often exciting moments can only be told by someone who was there. The conversations in many instances are imaginary but what was actually spoken was in effect the same.

It has long been a "spur" to this writer to recreate those forgotten scenes. Two years ago while watching *The Silent Service*, a TV program, Rear Admiral Dykers, USN (Ret.), introduced Vice Admiral Lockwood, USN (Ret.), as the "enlisted man's friend." I wrote Admiral Lockwood and described my idea for this book. His answer was an encouraging "Go ahead." A year later, I wrote the Admiral again saying the manuscript was finished. Without his subsequent help and encouragement, it is doubtful whether the book would have become printed at all. Therefore, I accord him every recognition and thanks that I can give in this endeavor.

Encouragement is something that I have been fortunate in receiving: My wife, Marie; mother, Pearl Wynn; Lottie (Rennels) Cervine; Evelyn Smith, M.A.; Alford O. Wilkinson, Ph.D.; William H. McEnroe, M.A., Ventura College; Claude F. Shouse, Ph.D., San Diego State College and many, many friends.

Now in 1997 I have decided to re-print this book because of further information and discoveries about the *USS Wahoo* which is outlined in the books new epilogue (see page 211). I wish to thank my many friends for encouraging me to pursue this third printing of my book and especially thank Donald Riley and Hollis Hayes my fellow residents and friends at the Naval Home.

Forest J. Sterling

Chapter 1

I sat on my sea bag in the shade of a palm tree and gazed moodily at the *U.S.S. Wahoo* moored securely to the north side of one of the U. S. Naval Submarine Base, Pearl Harbor, piers.

It was so peaceful on this October day of 1942 that I had difficulty believing that nearly the whole world was at war. A war that was a hazy nebulous something which kept daily newspapers headlined with urgent news of its consuming progress. Headlines that stirred emotions much the same as a good radio announcer can sway his audience with the rise and fall of events in a close baseball game without the reality of actual participation.

I pulled my eyes away from *Wahoo* long enough to make a visual search for the evidences of war and found them. A broad black band of mourning encircled the littoral shores of Pearl Harbor, bearing mute testimony to crude-oil vomitings from ruptured bowels of mortally wounded ships on the morning of December 7, the year before. Men in uniform and civilian Navy Yard workers were moving hurriedly in all directions. Familiar ship repair noises were all around me, made even more conspicuous because of the wartime urgency that bred them. Above Hickam Field I glimpsed several blimps straining in unsuccessful effort to snap free from their steel cable anchorages. And of course, there was *Wahoo* waiting patiently for me to come on board.

Twisting around, I could see a gray three-story building with screened porches, which was the submarine base main barracks. Towering over the building were coconut palms, whose fronds were suddenly stirred by the invisible mischievous fingers of a more vigorous zephyr shaking loose musical rustlings to please the ear. By twisting a bit further, I could see a portion of the Koolaupoko mountain range.

I tried to visualize the trade winds coming out of the northeast and striking against this volcanic barrier from the windward side of the island. The winds were carrying minute hitchhiking particles of moisture, which collected rapidly into cumulus clouds above the Pali. In an hour these clouds would unshackle themselves from the volcanic ridges and drift across Oahu Island, raining heavily on the verdant igneous slopes below, flooding the sugar-cane and pineapple fields. Countless rainbows would fill Nuuanu Valley in the process.

A steady warm breeze with a saline tang came from the direction of the jagged high mountain range, bringing with it the subtle scent, the sweet fragrance and delicate lure of tropical flowers accumulated along the way, seducing my olfactory sensory perceptions into a deceptive feeling of peacefulness. Where it caressed the bare skin of my face and arms, it tended to lull me into drowsiness.

There is a brief and relaxing sense of freedom that comes between assignments of duty. To prolong the sensation, I lit a cigarette as an excuse for delaying my reporting on board. Again I forced my attention back to *Wahoo* and studied her lines. She looked little different from the other submarines scattered along the piers but somehow, to me, she seemed to have a definite personality. At the moment she was not a pretty ship. She had great salt-encrusted sores along her hull and about her superstructure. She carried no life lines and her decks were barren of benches—for *Wahoo* had been stripped for action and there was no fat showing. *Wahoo* had just returned from her first war patrol. Her only identification was the large white numerals, "238," which stood out against a black background on her superstructure. Somehow she reminded me of a Viking ship, and I thrilled to the similarity.

I finished the cigarette, arched the butt gaily over a sign that read "No Smoking Permitted on the Piers," adjusted my white hat, thumbed the belt line of my dungarees, raised the soiled sea bag to my shoulders, and sauntered down the pier. Teetering across a wobbly gangway, I dropped my sea bag on *Wahoo's* deck, saluted the Stars and Stripes on *Wahoo's* fantail, and turned to the Gangway Watch. He returned my salute with military briskness.

I handed him a copy of my orders and waited while he retrieved a grease-smudged, green-backed notebook from a hidden niche somewhere about the deck gun. He began laboriously to copy my name, rate, service number, authority for transfer, and the time of reporting on one of the pages. While he was absorbed in this chore I looked him over. He was physically well-built and had a clean-cut serious intelligent demeanor. About his slim waist he wore a web military belt over clean, pressed dungaree trousers, to which was attached a well-used and time-polished holster. From the holster protruded the handle of a forty-five-caliber automatic. His clean white hat was squared and his shoes were polished to a mirror finish. In my seven years in the Naval service, I had become accustomed to the easy American slouch that most submariners affected, which could be snapped into military erectness on command, but here was a man who was the perpetual cadet. Above his shirt pocket I noticed the neatly stenciled letters of his name and rate, "Carr, W. J., GM1." He snapped the book shut and without looking pointed to the dog hatch. "Mr. Henderson is the duty officer. You will find him in the wardroom."

"Okay, thanks." I smiled at him and dragged my sea bag to the opening. Looking down I could see into the lighted depths of the control room. A smell of diesel oil came up to greet me with nostalgic delight. "Look out below," I shouted and handed my sea bag over to the control of gravity. It landed with a loud *whump* on the deck below, and I followed it down, aided by the more conventional metal ladder that was attached to the sides of the cylindrical shaft. At the bottom I turned and looked around.

The Below Decks Watch was seated on a high stool with both elbows on the chart table in the center of the control room. His chin was cuddled in the palms of his hands. His eyes had but recently lifted from a comic book, which lay open in front of him on the table, and he was staring at me. There was no expression on his poker face above which all the hair had been clipped. His shirt said his name was "Witting, R. L., F2" but he said nothing.

I stuffed my sea bag behind the emergency helm and looked about. My eyes wandered over the air manifold, the electrical switchboards, bow and stern planes, hull opening indicators (Christmas tree), and finally back to the Below Decks Watch. Witting had become reabsorbed in the perils of Bugs Bunny, and I decided to disturb him no further.

Relief crew sailors and civilian yard workmen were moving along the passageway with one or the other stopping now and then to look around speculatively and to jot scratchy notations in little black notebooks. Occasionally, a yard workman would come in hurriedly, glance at a paper in his hands, and then stretch his neck to look around or under or over some piece of machinery, valve, or pipe, or perhaps disappear down the pump-room ladder in search of a deficiency that had been reported. Aft, someplace, an automatic air-chipping hammer began a staccato which was shortly joined by the hiss of an acetylene torch. The smell of fresh paint was being added to the organized confusion.

I made my way to the open forward watertight door, threw a leg over the low oval-curved sill, bent my back and head sufficiently to duck through, and straightened up in the passageway leading into the forward

3

battery. On my left were green hanging curtains, which closed off the chief petty officers' sleeping quarters, and on my right was the closed door to the yeoman's shack. This small office, four by three by five and a half feet high, would be my own little bailiwick for some time to come. I resisted an impulse to look inside and instead went down the narrow passageway that was officers' country and was broken up into tiny staterooms with green curtains hanging loosely or pulled back from the door openings. Above me I could hear the purring of an overhead motor to the forward battery ventilation system. In here there was a slight acid smell that came from the batteries below deck. I removed my hat and stepped to an open doorway of the officers' wardroom on my left.

A young dark-complexioned officer was seated alone at the after end of a dark-green cloth-covered table, along each side of which ran leather upholstered benches that could seat eight officers. The officer's khaki shirt was open at his throat and two silver bars decorated the corners of his collar. He shifted about to face me, still clutching several pieces of official correspondence, which he had evidently been sorting into different piles in accordance with their importance. He raised tired brown eyes to my face and said, "Yes?"

I replied, "Reporting for duty, sir," and handed the lieutenant my orders and a sealed manila envelope containing service record, pay accounts, and health record.

The lieutenant looked at me absent-mindedly for a few seconds, as though his mind was still reviewing the contents of the correspondence, and then he seemed to awaken. Thrusting out his hand, he said warmly, "Welcome aboard."

I shook his hand and answered, "Thank you, sir."

He glanced at my orders and began to smile broadly. "You're a third-class yeoman. Can we ever use you! We haven't had a yeoman since *Wahoo* left Mare Island." He paused before looking at me again and explained, "The pharmacist's mate has been doing all the paper work. You'll probably find the office in something of a mess."

"Yessir," I said lamely, feeling vaguely puzzled.

"I'm Lieutenant Richie N. Henderson," he stated and opening up the brown envelope started thumbing through my service record. While he was doing this I glanced about the wardroom. Cabinets were fitted into both ends of the room, and from past experience I guessed that in the forward cabinet would be the officers' silverware and tablecloths while the after cabinet would probably contain books and navigation charts. An idle record player sat in a corner. An opening in the forward end of the room led into the pantry, and I could see the white-coated back of a colored steward moving about. A rack contained many creased and thumbed copies of magazines, and I noticed idly that they dated back several months.

"I see you have broken service," Lieutenant Henderson said.

"Yes sir, I came in, in '30, and got out in '37," I replied and as an afterthought: "It was all sub duty, sir. *Holland, Barracuda, Nautilus, Sail 40,* and *Canopus.*"

Lieutenant Henderson grinned and said, "Well, then, you shouldn't have much trouble getting things straightened out. You know where the office is, and there will be a Duty Officer here to sign correspondence each day. Most of the crew will be at the Royal Hawaiian Hotel for two weeks yet, so just make yourself at home."

I took my orders and records and retreated back down the passageway. At the yeoman's shack I cheerfully opened the door. Eight mailbags were jammed into this small space and each was bulging with mail. Sorrowfully, I softly closed the door and slipped into the control room. Witting was lost in a comic dreamworld and apparently did not see me dragging my sea bag along the deck as I plodded aft. Passing through the crew's messroom and on into the after battery crew's sleeping quarters, I found an empty top bunk under a ventilation blower and near the medicine cabinet. I tossed my sea bag on it and returned to the messroom.

A heavy-set sailor with sad eyes and a double chin was puttering around in the galley. When I paused at the door to look in, he turned and scowled at me. A cigarette was hanging from his lips. "Well, wataya want?" he questioned.

"I'm the new yeoman reporting aboard," I answered, waiting for a reaction.

"So?"

This was not the reaction I wanted. I said, "So you've got about the best-lookin' galley and messhall I've seen on a submarine."

"You ain't been on many submarines." He glowered back at me. "And besides, it's not a messhall, it's a crew's messroom."

"I stand corrected," I answered acidly, "but on the other subs I been on we always called it messhall."

"Only shore bases have got messhalls," he said adamantly.

"Okay, so it's a crew's messroom, if you want to get technical," I retorted angrily.

He stared at me a long time, and finally reaching down, he opened an oven door, drew out a baked ham, and cut off a large slice. Building a man-size sandwich, he pushed it toward me. His cigarette had burned close to his lips. He removed it simply by opening his mouth and letting it fall into a garbage pail. He leaned toward me confidentially. "My name's Rowls, and I'm the First-Class Ship's Cook on board. What I would like to know is will you take over typing my weekly menus for me? I ain't so good on a typewriter."

Munching on the sandwich and with a cup of coffee in hand, I returned to the ship's office. I emptied the mailbags, stacked the empty sacks under the small-arms locker, separated the magazines from the pile, took them into the wardroom, and dumped them on the table while Lieutenant Henderson looked on. An eager look came into his eyes as he noted the latest issues. There were several copies of each magazine, and I knew that they would find their way into the messroom via the chiefs' quarters before long.

I went back to the office and looked for an incoming mail log. Not finding any, I made one up and began to segregate the mail by bureaus and commands. I found a letter opener and started opening the letters I thought might be most important. By 0200, I began to feel weary and closed shop. I took my shoes off and climbed into my bunk boots-and-saddle without even a mattress cover and fell instantly to sleep. The night shift was working on *Wahoo* but I heard nothing. At 0830 the next morning, I had eaten and was working away completely absorbed in my new duties.

By the middle of the second week I could see results. Most of the correspondence had been answered. *Wahoo's* officers had returned to the ship on duty days and I met them all with the exception of the Commanding Officer. They would rough-write answers, sign smooth correspondence, and leave directions for whatever important items they wanted handled next. I found time to inventory my supplies and restock from the submarine base G.S.K. It was disappointing to discover I could not get paper clips or fasteners because of the metal shortages, but I solved the problem by going through the files and service records and accumulating a large box of both. Rubber bands I could do nothing about. Those I could obtain were of synthetic rubber and broke with the slightest stretch. I brought all back reports up to date and was thumbing through the men's service records, shaking my head at the carelessness and discrepancies I was finding, when I became aware that Lieutenant Henderson was standing at the door watching me.

"How's everything going?" he queried.

"I can see daylight," I grumbled, "but I'll never get everything done that has to be done before we go on patrol, sir."

Lieutenant Henderson spoke softly. "I think you've done a fine job. In fact, I told the Exec just that and suggested that you spend the next few days at the Royal Hawaiian Hotel. But of course if you're too busy . . ."

My eyes must have lighted up like a neon sign. "Sir, I wish to report that as of this instant the ship's clerical work has been brought up to date."

"Well, all right." Lieutenant Henderson laughed. "Shove off when you feel like it. The Exec has granted permission."

An hour later I stepped out of a taxicab at the entrance to the Royal Hawaiian Hotel. I checked in and found that it would cost me twenty-five cents for fresh linen. Next, I was assigned to a room on the third floor with windows facing out on Waikiki Beach and a view of the never-ending march of those famous white breakers. In the background was Diamond Head. Six beds in the room indicated that I would share this paradise with five other men, but somehow I did not seem to mind at all.

With a few deft motions, I applied linen to the bare mattress and converted it into a made-up bed. Pulling my white jumper over head and arms, I folded it neatly and began a search in my ditty bag for soap. I had taken but a few steps toward the spacious tiled bathroom when the door swung open and Witting walked in. In one hand he held a large paper cup filled with Coca-Cola and in the other was the ever-present comic book. "Take a swig," he ordered, handing me the cup. My Navy nose picked up the scent of grain alcohol, and I reached for it without hesitation.

"Sure," I answered, tilting the cup up and drinking half the contents. I handed the cup back and wiped my mouth on the towel I had over one arm.

"Let's go get another," Witting proposed.

"Lead on, kindly light," I replied, leaving my jumper and towel on the bed and following him out of the room down the passageway to another room. Inside were four *Wahoo* crew members sitting or sprawled in chairs and on beds. They looked at me curiously while Witting filled another paper cup from a gallon jug of mixed alky and Coke.

"This is the new yeoman, fellows," he announced. Pointing his comic book at a potbellied chief whose sparse hair contrasted sharply with a hairy chest, he added, "And this is Pappy Rau, Chief of the Boat." The other men he introduced as Wilcox, Chief Machinist's Mate; Lindhe, Pharmacist's Mate, First Class; and Hunter, Signalman, First Class. They began to talk in a rush of mixed voices.

"Howsabout thirty days' leave, Yeo? Can you fix me up?"

"What do I have to do to put in for the Fleet Reserve?"

"When's payday?"

"Who do I see about a transfer, Yeo?"

I knew then that I had met their approval and was accepted as a member of the *Wahoo* crew in good standing. I relaxed and started on a third highball.

Pappy Rau was apparently more interested in an old pipe he was smoking than in drinking. Even without the evidence of much good-natured bantering, I had but to look around to see that he was admired by everyone present. By listening closely, I soon found out that he was from New London, Connecticut, and had twenty-four years' service, all of which had been served on board submarines. He was, in the nautical vernacular, an old salt.

Somehow the conversation got around to how far away the sun is from the earth, and this led to a recent error one of the officers had made in charting *Wahoo's* position. The next step led into the idiosyncrasies of the different officers and then to those of various members of the crew. Someone mentioned a liberty he had made in San Francisco, which brought up the favorite subject of girls. Devillo Guy Hunter came in for a great deal of teasing about an episode in which he apparently had shot out lights along a San Francisco pier and was handcuffed to the periscope shears overnight to repent his behavior.

Shadows from the palms outside the windows lengthened and blended with the dusk and finally into darkness. Sailors came in and out of the room. Some were going to chow in the dining room, others were on their way to movies. Witting faded from the room with paper cup and comic book.

Curiously enough, little was said about the war, and nothing at all was mentioned about *Wahoo's* first war patrol until the party began breaking up. Then Hunter said in a loud voice, "Yeo, has anyone told you how we shot down that Jap Zero on patrol?"

"Did you guys get a Zero on the last patrol?" I asked excitedly.

"We sure did. It was like this. We was riding on the surface when this damn Jap plane came diving out of the clouds overhead. The Old Man took one look and ordered a crash dive. We went down at a forty-five-degree angle with this plane diving straight in on our stern, which was out of the water. Well, sir, the Old Man did some quick thinkin' an' do you know what he did?"

"I haven't the faintest idea," I answered, getting suspicious.

"Well, he fired the stern tubes, and we knocked that plane right out of the air."

When the laughing quieted down, I said, "I just remembered something. I gotta go take a shower," and made a hasty exit.

The next two days I spent wandering through the streets of Honolulu, swimming or sunning on the beach, taking in movies, and finally getting drunk with the crew on the last night at the hotel. On the following morning a Navy truck loaded up *Wahoo's* crew, and we went aboard a *Wahoo* that had been made ready for war. Like a mother hen she was clucking her chicks aboard.

Chapter 2

W_ahoo_ was nearly ready to fight again. On her first war patrol in the Carolines, she had sunk a Japanese freighter, and now she was restlessly flexing her mechanical muscles in preparation for another foray into enemy waters. It would take three days of human testing and drilling to make her absolutely ready and able. I kept pace, taking up orders and records of new men, typing last-minute reports, keeping the correspondence moving, and making up an accurate sailing list. I put off the crew's personal problems with but two exceptions. If a man wanted government insurance or an allotment made out, I dropped whatever I was doing and took care of the matter immediately. I knew that some of the slighted personnel thought I was an officers' yeoman, but I was too busy to worry about it. My collateral duties as unofficial Chaplain could wait. Then too, the Executive Officer, Lieutenant R. H. "Dick" O'Kane, could get alarmingly purple in the face whenever his work did not receive precedence over all other matters.

On the morning of November 8, 1942, Pappy Rau came into the after battery compartment, turned the lights on, and began screaming, "Reveille, hit the deck!" He paid us this personal compliment because *Wahoo* was ready for sea. I sleepily crawled from my bunk, opened my locker, and took out clean skivvies, dungarees, and a new pair of moccasins. Groping my way through other members of the crew in various stages of undress, I waited patiently for someone to vacate a washbowl and finally was able to get to one long enough to clean my teeth and slosh some water over my face.

In the messroom, I was luckier in finding a plate and in a few moments rapidly reduced a plate of bacon and scrambled eggs to nothing more than a pleasant memory. Rowls and the messcooks were urging everyone to eat up and get the hell out of the "messhall" so they could start cleaning up. I poured a cup of coffee and balancing it with one hand reached high for a rung on the ladder leading up the after battery hatch. By stepping up a rung, bracing my feet and reaching for the next rung, I managed to reach topside without spilling a drop of coffee. I sat down on a cleat near the conning tower·fairwater, which was still damp with morning dew, lighted up a cigarette, and sipped from the cup. Some musicians carrying instruments straggled along the pier and gathered into a close group exchanging conversation and smoking cigarettes. On the bridge someone shouted, "Station the maneuvering watch." I walked over to the after battery hatch, swallowed the coffee left in the cup, and shouted below, "Cup coming down." I saw the white blur of a face looking up and dropped the cup. Two hands reached up, fielded the cup, and the face disappeared.

Leisurely I climbed the side of Wahoo's superstructure and crawled onto the cigarette deck. Benjamin Fertig Krause, Signalman, First Class, handed me a coil of rubberized telephone line, which was already plugged in, and a battle telephone talker's headset. He winked at me and hurried below to take care of another of his many errands. Krause was an energetic sailor, always in search of something that had to be done.

Ensign J. B. Griggs III, newly commissioned after three years at the United States Naval Academy, was on the bridge. I wondered if he had reached his twentieth birthday. He appeared to be nervous in his first contact with real responsibility, and he was making every effort to be alert if an opportunity should present itself that would require him to make a decision. Unfortunately, Wahoo's crew were so well trained that he found little opportunity to use his authority.

I uncoiled enough line to allow myself a position on the starboard side of the cigarette deck to see better what was happening on the pier. A large crowd of well-wishers had gathered. The SubPac band was gathered in a semicircle, and its members were receiving instructions from the Chief Bandmaster. Above me two lookouts had taken their places on platforms alongside the periscope shears and were lounging nonchalantly against the guardrails. They were wearing foul-weather jackets, and their blue-dyed hats were turned wrong side out on their heads. They, too, were curiously watching the build-up of excitement as the time for departure came near. A searchlight started clattering away as Simmonetti, Signalman, Third Class, began signaling the orange and white checkered signal tower at the Naval Base. On the dock, four children began to run in circles, screaming as they chased each other about the legs of bystanders. A dungareed sailor cupped his hands and shouted to a *Wahoo* sailor standing in a group on the fantail. He must have said something insulting about the *Wahoo*. There was too much noise for me to hear, but several *Wahoo* sailors took up the challenge and their actions pantomimed the impression that the *Wahoo* was the best damn submarine in the Navy and was going to sink every carrier in the Japanese fleet. A commotion near the gangway drew my attention in that direction, and I saw a group of officers come on board, led by a four-stripe Captain. They were met by *Wahoo's* Skipper, Lieutenant Commander M. G. Kennedy, and the prospective Commanding Officer (PCO), Lieutenant Commander Dudley Walker Morton, and Lieutenant O'Kane and one or two other *Wahoo* officers. A great deal of saluting went on before they started shaking hands and laughing at each other's repartee.

The Skipper said something to Lieutenant R. W. Paine, and he in turn glanced up at us on the bridge before hurrying our way. Lieutenant Paine spoke in low tones to Ensign Griggs on his arrival. "Your father would like to see you for a few minutes. I'm relieving you." Griggs scampered down the ladder and onto the quarter-deck. I watched them salute each other and then shake hands. Captain Griggs began talking to his son, who stood before him shaking his head in serious and obedient affirmation.

Krause came rushing up and stopped long enough to look down at the father and son combination. "That's Captain J. B. Griggs the Second, Chief of Staff, ComSubPac," he informed me before hurrying off again.

I had been automatically relaying reports to Lieutenant Paine, and I now reported, "All stations manned and ready for sea, sir." He in turn was alertly testing the annunciators. He acknowledged my report with "Very well."

When I looked down on deck again, the officers were departing from *Wahoo*. On the deck the band began playing "The Hawaiian War Chant," and the music made me feel proud that I had been selected as a *Wahoo* crew member. I could even imagine *Wahoo's* bow rising out of the water in similar elation.

Lieutenant O'Kane came below me and shouted upward, "Is the sailing list ready, Yeo?"

I pointed at Lindhe at the gangway and replied, "Yessir, Lindhe has it."

He turned and shouted to Lindhe, "Get the sailing list off."

Lindhe's reply, "Aye, aye, sir," drifted back, and I watched Lindhe hand the manila envelope that contained the names and home addresses of all crew members to a mail orderly waiting on the dock.

Sunlight broke loose from behind the submarine base buildings and flooded the scene with a new brilliance. *Wahoo's* Commanding Officer, Lieutenant Commander Kennedy, came on the bridge and took the conn.

He was followed on deck by Lieutenant Commander Morton and Lieutenant O'Kane. Orders began to pass rapidly. The gangway was pulled in, lines were singled-up and flaked on deck. Finally only the mooring line that held Wahoo's bow to the pier remained. Lieutenant O'Kane shouted, "Watch your eardrums," and the siren shrieked. Simultaneously, the bowline was thrown off the bollard on the pier and landed with a splash in the water. The Colors broke out on the cigarette deck flagstaff, helped by Krause, as the Union Jack forward and the Ensign at the stern came down. A whistle sounded. On deck, Pappy Rau was directing two men to secure the gangway to the side of the superstructure. Aft, diesel engines came to life with a roar, blue clouds of smoke sprang from the exhausts and turned to white, hiding the fantail and pier temporarily. Fumes of carbon monoxide swept the ship, smarting my nostrils. Wahoo began to vibrate as the screws dug in, and as they began to churn, Wahoo moved slowly and smartly astern.

I looked out at the people on the dock and became aware that they were waving and calling out good luck and good hunting omens to Wahoo. The band was now playing "Aloha."

Wahoo backed clear of the pier and turned. She shook as the screws reversed, stopped and then headed proudly out Pearl Harbor Channel.

On the pier, the spectators were straggling off to their routine jobs, and on the Wahoo, I stood watching with my stomach churning in excitement. There was a sudden silence about the ship, and I noticed everyone who was topside looking to starboard. I followed their gaze and saw the overturned hull of the U.S.S. Arizona. Without signal I saluted, and only after I dropped the salute did I realize that everyone topside had done likewise. Krause was two-blocking the Colors, after having dipped the flag in a Wahoo salute. I found myself wishing that on this patrol Wahoo would in some small way help to atone for the sacrifice made by the men still entombed aboard the Arizona.

The order, "Rig ship for sea," was given, and deck hatches began to slam shut. Soon I could see no one on deck except the officers and men manning the bridge.

Wahoo reached harbor entrance and turned right toward Barber's Point. The welcome word was given to "Secure the maneuvering watch." I coiled the electric cord, pulled the plug, and went below into the conning tower. Here I put the phone set away and lowered myself down the ladder into the control room and went on into the crew's messroom. A pinochle game was in progress. I drew a cup of coffee and sat down at an empty table. There was little roll to Wahoo, but I could feel her moving forward purposefully.

Krause came in and sat down across from me. "Griggs' hat blew overboard," he stated.

I looked at him blankly, not comprehending.

"Don't you see?" he went on patiently. "His name is in the hat. Suppose it drifts ashore and is picked up. We're under radio silence, and ComSubPac might think we got sunk by a Jap submarine. They won't know for sure until we pull in off of war patrol."

Chapter 3

Krause and I sat talking about Griggs' hat when we were interrupted by Hunter bustling into the messroom.

"Hey, fellows, we're going to the Solomons and Bougainville," he began loudly.

Krause said aside to me, "He's been working on the navigational charts. He ought to know."

The pinochle game came to a halt while everybody took time out to do some speculating.

"Boy, we ought to run into a lot of Jap shipping down there."

"Hey! Hunter, ain't the Marines still at Guadalcanal?"

I babbled to Krause, "Maybe we'll run into a Jap carrier, huh?"

Krause looked at me sourly and answered, "Well, if we do we'll run into a whole hornet's nest of destroyers, too."

I thought that over. "That's not good?"

"Oh, it's all right if we get a crack at a carrier, but don't kid yourself, we'll get plastered plenty with depth charges at the same time."

"Aw," I replied, "they don't have an ash can that's got the *Wahoo's* name on it." But the idea made me uncomfortable.

I looked at the clock and saw that it would be a half hour before noon chow. "I'm going to turn in." The lulling motion of *Wahoo* underway, the fresh sea air blowing into the compartment, and the excitement was making me drowsy.

At my bunk I kicked off my moccasins, looked around in the semi-darkness, and saw several of the crew in their bunks still in their dungarees. Next to me was Kohut, Machinist's Mate, First Class, already snoring loudly, and across the passageway Lindhe had his back toward me, to all appearances fast asleep. I crawled into my sack and was soon blending my baritone snore with the harmonious group.

A beam of light forced its way through my closed eyelids and at the same time a rough hand began shaking my elbow. I opened my eyes and pushed the offending flashlight to one side.

"Time to go on watch," a rough voice was saying. "It's 1530 and early chow's down."

I poked my nose over the edge of the bunk, and when my pupils adjusted to the dim light I saw the burly form of Joe Vidick, Electrician's Mate, Third Class, looking at a piece of paper in his hand with the aid of the flashlight.

Even though the watch came as a surprise, I had never been hard to get up to go on watch, and so I threw my legs over the edge of the bunk and sat up. Vidick, satisfied that he had awakened me, went off looking for the next name on the list.

I stumbled sleepily into the crew's messroom where the lights were blinding after the near darkness of the after battery sleeping compartment.

Someone jeered, "About time you got out of that sack. Want to sleep your life away?"

I answered blindly, "Aw, shut up." There was a great deal of laughter, and I sat down heavily and stupidly to an empty plate. By the time I had finished supper I was fully awake. I took my mess gear to the sink and pushed it between the suds-immersed arms of James H. Allen, Seaman Second, who was messcooking. Then I made my way forward into the control room.

Pappy Rau, in skivvy shirt, was waiting for the oncoming watch standers' arrival. He looked up, grinned, and put a check mark after my name on the watch list. "You need some fresh air," he announced. "Take the port lookout."

"So, all right," I retorted. I took a wool-lined submarine jacket from a locker, chose a pair of binoculars from several on the top of the gyrocompass table, stuffed some lens paper in a pocket, and climbed into the conning tower. I called up the hatch to the bridge, "Permission to relieve the port lookout, sir?"

The answer came back promptly, "Permission granted."

I went on up the ladder to the bridge and then climbed the periscope shears to the port lookout station. David Veder, Seaman Second, was on watch.

Wiping the lenses of the binoculars, I looked through them at the propeller guards on the fantail and adjusted them. Veder, without lowering his glasses, continued to scan the ocean. "Gosh, I'm hungry," he muttered. "What'a we got for chow tonight?"

I picked up the position he was looking at and answered, "Roast beef, mashed potatoes, green peas, and gravy, you're relieved."

Veder dropped his binoculars to dangle from the end of the strap around his neck and started below. ·

"Ice cream for dessert," I called after him. I spotted an unusual white-cap and watched it until it smoothed out into bluish-green ocean again. Then I took up the routine duty of scanning the sky, horizon, and ocean and let my thoughts run wild in the meantime. I had the consolation of knowing that this would be a dogwatch and that I would be relieved at 1800.

Two days slipped by and there were more watches. Watches on look-out, messenger watches in the control room, helmsman watches at the steering wheel, radar watches, sonar watches, and when there were no watches, there were drills—battle stations surface, battle stations submerged, fire, collision, and depth-charge drills. *Wahoo* was toughening her crew and we were learning to be ready for any emergency.

In-between times, I found time to play pinochle and acey-deucey, read, listen to the record player, join the inevitable bull session, and sleep. James P. Buckley, Radioman, First Class, managed to have a daily news bulletin at the breakfast table. I began to learn personal items about the crew. There was Lynwood Deaton, Torpedoman Second, and Dalton Keeter, Machinist's Mate First, and the ship's leading entrepreneurs. I learned that Dean Hayes, Electrician's Mate, Third Class, was a Canadian from Victoria, British Columbia, and that Robert Jasa, Fireman, was from Wahoo, Nebraska. Little things, but information that welded me closer to the crew.

On the fourth day at sea, the drills slacked off and I began to worry about the condition of the men's service records, and for the first time since getting underway I went to the wardroom. I found Lieutenant O'Kane playing cribbage with Lieutenant Commander Morton.

"Sir," I said, "I would like permission to take the men's service records into the messhall, show each man his record, and get them to help me straighten them out."

"That's a good idea," Lieutenant O'Kane replied. "And while you're at it give me a list of the men who are eligible for next higher ratings."

"Yes, sir." I was only too happy to comply. Turning to leave, I noticed Lieutenant Commander Morton looking quizzically at me. Remembering him from Asiatic duty days, I did not think that he remembered me, and I guessed that he must be wondering where he had seen me before.

I took three drawers of service records into the messroom, set them on a table, drew a cup of coffee, laid a pad of ruled paper in front of me, and made a little speech. My actions had drawn a curious and eager audience.

"Hear ye, hear ye, today has been set aside as Judgment Day. All ye who are heavily laden with personal problems may now lay your cares upon the yeoman's broad shoulders, and he will do his best to foul ye up worse than thou art."

After every man in the crew had a chance to review his service record, I was amazed at the pages of notations on the pad, each representing a correction to be made or a request to be fulfilled. There were entries that should have been made but had not been entered, beneficiary slips that were out of date, and errors to correct. I spent the next two days between watches bringing the service records up to date. I turned in a list of men eligible for next higher rating to the Executive Officer and received his thanks.

Returning to the office, I lit a cigarette. All the baskets were clear, and as far as I could see, there was no more clerical work to be done until we headed for port again. It was quiet in the office, and I relaxed by daydreaming of the telephone operator I had met in Los Angeles shortly before leaving the States. A bolt of lightning landed on my back and drove me into the typewriter. The dream exploded. Disentangling myself from the typewriter keys, I raised myself angrily with doubled fists, turned, and froze ludicrously in that position. Lieutenant Commander Morton literally filled the doorway, and he was grinning maliciously at me.

"Go ahead and strike me," he invited, pointing to the insignia on his collar.

My backbone felt as though it had been disjointed by a chiropractor. "No, thanks," I answered dryly, "besides outranking me you're a lot bigger'n me."

"Where have I seen you before?" he asked seriously.

Feeling that this would be a good chance to get even, I retorted, "If you could remember as far back as '34, '37, you'd know."

"China station," he exploded and then said, thoughtfully, "but you weren't a yeoman then, were you?"

"No, sir, radioman, third class. I was on the *Sail 40* for a while and then the tender *Canopus*." And I added, "You was only a shavetail ensign."

"Yeah," he grinned. "You didn't by any chance see the fighting cocks I had in Manila, did you?"

"No, sir." I was beginning to warm up to his magnetic personality. "I spent most of my time there at Moppy Joe's, the Silver Dollar, Santa Anna's, Legaspi Landing, or the Dreamland at Cavite."

He asked, "How do you like the *Wahoo*?"

"I think it's a swell boat, sir. I like it."

"How did she act on her last war patrol?"

"Oh, I wasn't on board. I just came on board at Pearl Harbor, Mister Morton."

He grinned. "Don't call me Mister Morton, call me 'Mush.' That's my nickname for 'Mushmouth.' It's the name they gave me at the Naval Academy—I like it."

A rapport was established between us.

"Are you going to be *Wahoo's* new Skipper, Mister—er—'Mush'?"

"It's not definitely settled yet." He evaded my question. "But she's sure a swell piece of fighting machinery. If I get her to command, we'll give the taxpayers their money's worth in sunken Jap shipping, you can bet your last dollar." His eyes shone and his enthusiasm radiated confidence and vitality.

I found myself willingly drawn into his sphere of commanded loyalty. The usual formality of officer-enlisted-man relationship diminished rapidly, but it was no longer needed. I knew that from then on "Mush" Morton's slightest wish would be my command.

On an impulse I said, "You give the word and I'll follow you to the bottom of the sea, sir."

"You might do just that," he said good-naturedly. "We won't always have the situation going our way, but we'll sure give 'em hell with what we've got as long as we've got it." He started to turn away and then stopped with another thought. "Yeo, when I get command, I want nothing but the best in submariners. In my estimation you're the best damn yeoman in the submarine fleet, and I want you in my crew."

I could not help being overpowered by his flattery. Any resistance I might have had to this officer's leadership was now entirely dissipated.

Chapter 4

Wahoo was moving steadily south and west, and we were but a few hours from our patrol area.

I had come off the midwatch and was eating a sardine and onion sandwich. Each night Paul Phillips, Ship's Cook, Second, did the baking and it was fascinating to watch him. He had finished with the bread dough that was waiting in bread tins to be shoved into the oven and was stirring with a big spoon a large dishpan of mincemeat. The spiced mincemeat was sending out invitations to the palates of any man up and around at that time of night. Ensign Griggs and Ensign G. A. Misch, from Tujunga, California (the latter had all the qualifications for an All-American football player), slipped quietly into the crew's messroom and blocked the door to the galley.

"Hi, Cookie." They greeted Phil simultaneously.

Phillips began to ladle the mincemeat into pie tins, apparently not seeing the new arrivals.

Misch sniffed appreciatively and made a statement. "A man really gets hungry after coming off that cold bridge at night."

"You bet," Griggs chimed in, "and there's nothing tastes better than mince pie at midnight." He was peeking around Ensign Misch's burly form to see what was going on.

A long silence followed in which Phillips turned his back on them while busily rolling out piecrusts. He looked through the galley aperture at me and winked.

The two ensigns fidgeted at the doorway, and finally Misch cleared his voice and said very authoritatively, "Phillips, howsabout a mince pie and that's an order."

Phillips looked around at them very much surprised and said, "Oh! good morning, sir, I didn't notice you standing there."

Ensign Misch, somewhat mollified; commanded, "Howsabout a mince pie for two hungry officers?"

"I'd be glad to, sir," Phillips replied politely, "but right now the bread is baking." He opened the oven door and showed them brown loaves.

Crestfallen, the officers prepared to depart.

"But I just happen to have a pie that hasn't cooled off yet."

Both officers swung back to the door as Phillips drew off a dishcloth in the corner and displayed a tempting, delicious, and steaming brown mince pie. They quickly accepted it like little boys and hurried forward to the officers' wardroom with their prize.

Phillips came out of the galley, sat down across from me, and we both laughed while I lighted up a cigarette.

"They sneak in every night for a handout," Phillips explained. "I always have something ready for them. The Old Man doesn't want them eating between meals."

"I reckon they've got growing pains," I observed.

We both laughed again and then I turned in to my sack.

Sometime before daybreak, November 20, 1942, Wahoo arrived on station. I awoke long enough to listen several seconds after the diving Klaxon sounded and felt the foot of my bunk rising as Wahoo took a down dive. Wahoo leveled off and I waited to see if she would settle by the stern. When she remained level, I went back to sleep after reflecting briefly that out there on our starboard or possibly on our port beam, not too far away, lay Bougainville. I tried to visualize U. S. Marines fighting Japanese soldiers in the Solomon Islands tropical jungles, but the effort was too much at that time of morning.

Wahoo changed her tactics. Where before she had been practically continuously on the surface, she now surfaced only at night to have her batteries recharged, so that she could hide beneath the seas on the following day. There was always the hope that a Jap convoy or ship would stray her way. The way of life inside her hull changed, too. Now, instead of lookout duties during the day, there were periscope "looksees" and sound watches, helm and diving stations, maneuvering stations, and telephone talkers. I found myself learning the intricacies of underwater sound fast.

Another internal change was felt when the Commanding Officer had a cot placed in the conning tower and began sleeping there.

Shortly after arriving on station, I caught a midwatch on the sonar gear. In the control room I was warned to move quietly and to speak in whispers in order not to disturb the Skipper. Moving cautiously up the ladder, I poked my head into the dim reddish glow of the conning tower and received permission from Ensign Misch to relieve the sonar watch. I tippy-toed to where Lindhe was impatiently watching for me and received the earphones.

"Keep sweeping all around and make your reports to the Junior Officer of the Deck every half hour," he whispered.

"Okay," I answered and assumed the watch. I swung the underwater sound receiver fully around and finding all clear glanced surreptitiously about. In the faint red haze I could make out the helmsman, with his back to me and his hands outspread on the steering wheel, making slow adjustments to the rudder to maintain *Wahoo's* designated course. Big Misch was leaning into the curved bulkhead with his head down in thought. I twisted around and saw the bundled form of the Captain in his cot with his back turned to me. An arm lying outside the blanket told me that he was fully clothed.

I turned back and concentrated on the fish traffic, which was making the earphone diaphragms vibrate incessantly with fish gossip. I became involved in my own thoughts and did the job automatically and reflexively. When the first half hour was up, my subconscious mind gave me warning, and after a quick look at the chronometer's luminous dial, I glanced in Ensign Misch's direction. He was looking at me expectantly and I whispered, "All's clear on the sound gear, sir."

An instant later a hand gripped me tightly on the shoulder and the Captain's voice boomed in my ear.

"*Where? Where away? What bearing?*"

I looked up startled into his frowning face, so close I could distinctly see that his eyes were dilated. My first thought was that the Captain had heard something I had missed. I began to dial frantically before I realized that this was an impossibility. Twisting under his grip, I looked at him again. I saw understanding come into his eyes, and he turned away muttering to Ensign Misch before descending the ladder.

"I must have had a nightmare."

When his head disappeared below the deck, Misch turned to me and grinned wryly, while Appel, Seaman Second, on the helm, who had turned around at the commotion, let *Wahoo* get five degrees off course.

The rest of the midwatch passed quietly and uneventfully until I was relieved by Ater, R. W., Seaman Second, who came from Allegan, Michigan. I went off watch with a clearer realization of the tremendous responsibility that goes with the command of a Naval war vessel in time of war.

In the messroom I decided against a cup of coffee but sat down on one of the deserted benches. Phillips was busy with his baking chores so I just stared at the scattered pinochle cards, the four cups with coffee sediment and one with a used tea bag. A tattered *True Detective* magazine lay on the table. I was tired, surely, but it was more than that. I stood up suddenly and said to Phillips, "Is it my imagination or is there tension on the crew of this boat?"

Phillips looked at me, wiped his floured hands on his cook's apron before replying, "Oh, sure, it's always like this on station."

I figured that he should know because he was a veteran of *Wahoo's* first war patrol. I was puzzled because I thought I detected a fleeting scared look on his face as he spoke. Shrugging my shoulders, I decided to give the thought a rest and turned in.

Wahoo continued her nocturnal prowling and daily submergence. Days went by and nothing happened, although *Wahoo* restlessly prowled and watchfully waited and "preyed" fervently for enemy shipping. Tension grew inside the boat.

I was playing pinochle with Bair, Arthur I., Seaman; Davison, William W., Motor Machinist, Second, from Fair Haven, New Jersey; and Frasch, Oakley R., Machinist's Mate, Second, from Lancaster, Ohio. I was about to meld three-hundred pinochle when the "battle stations submerged" chimes began. If a magician had moved his wand over the table, the men could not have disappeared quicker. There was a *swish, swish, swish,* and I was left sitting at an empty table with a handful of cards and a monel ash tray that smoked with abandoned cigarettes. I had not been assigned a battle station, so there was nothing for me to do except to continue sitting. Men were jostling each other in the passageway hurrying for stations, and when it quieted down, there was only Rowls, Phillips, myself, and Carter, James, a Radioman Striker, from Monroe, Louisiana, in the crew's messroom. Carter had donned a telephone talker's headset and was sitting with his back to the bulkhead with his legs stretched out on a bench.

"Crew's messroom rigged for battle stations," he reported into the talker.

There was a long wait in which the only sounds were muffled orders emanating from the conning tower and corresponding movements in the control room as they were carried out. A long jointed rod passed through the crew's messroom connecting the stern diving station in the control room to the stern planes. Frequently it would spring into action, twirling rapidly either clockwise or counterclockwise as needs dictated, to keep *Wahoo* at regulated depth. It sounded very noisy to me, and I wondered if an enemy destroyer could pick it up on their sound gear.

Of a sudden the loudspeaker came on, and O'Kane's voice could be distinguished angrily calling out, "Secure from battle stations! Secure from battle stations!"

Wahoo began to vibrate with more speed, and shortly the messroom was filled with milling men again. I could catch scattered phrases of conversation in what seemed to be a unanimous heated discussion.

"Sure was dark up there with . . ."

"Hell, we wuz right on top of her. She : . ."

"You know what I think? Her fathometer . . ."

". . . lightning flashes all around the horizon."

"The Old Man oughta . . ."

". . . big oil tank . . ."

". . . and he said it was echo-ranging."

When the voices finally subsided, Hall, James C., Torpedoman Striker, from Tampa, Florida, came over to the table.

"What day is today, Yeo?"

I pulled out my wallet and looked at a card calendar. "Why, it's November thirtieth," I answered. Then in surprise, "Whatin'el happened to Thanksgiving?"

Hunter, sitting across the table, piped up. "We been fightin' a war, yuh damn fool. Haven't yuh heard about it?"

Hall joined him in laughing at me.

"Well, if you're so smart, what happened just now up there and where are we?"

Hunter replied with guile. "It's simple. We been patrolling the Buka-Kilinailu Channel since we been on station and tonight we made a contact."

"Yeah," I urged, "and so?"

"So," he went on, "we got in close to this big oil tanker and she began to echo-range on us."

"Yeah, go on . . ."

"Well, the Japs have got lots of oil tankers and we're looking for battle-wagons—so we just naturally broke off the attack."

"Aw, go to hell." I gave him the best answer I knew, not knowing whether to believe him or not. He gave me a Mancos, Colorado, horse-laugh and left the crew's messroom.

Krause came in and by way of salutation I asked, "What are we going to do now?"

Not the least surprised, he answered, "We're going to start patrolling between Truk and the Shortland Islands in a couple of weeks. Maybe we'll get a chance at that carrier you've been asking for."

"Well, if we do," I muttered, "I hope it ain't got no echo-ranging gear."

Vidick came bustling up, handed me a pair of red goggles. "You go on watch in fifteen minutes," he said mechanically and hurried away with three more pairs of goggles dangling from his fingers.

Wahoo made no other contacts for several days. Each day was a routine unto itself, but minor experiences and revelations kept them from being monotonous. On an afternoon in early December I grew weary of the crowded messroom and left it to go forward to the yeoman's shack. I paused on the way out to listen to an excited radio announcer say something about ". . . it has been a year since the Japanese bombed Pearl Harbor and now General Montgomery's Eighth army is attacking Rommel's forces in Libya . . . battle of El Alamein . . ." I wondered where exactly Libya was and what the American forces were doing.

I started past the radio shack and paused as I heard a practice oscillator making code. Standing in the doorway, I could see Buckley, who came from New London, Connecticut, on radio watch. Although there was a radio silence, the frequency still had to be guarded. He was sitting with earphones cocked up above his ears and sending practice code to Carter. He glanced up at me and without pausing kept on sending, "Y-E-O I-S A-S F-U-L-L O-F F-E-C-E-S A-S A X-M-A-S T-U-R-K-E-Y."

"Oh, yeah?" I answered. "Coming from a 'radio twigett' that's a real compliment."

Carter and Buckley both looked at me in surprise and consternation.

"Where did you learn the code?" Buckley snapped.

"Oh, was that code?" I replied sweetly. "I thought it was some banana-boat operator learning how to send."

"N-U-T-S," the oscillator rattled rapidly.

"And nuts to you, too," I replied. "I used to be a radio operator before the Navy discovered I was a boy."

I was pushed aside by Lieutenant C. C. Jackson II, *Wahoo's* Communication Officer. "What's going on here?"

"Nothing much." I beat Buckley to a reply. "I've just been teaching your eunuchs the international Morse code, is all."

Buckley growled, "He usta be a operator in the old Navy, sir."

"Really?" Jackson was impressed. "We're short of watch standers and . . ."

"I gotta be going, sir," I answered hastily. "Got a lot of work waiting in my pending basket. Something the Exec wants out right away, sir. Be seein' yuh."

It was quiet in the office and I shut the door for more privacy. I had lost all desire to write letters that might never be delivered, so instead I retrieved a *Reader's Digest* and began reading. Besides, there was nothing in the action or pending basket to do anyway.

Three days later, I came off the helm watch at noon, ate a lunch of fried liver and onions, and turned in for some sleep before I would catch the 1800–2000 watch and the 0400–0800 watch after that.

When the general alarm went, the insistent *bong, bong, bong* brought me upright in my bunk. After the rush of stampeding humanity passed by, I crawled out and made my way into the glaring light of the crew's messroom. A glance at the ship's clock showed the time to be going on to 1600. Rowls, Phillips, and Carter were already there and a glance at their faces verified the excitement that was stirring my stomach. I drew a cup of coffee and sat down across from them to await whatever would happen. Watching the others smoking reminded me that I was going through one of my periodic "breaking-the-habit" ordeals and proudly remembered that it had been ten days since I gave my cartons of cigarettes away. The strain of waiting began to tell. I became aware of a familiar sensation. It was the way I used to feel in high school football just before the referee's whistle would blow and I would run to kick the ball.

Carter, lazily sitting in his corner, made a quick movement to press the earphones closer to his ears. He glanced at us while he listened to scratchy sounds. When they stopped, he relayed:

"There's a big convoy up there, six or eight ships. Looks like a couple of escorts, one forward and one aft. We're making an approach."

I was amused by a thought of how similar submarine warfare was to hunting. The game is located and then a person sneaks up on it and shoots. But, suppose the game turns out to be a big grizzly bear and you only wound him. That was not so good.

It seemed like an hour but the clock indicated that only twenty minutes had passed. I began to wonder if there really was a convoy or if this was just another drill. I began to relax. Carter's voice startled me into tenseness again.

"They're opening the outer doors of the forward torpedo tubes."

I thought of the sleek bronze war-headed torpedoes in the torpedo room and wondered how much damage they were actually capable of doing. I had a mental picture of the torpedomen standing by the tubes and chain-falls.

Wahoo's bow shuddered and the jolt carried back through her frame. Rowls and Phillips craned their necks to watch with fascination the second hand on the clock. Carter announced superfluously, "One's been fired."

Mentally I could picture the torpedo just beneath the ocean's surface, leaving a widening white trail behind it going toward a large ship.

Wahoo shuddered again, followed by Carter crooning tonelessly, "Two's away."

I glanced at the two ship's cooks watching the clock raptly and frowned at their concentration. My insight clicked and I knew that they were timing the torpedo runs.

Three and four were fired after brief waits.

A voice carried through the bulkheads and I heard distinctly, "Up 'scope!"

The quiet was broken now, and sounds of scurrying feet, faint clanging noises forward, and movement in the control room added to the excitement.

"One minute," Phillips was shouting. "She ought to be going."

Wham. I jumped.

"It's a hit!" The whole ship shouted in unison. *Wham.* "Another!" *Wham.* "Three hits!"

There was a brief silence as we waited for the fourth. When it did not materialize, bedlam broke loose. Men could be heard shouting and rebel-yelling throughout *Wahoo.*

"Rig for depth charge! Rig ship for depth charge!" The urgent voice of Lieutenant O'Kane was loud on the compartment speaker. I realized then that I had leaped up and was shouting excitedly with the rest of the crew. But now, as silence came quickly following the Executive Officer's command, I could feel *Wahoo's* decks dipping at a growing angle, which was accentuated by a lone coffee cup sliding and clanging against the metal end of the sink.

Phillips was quick to close the ventilation system, while Rowls secured the main induction stop valve, and I ran to slam shut and secure the watertight door between the control room and the crew's messroom. I dogged it with quick turns of the double handle. Carter was speaking into his talker. "All secured in the after battery." There was absolute quiet inside the ship when I sat down again. *Wahoo* was still diving.

I had thought a lot about depth charges and seen movies of depth-charge conditions, but the explosion that went off above my head caught me totally unprepared. The shock shook the boat. In the crew's messroom, lights went out, followed by audible *pops* that sounded like a rifle firing in the compartment. I was shaken so hard my head snapped. Small loose objects whistled through the pitch-darkness, and huge segments of overhead cork propelled downward on my head and shoulders, scaring me more than any harm they did. The detonation was followed in quick succession by two more, with each throwing me bodily against trembling mess tables. Then all was silent again and *Wahoo* was leveled off at a considerable depth.

A blue light flooded the compartment and I could see Carter standing by the emergency light, his hand leaving the switch. Rowls was picking himself up from the center aisle, and Phillips was standing with his legs braced holding on to the sides of a table. The crew's messroom was a shambles of debris and the air was filled with dust. I found myself wondering dimly where the dust came from. I started to take a step and felt glass crushing beneath my foot. Looking down stupidly, I saw fragments of electric light bulbs littering the deck. I pondered with awe at the force that had untwisted them from their sockets.

Phillips moaned something in a low voice and I turned to him. He repeated himself, staring at me vacantly with dilated eyes, "More depth charges. There's going to be more depth charges."

We braced ourselves as three more bursts shook us savagely with a repeat performance of the first charges. The ferocity of the shaking seemed in no way abated. Blessed silence came again and I could hear Carter on the phone calmly reporting the damage but no leaks.

Carter came to life with an exclamation. "We're diving right under the torpedoed ship!" He was interrupted by more depth charges shaking the boat but this time they were farther away. We waited tensely for the next explosions, and I tried to picture the barnacled bottom of the sinking ship that Wahoo was cruising beneath. The explosions went off and seemed farther away. Apprehensively, I asked Carter, "Are we under her yet?"

He repeated my question into the phone set and waited for an answer. In a few seconds he turned and said, "All clear. We're on the other side now." He paused, adjusted the phones, and spoke again. "We got a large freighter about 9,000 tons. She's sinking fast. The Japs have been dropping depth charges right in the middle of their own survivors."

I remembered belatedly feeling Wahoo easing back to the surface and knew that the Skipper must be making observations through the periscope.

My nerves began to settle and I noticed Phillips was missing. "Where's Phil?" I asked Rowls.

"He got sick. Always does when the depth charges go off. He's probably in the washroom."

Sweat began to run in rivulets down the sides of my cheeks and neck. "God, it's hot in here."

"It'll get hotter'n this before we're through," Rowls predicted.

"Can I have one of your cigarettes, Rowls?"

"Thought you quit smoking. Remember? Only this morning you said I was a nicotine fiend with no will power."

"Aw, to hell with that," I growled. "That was this morning. Howsabout a cigarette?"

I smoked it about half through when several more depth charges went off, closer this time.

The watertight door swung open and Lieutenant Henderson came in with a flashlight. 'How's things in here?" he asked.

"Not so good, sir," I answered respectfully. "We got a good shaking up."

He flashed the beam along the pipes and and then up into the after battery hatch. "Smoking lamp's out," he commented casually without looking at us. "I suggest you men who don't have a battle station get into your bunks. We're going to be down for some time."

"Yes sir," Rowls and I both answered.

He went aft toward the engine room.

I followed him as far as the sleeping quarters and after dusting off my bunk and taking off all my clothes I climbed in. I peeked over the edge and could make out Phillips' form in a lower bunk. I suddenly felt sorry for him and at the same time was surprised at the way I came through my first depth charging. More explosions hurt my eardrums and rattled bottles in the medicine cabinet in the corner but did not shake a growing inner certainty that *Wahoo* was not going to be sunk. Cork came powdering down and stuck to my profusely sweating skin. Depth charges kept going off periodically. Some were close and others farther away. I had a curious thought trying to imagine how it would feel to have tons of water cascading through a ruptured hull into the compartment. Would death come quickly or slowly? Then I said softly to the darkness, "Thank you, dear God, for bringing us through safely," and went into a drugged sleep.

Cool air from the ventilator above my head caused me to shiver into wakefulness. I lay there a few moments listening for depth charges before realization came upon me that the roaring of *Wahoo's* diesels was an indication that we were riding the surface. I jumped down, took a hasty shower, and returned to the crew's messroom. It was 1930 by the bulkhead clock, and in fifteen minutes I would have to relieve one of the lookouts on the bridge.

It was crowded in the messroom and everyone was holding a postmortem on the recent attack.

Holman, Earl T., Machinist's Mate, First, from Sacramento, California, was the closest and the loudest and I could hear him shouting, "I counted over fifty depth charges before I stopped counting."

I shouldered somebody aside and opened the hatch to the dry-stores storage room saying, "Don't be a Marine all your life," and started below.

Simmonetti, from Fall River, Massachusetts, answered Holman. "There were seventy-eight. I counted them for the ship's log. Forty of them were damn close, too."

"Our information was that those tin cans only carry twelve depth charges, but, boy, is somebody mistaken," added Hunter.

I searched around, found a couple of cans of tuna, and climbed back out of the hold, turning the lights off as I came.

Holman questioned, "How many ships was there?"

Hunter said, "Three freighters and two destroyers. The Old Man picked the largest freighter to fire at."

"It sank, too, at 1815," supplemented Simmonetti.

I moved into the galley and used the can opener on the tuna tins, then

I got a jar of mayonnaise and pickles from one of the cabinets and pushed my way back into the crowded crew's messroom.

"Clear the way," I yelled, "messcook coming through."

A space opened up at one of the tables without anyone hardly doing more than glance at me.

". . . the Old Man said them ships scattered in every direction when those fish hit," Hunter was saying.

Industriously, I mixed up a large bowl of tuna salad and left it on the table to go get some slices of bread. When I got back, I looked in dismay at the empty greasy finger-streaked bowl and twisted around angrily. "That's a helluva way to treat a guy going on watch."

The noise stopped and everyone turned my way in innocent surprise.

"What's the matter, Yeo?" the Chief Electrician's Mate, Edward Jesser, from Southgate, California, crooned softly. "Did some nasty old person steal your pap?"

"Aw, the whole bunch of yuh can go to hell," I snapped.

"Time to go on watch," Vidick said tonelessly as he handed me a pair of red goggles.

"And you can go to hell, too," I flared back, completely frustrated. I slammed the goggles down over my eyes, drew a cup of coffee, and found a corner to sulk in while everyone laughed at my discomfiture. Seeing Laffin, Sylvester J., Torpedoman First, from Seattle, Washington, across the table, I wheedled, "Howsabout one of your sea-stores cigarettes, Laff?"

"Sure," he said, "but only this morning you was telling me the cigarette habit could lead to cancer."

"Well, I might as well have cancer along with the rest of yuh. You've already given me ulcers," I retorted.

I finished the coffee and cigarette and started out.

Hunter was saying, ". . . I never seen the Old Man so brave. It was as if . . . "

I did not hear the finish as I ducked through the door into the control room on my way to relieve the watch.

Four days faded into history. *Wahoo* continued her vigilance while her crew, still tense under the strain but much heartened after their conquest of the Jap freighter, went about the daily business of watches, necessary sleep, recreation, and enough horseplay to break the monotony.

I started a personal letter in the typewriter and got as far as the date, December 14, 1942, when I was stopped by Lemert, Richard H. M., from Minneapolis, wanting to know if I would be his partner in a game of pinochle. I gladly left the letter languishing in the mill and went aft with him, but on arriving in the crew's messroom we found two other players had taken over the game. The mess tables were still damp from their morning scrubbing. After some heated arguing, which we did not win, Lemert went aft to the engine rooms.

I sat down in the corner hoping someone would drop out of the game or enough other crew members would come in to start another game. Finding a Western magazine, I got involved in a range feud in which about fifty ranchers and their thousand or so ranch hands, a few hundred rustlers and gunmen, not to mention the thriving town of Formaldehyde and a whole "passel" of Indians, were lined up against me and my three trusty sidekicks. This made it about even odds. We were riding into town for a showdown when I was rudely brought back to *Wahoo* by the loud strains of "Sock 'em down, Winsocki, sock 'em down." I glanced irritably up to see O'Brien, Forest L., Electrician's Mate Second, from Vallejo, California, standing by the record player. He winked down at me and turned the volume higher. My eardrums were ringing.

"Shut that damn thing off," McGill, Thomas M. J., Machinist's Mate First, from St. Pauls, North Carolina, one of the card players, shouted. "Do you want to deafen us?"

O'Brien turned to him. "Why? I like good music, don't you?"

"Hell, yes," yelled McGill, "but I don't like it so loud they can hear it in Tokyo."

O'Brien turned the volume low and sat down near me. "Let's talk about something."

I gave a sigh, turned down the corner of a page, and shoved the magazine into my hip pocket.

"Okay, *Forest*." I emphasized his name because it was the same as my own. "Upon what subject shall I fill out the missing blanks in your erudition today? I know," I went on, "you got a letter from your wife at the last mail buoy wanting you to increase your allotment."

"Naw, nothing like that." He looked around at the silhouettes of Japanese ships pasted thickly on every available space in the ship. "What do you think about them damn pictures?"

"I hate 'em," I replied promptly. "Are we really expected to memorize all the Jap fleet?"

"Sure. Haven't you got them memorized yet?"

"Hell, no, and I don't think anybody else has either, including the officers."

"Well, if you want to qualify on this boat, you better."

I said dreamily, "I can see myself now. I'm on lookout. See! I'm looking at the horizon through my binoculars. See! Suddenly I spot a tiny speck on the ocean rim! I am very calm. The Captain is on the bridge. I turn to him while I point dramatically at the horizon.

"Ship ahoy!" I sez.

"Where away?" The Captain sez.

"Two points abaft the starboard beam, sir."

"I don't see," the Captain sez. "What's it like?"

"It is a Japanese cruiser, sir, of the *Suki-Yaki* class, 25,000 tons, sir. It has thirteen eight-inch guns. One is pointing astern and a broadside is zeroed on us, sir. Bearing on the bow is now zero degrees, sir. Making about thirty knots . . ."

I became aware of six or seven sailors around me grinning broadly, and towering over them was Ensign Misch, the happiest of all. Embarrassed, I tapered off meekly, "Shucks, fellers, it warn't nothin' really."

O'Brien jumped up and increased the volume on the phonograph, "Sock 'em down, Winsocki, sock 'em down."

"Clear the messhall, you bums. It's time to set up for noon chow." It was Rowls raving. "Give the messcooks a chance."

I was glad of the interruption.

We had country-fried steak for lunch and I ate hungrily. Minutes later, I was in the conning tower relieving Lindhe from the sonar watch.

"What's new?" I asked brightly.

"Nothing," he said sarcastically. "You're late in relieving as usual."

"Two minutes," I answered. "Next time I'll relieve you on the hour and then you'll have something to holler about."

He grunted. "Keep a sharp lookout, the fish are really bad today," and he went below.

I settled down to routine listening with corresponding half-hourly reports. Lieutenant Paine was the Duty Officer. I noticed that every twenty minutes he would have the Diving Duty Section bring *Wahoo* to periscope depth; take a quick sweep or two around, and then bring her down to a deeper depth than usual.

Conditions were normal on the sonar gear except that there seemed to be more scattered rain squalls than usual on the surface. About the middle of the watch, I heard an extra heavy squall bearing zero-three-zero degrees.

"Mr. Paine," I reported, "I hear a terrific rain squall on the starboard bow. It must be hailing there the way it sounds."

"Switch to the sonar loudspeaker," he ordered.

I threw the switch and the sound was made audible without the use of earphones. He listened to it with a puzzled expression on his lean handsome face. Glancing at the clock, he frowned thoughtfully.

"There's ten minutes to go before periscope time. I think I'll run her up though and take a look." He ordered *Wahoo* up. When the ship obeyed, he pressed the "scope pickle" and followed the eyepiece up where it cleared the tubular periscope well. He swung the 'scope around and back to steady on the starboard bow. With a startled exclamation he pulled the periscope down halfway, leaped to press the general alarm button, and shouted into the voice tube, "Control, notify the forward torpedo room to open the outer doors on the double!" The last words were hardly out of his mouth before he was racing back to the TDC (Torpedo Data Computer).

I sat stupidly through these unexpected actions, but now I twisted the sound gear lever back and forth and across the rain-squall area. It sounded the same to me only louder. Subconsciously I could hear the battle stations gong chiming away. A commotion sprang up in the boat, followed by Captain Kennedy literally bursting into the conning tower.

"Submarine, Captain. A Jap sub is up there on the surface," Lieutenant Paine reported while he continued spinning handles, twisting dials, and snapping toggle switches on the TDC. "She's going to cross our bow at about 1,000 yards."

Captain Kennedy had not wasted any time. He was 'scoping to look the situation over. He was followed by Lieutenant O'Kane, Lieutenant Commander Morton, Krause, Simmonetti, and several others. Buckley reached me and took over. The sonar was his designated battle station.

"What is it?" he asked excitedly.

"It's a Jap sub bearing about zero-three-zero degrees," I replied somewhat in awe. Now I could hear the distinct sound of propellers beating the water on the loudspeaker. Amplified, they sounded right on top of us. One of the officers shouted, "Turn that damn sound off," as I shinnied down the ladder. The sound clicked off. Below, I noticed Lieutenant Grider being relieved by Lieutenant Henderson, Pappy Rau standing by the Christmas tree, and the skivvy-shirted backs of the bow and stern planesmen. Pappy Rau turned his head and queried, "What is it?"

"A Japanese submarine," I almost whispered.

Everybody looked apprehensively at the overhead, even though they knew that they could not see the submarine. I walked on back into the crew's messroom where I had to tell Rowls, Phillips, and Carter again that it was a Japanese submarine. Phillips looked as though he was going to be sick and hurried through the after door. I sat down and made motions with my two fingers in a sign language request for a cigarette. Rowls complied by tossing me an unopened pack with a grunted, "Keep 'em, I got more."

"Hope no planes spot us. We're laying off the Buna airfield," Rowls offered.

"So that's it," I answered, peeling the cellophane from the pack and extracting a cigarette. "I wondered why we was laying so deep this afternoon."

"Yeah," Rowls replied. "Them planes can spot a submarine silhouette in these clear waters a mile away."

I got a light from Rowls' cigarette and noticed my hand shaking a little. Now that my job was finished and I had nothing to do but wait, I was beginning to get nervous.

The sudden jolting of *Wahoo's* hull, followed by the rumble and hiss of high-pressure air up forward, contracted my stomach and intestines into tense knots. This time my eyes focused simultaneously with Rowls' on the clock's second hand. We stared at its slow movement as though we were hypnotized. Without realizing it, I was at the same time holding my breath. When the second and third "fish" left the tubes, I paid little attention to *Wahoo's* vibrations, only vaguely to the fact that they were fired seconds apart. The second hand had not completed its circuit before an unusually loud explosion caused me to involuntarily grip the table. I looked quickly at Rowls and let my breath go in a rush. "Whataya think? A premature?"

Rowls opened his mouth to speak and his countenance froze in that ludicrous position—interrupted by an equally loud explosion. His eyes bulged.

"We got 'er! It's a hit!" someone screamed from the direction of the control room. Pandemonium broke out in the boat. Rowls started shouting and whooping while Carter and I did an Indian war dance.

Crash! My eardrums burst and we were shocked into goggling statues. This time there was no doubting that the explosion was directly overhead. *Wahoo* shook as she was driven deeper, already in a dive angle, by the explosive force.

"What was that?" we asked in unison.

Carter clutched the headset to his ears. "A plane dropped an aerial bomb on us." He listened again as Rowls and I anxiously waited. "He must of been right above us when the torpedoes hit." Then into the talker, "No leaks or damage in the after battery."

Wahoo had pulled the plugs and we were headed for bottom. A large dishpan fell with a heavy metallic clatter to the deck in the galley. Already nerves on edge, we jumped at the noise. It was banging and ringing as Rowls hurried to grab and secure it. After what seemed ages, *Wahoo* leveled off and the command came to "Rig for depth charge! Silent running. Rig for depth charge! Silent running."

We settled down to waiting again. I noticed in surprise that half the pack of cigarettes was smoked. With the boat noiseless again, I became aware of another noise outside the hull, explosions and breaking-up sounds.

Carter made his usual preparatory movements for listening to the headset. Catching the movement from the corner of my eyes, I swung to face him.

"That's the Jap sub making all that noise. Her compartments are caving in and her warheads are exploding under the deep pressure of the sea," he announced excitedly and triumphantly.

When several minutes went by and there was no recurrence of the aerial bombing, Rowls answered my unspoken thoughts. "Guess he only had one bomb."

We stayed on silent running, and finally my finger searched the inside of the cigarette pack and found no cigarettes. Rowls tossed me another pack without comment. None of us had spoken a word in the interim.

Someone blew into the mike of the ship's speakers a couple of times and all was quiet again. After a short interval, Lieutenant O'Kane's voice boomed out of the speaker. "We're going to surface for a looksee. Everybody stand by for an emergency dive." *Wahoo* took a slow steady up-angle as air roared into the ballast tanks. The nape of my neck began to itch as the short hairs stood on end.

"Gosh, I hope those planes don't spot us," I muttered under my breath. Rowls looked at me and nodded agreement.

Wahoo leveled off and stayed there. After a few seconds, the loud speakers sprang into action again. "Secure from silent running. Secure from battle stations." It was a most welcome command.

Almost immediately, the crew's messroom filled with excited men. I wanted to stay around and brag about making the contact on sonar, but I had thirty minutes to do on watch yet, so I made my reluctant way back to the conning tower and relieved Buckley.

Lieutenant Paine was still there, his eyes sparkling and face flushed with excitement. As soon as I was squared away, I turned to him.

"Was it a big sub, sir?"

"You bet. It was one of the Japanese fleet type with the letters I-2 and a large Rising Sun painted on the conning tower. The bridge was crowded with brass hats. They hardly knew what hit them, they went down so fast."

"How far away was it?" I asked, wide-eyed at the mental picture.

"Seven hundred fifty yards," he answered gravely. "Did you hear it breaking up on the way down?"

"I sure did, sir. It kinda brings home what could happen to us when we're riding on the surface, doesn't it?"

We both fell silent thinking about the consequences and I turned my attention back to the sound gear.

When the minutes had dragged by, I was relieved by Morris, James, Seaman, from Watertown, Massachusetts. I went down into the crew's messroom to the evening chow confusion: knives, forks, dishes rattling, everyone talking, feet shuffling on the deck, mixed smells of wieners, sauerkraut, and boiled potatoes permeating the compartment, an odor of strong soapsuds in the sink. I sat down to eat.

I nudged Vogeler, Lonnie L., seaman second, from Sedalia, Missouri, who sat next to me, and cleared my throat importantly. "I was on sonar watch when . . ."

"Hey, Yeo, if you'd gotten outa your sack long enough this afternoon you'da had some excitement," interrupted Hunter.

"Oh, yeah?" I answered heatedly. "Well, for your information . . ."

Lindhe tapped me on the shoulder and demanded, "Pass the spuds."

I picked up the tureen of steaming potatoes and passed them over my shoulder to him. When I turned around, Hunter had finished chow and was leaving the crew's messroom. "Hey, Hunter," I shouted, but there was so much noise that he apparently did not hear me. I turned back to Vogeler. "I was on sonar watch when . . ."

"Hey, Yeo." Holman shoved an empty tureen under my nose. "Ask Cookie to fill this up again with wieners."

I set the pan down with a loud bang on the serving shelf and hollered, "Wienies." Turning to Vogeler, I reiterated, "I was on sonar watch when . . ."

Vogeler said, "Sorry, but I'm late in relieving the watch. I gotta be going."

"Aw, hell," I muttered and attacked viciously the wiener on my plate.

Pappy Rau at another table was conversing. "Those aerial bombs explode upward. I'm glad it wasn't a depth charge. Those Jap sailors must of . . ."

I sat gloomily through the rest of the meal. How in hell, I thought, can a guy get to be a hero if no one will listen to you? Then I fell to cogitating on conditions aboard a Japanese submarine. I wondered what kind of food they ate. Rice? Tea? *Asahi* beer or *saki*, most likely. Bet the yeoman has a "wing-ding" of a time typing up reports on a Japanese typewriter.

"You can't stay here all night," Rowls was growling. "Give the mess-cooks a chance to clean up, willya?"

I picked up my mess gear and dropped them into the sink on my way out.

Several days passed and the only occurrence to change *Wahoo* lives was to begin patrolling along the Truk and Shortland Island shipping route as Krause had foretold. But since these changes originated with the "Great White Father" at SubPac, Krause was given little credit for his occult powers, especially since the rest of the crew knew for certain that quartermasters and signalmen are not so smart as they are fortunate.

On this particular morning, or noon as it turned out to be, Vidick shook me so hard I came out of the wrong side of the bunk fighting mad. He left the words, "Time to go on watch," hanging in the darkness behind him, and like the "shadow" dematerialized into the passageway going forward. Instead of a haunting laugh or whistle, all I could hear were snores from my more fortunate shipmates.

I'll kill that oaf, I made a solemn vow to myself. Then I pictured myself weaving in-and-out, a right to the jaw, the lethal left cocked and ready, but lo and behold! Vidick falls forward like a giant pine and crashes slowly to the deck. I place my foot on his neck and pound my chest.

"Second call, Yeo. Time to go on watch." The imperturbable voice of Vidick reached me out of the darkness and I heard his footfalls pounding away.

On the way to the crew's messhall, I wondered if there was a connection between Vidick having come from Flint, Michigan, and the "Gibraltar of Frustration" symbolism he had assumed in my mind.

My nostrils informed me that we were having fish and meat loaf for lunch. I took a cup from a cabinet, dipped a couple of heaping teaspoons of cocoa into it, and dissolved it into steaming chocolate with hot water from the coffee urn.

There was a soiled mimeographed copy of the *Wahoo Daily Gazette* on one of the tables, and I punched my way into the crowd, rescued it, and came back out, having spilled only a few drops of hot cocoa down Hunter's neck. He screamed but was so packed in that he could not get at me until after I was safely out of reach.

Lindhe was vitriolic in his prerelieving speech, and I made a mental note to kick him right in the britches when we got ashore. This was not my day. I could readily discern that.

I listened all around, and when I could hear nothing but jabbering fish around the entire circuit, I reported "all clear" to Ensign Griggs, who was waiting for Lieutenant Paine to relieve him. Then I pulled out the morning news and while dialing around began to read. "German troops were reversed at Kasserine Pass . . . Rommel's tanks skirmishing in North Africa . . ."

"Get rid of that paper, Yeo." Griggs growled into my ear.

"Yessir," I answered, cramming it, not without bitterness, into a hip pocket. "This sure ain't my day," I ruminated sadly. I sipped on the cocoa, which had become cold and was not sweet enough. It tasted terrible. I started to dump it down a drain but changed my mind when I saw Ensign Griggs looking at me.

The noises of trillions of fish, shrimp, and sea denizens of every biological description (I was not sure about barnacles), I was convinced, had been organized into a union whose sole purpose was to disguise alien noises so that bewildered and neophyte soundmen could not recognize them. I was positive of this fact, but since nothing was going right this day, anyway, I accepted it philosophically.

Lieutenant Paine relieved Ensign Griggs and he went below. In a little while Lieutenant Paine came over beside me. "Going to find any more subs today, Yeo?"

I answered gloomily, "I wouldn't know a ship's screws from a pin dropping in a boiler factory, sir."

He turned one of the earphones outward and listened carefully. "It really is bad, isn't it? Well, keep listening and if anything unusual happens let me know."

I took this opportunity to satisfy a curiosity. "Are you really from Fort Smith, Arkansas?"

"Yes," he answered, a little surprised. "Why?"

"I don't know. It's only that I always think of Arkansas as being a rugged, hillbilly place overrun with razorback hawgs," I said, embarrassed.

He laughed easily. "Well, some parts of Arkansas are more civilized than others and Fort Smith is one of them." He turned toward the helmsman as Krause came into the conning tower and began to write in the quartermaster notebook. Suddenly my mouth went dry as a heavy air bubble seemed to scare the fish away. I looked quickly at the dial and saw that the indicator was pointing abaft the starboard beam.

"What is it?" Lieutenant Paine and Krause, who were keyed to the slightest out-of-the-ordinary movement, were flanking me.

"Somebody blew the head," I answered sheepishly. "For a minute there, I thought it was a torpedo tube firing a fish at us."

Both relaxed, laughing at me.

"This just ain't my day," I complained. Saliva began to flow into my mouth again and I slumped over, getting a mental picture of a torpedo heading *Wahoo's* way. What if it had been a real torpedo being fired? I began to dial, listening with more care to the heavier and odder sounds.

The air seemed heavier, denser, and foggier in the conning tower. An underwater quietness seemed to push against the sides of the bulkheads. Water condensed and dripped down the sides. Dullness of the monotony of fish sounds relaxed me into careless dialing again. Goose pimples popped out on my goose pimples as I caught the Wh-r-r-r of what sounded like a speeding torpedo at one-eight-oh degrees.

Lieutenant Paine and Krause were immediately at my side again. I threw on the switch to the loudspeaker wordlessly. Lieutenant Paine listened briefly and uttered the first curse word I had yet to hear him use. "Tell those damn fools in the after torpedo room to stop using the chainfalls without first requesting permission from the conning tower." Krause leaped to the intercompartment phone and almost immediately the noise stopped.

"I shoulda stood in bed," I moaned.

Lieutenant O'Kane came into the conning tower, and he and Lieutenant Paine conversed, looking obliquely at me and giggling like two schoolgirls. I could feel the blush rising on the back of my neck.

Krause started below and stopped with his head above the deck. "Would you like a cup of coffee, Yeo?"

"Yeah," I answered, "make it blonde and sweet."

Lieutenant O'Kane said, "Get me one,.too."

Krause, who had started down the ladder, turned back and answered, "I am not a mess attendant, sir, but I'll tell James that you want a cup of coffee."

I looked from Krause in stunned surprise to Lieutenant O'Kane.

O'Kane shrugged his shoulders and said, "Very well." Then he turned back to checking the ship's rough log.

In a few minutes, Willis James, from New Orleans, Louisiana, entered the conning tower with coffee for the executive officer, followed by Krause with a cup for me.

I just got settled good with the hot coffee when I picked up a *scrape, scrape, scrape* on the sound gear. In exasperation, I turned on the speaker again. Paine and O'Kane both listened. Lieutenant Paine shouted down the hatch into the control room, "See if someone is using a wire brush in the crew's messroom." There was a movement below, a brief wait, followed by the noise on the sonar gear stopping. Pappy Rau's voice came up through the hatch, "A messcook was scraping some corrosion off a pipe in the messhall."

"Well, tell him to knock it off," Lieutenant Paine ordered.

"Aye, aye, sir," replied Rau.

I hung my head in resignation to fate. My wrist watch had quit running the night before and so I looked at the clock. Only one hour and fifteen minutes of the watch had passed.

Even the fish began to show their hate for me by getting gradually louder. Then one fish, evidently much bigger than the rest, came closer. He kept getting louder with his *clopity, clopity, clopity* lazy movements. At first I pictured a shark and then a courting whale, and then I snapped out of it. This was not a whale. This was a large ship's screws I was listening to. Stuttering, I began to report, "Ship's screws bearing all around the compass, sir!" I threw the switch to the speaker.

Lieutenant Paine listened doubtfully. He up 'scoped, looked all the way around, and settled on an object. Presently he lowered the 'scope and moved over to the voice tube.

"Control, send a messenger to tell the captain that we have contacted a Japanese hospital ship."

He came back to the sonar and listened to the propeller pitch. The Captain arrived promptly, followed by Lieutenant Commander Morton and the quartermasters, who always seemed to get the word by mental telepathy.

Each officer took a turn at the periscope.

Captain Kennedy had been standing by thoughtfully. "Did anyone see any troops lounging about the decks?" When he received a chorus of negative replies, he said to Lieutenant Paine, "We will stay out of her way. Go deep until she gets away and don't let her see the periscope."

"Yes sir," Lieutenant Paine acknowledged.

When my relief released me from the duty, I went below and hit the sack. I had had enough of that day.

A week went by. *Wahoo* had been to sea six weeks and five days. The thought of leaving the patrol area for a safe harbor was beginning to be the most popular topic of the *Wahoo* crew's conversations.

I caught the morning 0800–1200 watch. It was a serene watch with only the fish objecting vociferously to *Wahoo's* trihourly up and downs and imitation of a porpoise. The Japanese had business elsewhere.

Ater was smoking a cigar when he relieved me on the noon watch.

"What gives with the cigar?" I asked politely. "Did somebody have a baby?"

"Yeah!" he answered contentedly. "About two thousand years ago."

I got it right away. "Christmas?" I could hardly spare the time to get below. In the crew's messroom, Phillips and Rowls were greeting each crew member with a "Merry Christmas and I hope you live to see a hundred New Years." They solicitously escorted me to a seat and waved me ceremoniously down. Rowls picked up my plate and carried it to Phillips who took it into the galley. He returned, handed it to Rowls, who set it down gently before me.

The plate was heaped with mashed potatoes, gravy, oyster dressing, white and dark turkey meat, and green peas. On the table were celery, olives, pickles, radishes, green onions, hard candy, and cigars.

Rowls said, "We have chocolate, tea, milk, lemonade or coffee. What would you prefer? And when you finish, we have frozen strawberries and whipped cream for dessert. Anything you don't see just ask for it."

My answer was muted by the amount of food a mouth can hold, but Rowls and Phillips seemed satisfied with the answer.

I was glad that I had no watch that afternoon. I turned in and slept soundly. When I rolled out for evening chow, we had pumpkin pie with whipped cream. I went to the office and scrounged around until I found some yellow obsolete forms. Coming back to the crew's messroom, I made a big ceremony out of giving them to Rowls.

"What's these for?" he asked.

"Those," I informed him majestically, "are re-enlistment forms. You can ship me over whenever you're ready."

Veder stuck his head in the door and hollered, "Hey, Yeo, the Exec wantstaseeya!"

"Okay," I answered, "I'll be right in."

I made my way forward noting that the tension had lessened and there were more smiles and easier banter among *Wahoo's* crew members. At the doorway to the wardroom, I paused and glanced in. Since *Wahoo* was still on area and submerged, all her officers were in the wardroom with the exception of the OOD and the Diving Officer.

Captain Kennedy sat at the head of the white linen-covered table, which held the same food that the enlisted men ate, the only difference being in the silverware, plates, cups, and saucers with the tiny blue anchor decorations on which it was served.

Lieutenant O'Kane was sitting next to the door with Lieutenant Commander Morton across the table from him. He turned at my entrance and said pleasantly, "Merry Christmas, Yeo."

I answered, "Merry Christmas, sir. You sent for me?"

He said, "Yes," while absently fishing for a paper on the shelf back of the Captain. "We're going to be leaving area and heading in tomorrow. You might as well get started on the roughs for the War Patrol Report."

I acknowledged this information with "Yes, sir." Then I took the plunge and asked casually, but ended up with a quiver in my voice, "Any dope where we're going, sir?"

The Executive Officer looked at the Captain and received an almost imperceptible nod. He said, "You can tell the crew that we are going to Brisbane, Australia."

I barely checked the impulse to shout.

Lieutenant O'Kane found the paper he was looking for and said, "Here's a little Christmas present for some of the boys. Backdate it to one December."

My eyes dropped down the list and I saw my own name at the bottom for second class. "Thank you, sir. I'll get right on it."

The officers laughed at my excitement, apparently enjoying vicariously the thrill that goes with an advancement in rating.

I backed out, turned slowly, and charged down the passageway into the crew's messroom.

"Hey, fellows, we're going to Brisbane, Australia. Hey, fellows . . ."

Hunter interrupted me skeptically, "What's this bum dope you're putting out?"

"It's true," I shouted triumphantly. "The Exec just told me. We're going to Brisbane, Australia."

For once I had outscooped the quartermasters and I was riding the crest of events. Hunter left the messhall apparently to check up on my scuttlebutt, but there was a group of shipmates wanting details and I was prepared to accommodate them. I was basking in the limelight and it felt good.

When my popularity began to wane, I orated to my spellbound audience, "In the future, please address me as Yeoman, Second Class, and if you come up through the chain of command, radioman, mess attendant, messcook, seaman second, seaman and yeoman third class, I may be able to do something personally for you."

This was greeted with jeers, and I noticed Buckley was jeering the loudest.

I broke out the list the Executive Officer had given me and read it Roman scroll fashion. "Through the authority vested in me by the XO and CO and the magic powers of BuPers, I hereby declare that Santa Claus has left some of you the following presents: Berg! Front and center! from Seaman Second to Fireman Third; Carter, Seaman to Radioman Third; Gerlacher, Seaman 'duce' to Seaman; Glinski, Fireman 'duce' to First; Johnson, K. B., Torpedoman Second to First; McSpadden, Torpedoman Third to Second; Muller, Machinist Second to First; Parks, Fire Controlman Third to Second; Terrell, Seaman Second to First; and Vidick, Electrician's Mate Third to Second."

At the last-mentioned name, Vidick reared his ugly visage above the masses and croaked in Mephistophelean tones. "Time to go on watch, Yeo. Pappy Rau says that, if the Exec is through with you, you had better relieve the sonar watch." The way he said it made me think of a movie Zombie reciting from memory.

I said cheerfully, "Tell Pappy I'll be right in." These were magic words that reversed his mechanism, and Vidick clanked back to the control room.

The next morning *Wahoo* left station. She left while submerged and so there was little difference in the crew's routine except that whatever was done was done with alacrity. That night on the mid-to-0400 lookout watch, I enjoyed being up on the surface even though the phosphorescent trail left by *Wahoo's* forward drive worried me. I wondered how far away it could be seen. *Wahoo* was not just idly charging batteries, she was headed for the "barn" with determination.

Near the end of the watch, Lieutenant O'Kane and Krause came onto the bridge. The Executive Officer had a sextant, and they stood around pointing at different stars before checking *Wahoo's* position. They went below, and I began thinking of the old sailing-boat days and wondering what their navigational problems must have been like. I thought of my yeoman duties. My routine had changed on leaving station. Now I was standing four-hour watches, sleeping four-hours, and putting in four more hours in the office, typing, retyping, and making additions or deletions to the War Patrol Report. In addition, the Junior Officers were inspecting *Wahoo* for deficiencies that would need correction during the coming overhaul period and making up long lists of repairs or alterations.

I had my minor clashes with them all. Each seemed to think that his work was more important than anything else. They would come barging up to the office door with "Yeo, get this out right away, or immediately, or if not sooner." I, very diplomatically, would smile, say, "Yessir," and when they were gone, would drop their work into the "pending" basket.

Two officers I did not fool. One was Lieutenant Henderson and the other was Lieutenant Paine. They took another tack with me. Either one would come up with his work hidden behind his back.

"How busy are you, Yeo?"

"I'm snowed under."

"You know, I wouldn't be a yeoman for anything. You sure get it piled on when the work starts."

"Well, you know how it is. War patrols and work lists and . . ."

"Yes, I certainly do. By the way, if you could find time to get this report out" (flourishing it in front of my face), "I'd sure appreciate it."

Thoroughly softened up, I would answer submissively, "Yessir, I'll get on it right away," and I would drop the work into the "action" basket. They even went a step further and offered a compliment when I finished the job. Oftentimes, I found myself working on a purely personal like or dislike basis, but I made certain that the War Patrol Report received first priority.

Everyone aboard *Wahoo* was mentally crossing off calendar dates with the knowledge that her EDA (estimated date of arrival) was December 31.

On the 30th, I came off the 1200–1600 watch, ate hurriedly and proceeded to Lieutenant O'Kane's stateroom. He was evidently waiting for me because he handed me the entire rough of the war patrol. "How long will it take you to do this in the smooth on mimeograph stencils?" he asked.

I did some mental arithmetic. Doing three or four an hour would take— "About six or eight hours, sir," I replied.

"When's your next watch?"

"Twenty to twenty-four hundred," I answered.

"Well, get on that patrol report and stick with it until you get it finished," he ordered. "I'm taking you off the watch list as of now."

"Thank you, sir," I replied and hurried to the office to get started.

I typed steadily without pausing, so interested in the final report and what I was doing that the time sped quickly by.

"Time to go on watch." Vidick was standing in the doorway.

"Oh, go to hell," I growled irritatedly. I looked up and saw the disbelief on Vidick's face before he disappeared into the control room.

Dammit, I thought, I better get in there and tell Pappy Rau I've been taken off the watch list.

I jumped up and ducked through the oval watertight door into the red-tinted darkness of the control room. Pappy and Vidick were standing by the gyrocompass. I walked over to them and opened my mouth to speak.

"Pappy . . ." I saw his fist ball up and start toward me with startling speed, getting larger as it came. Instinctively I leaned backward for the punch. Rau's fist traveled faster and a blinding flash of light blotted out everything for a second. I could feel myself being propelled backward into the air manifold. Sharp metal objects dug into my rib cage and pained me back into consciousness. Somehow I maintained my equilibrium and bounced back like a boxer off the ropes. My instinct was urging me to strike back. I stood crouched and waiting. Pappy just stood looking steadily at me with his dark brown eyes not showing any expression.

It came to me that Pappy was a tired man. The patrol with all its nerve-racking responsibilities as Chief of the Boat had finally come to a climax in that one resounding blow. I turned and made my way past O'Brien, who was watching me strangely, and on back to the washroom. There I stripped, turned on the cold shower, and stepped under it.

The water was chilling and in a little while I was shivering. I stepped out and dried off, located clean skivvies and dungarees, and dressed slowly. I decided that I would ignore the argument and go on watch. I would wait and see what Pappy's next move would be.

Returning to the control room, I said to Pappy, "Okay, I'm ready to go on watch. Which lookout?"

He said indifferently as though all his energy had been used up, "You don't have to go on watch. You've been scratched from the watch list."

I waited around uncertainly but Pappy wouldn't look at me. I went back to the office and began typing where I left off. A slight noise behind caused me to swing about sharply. Lieutenant O'Kane was standing where he could read over my shoulder.

"How are you coming?" he asked pleasantly.

"All right, about five more pages to go."

"That's fine," he said absently. "Did I hear a racket out here a few minutes ago?"

I looked him straight in the eye. "I don't know what it could of been, sir. I didn't hear anything."

He smiled at me strangely and went back to the wardroom. Someone coughed behind the CPO quarters' curtains. I returned to the typing of the War Patrol Report. When it was finished, I cleaned out the action and pending baskets. I wanted everything to be caught up when *Wahoo* arrived in Brisbane. I was looking forward to getting good and drunk. It was 2330 when I closed shop.

Passing through the control room, Pappy Rau stopped me. "Yeo, would you take the midwatch on the radar? We're short of radar watch standers and we have to be extra alert through here."

"Can I grab off a sandwich and a cup of coffee?" I asked.

"Sure can," Pappy replied quietly.

In a little while I was standing in front of the radar screen watching the "grass" flicker up and down, waiting for a "pip" to show.

About 0300 I reported a radar contact to Ensign Misch on the bridge. It turned out to be land and was no surprise to him for he had been expecting the report.

At 0400 I was relieved of the radar watch by Tyler, Ralph O., from Oelwein, Iowa.

I stopped in the crew's messroom, which was crowded with men for that hour of the morning who were too excited to sleep anyway. One of the mess tables was covered with night rations, and there was a steaming pot of soup on the galley range. A large can of Vienna wieners was open and only one or two were gone. I sat down and finished them off.

"Station the maneuvering watch, station the maneuvering watch," the loudspeaker commanded. I went out into the control room and got a submarine jacket before I climbed to the bridge. Dawn had broken and I could see the dark outlines of land and trees on the beach. The smell of vegetation was strong in the air. It was an early morning odor that released a tingling sensation into my blood stream and crowded out any thought of being sleepy that I might have had. I plugged into the bridge telephone talker's circuit and stood with both hands in my pocket just looking. A plane flew in low and zoomed over us. Simmonetti was quick to flash it a recognition signal on the bridge blinker.

I fell to lucubrating about the Japanese submarine we had sunk. She had been riding on the surface into a friendly harbor. Below decks the Japanese sailors must have been planning their liberties just as I knew the *Wahoo* crew were. I looked apprehensively toward the open sea but could see nothing that looked hostile. I wished we were safely in.

Soon *Wahoo* was turning into a wide expanse of water between funny lace-foliaged trees. The water here was a muddy brown that contrasted with the green and blue of the ocean. Captain Kennedy, Lieutenant Commander Morton, and Lieutenant O'Kane came onto the bridge. *Wahoo* penetrated upstream a short distance and met a tugboat coming bow on. Looking down on deck, I saw Pappy Rau, Carr, and several others exercising by walking up and down. The word for "Stations for coming into port" had been passed a few minutes earlier.

The tugboat swung into a half circle when abreast of *Wahoo* and rode upstream alongside. A sailor on the tug tossed Wach, Ludwig J., from Littleport, Iowa, a line and he looped the eye over a cleat. A slight civilian wearing a bowler hat and carrying an umbrella leaped across to *Wahoo* and came quickly up to the bridge. Wach threw off the line and the tug slewed away but stayed within hailing distance of *Wahoo*.

Captain Kennedy met the Harbor Pilot as he came onto the cigarette deck. They introduced themselves and the Captain then introduced him to the other officers. I could catch their conversations but the pilot's name eluded me.

"I'll take over now, Captain, if you wish?"

"Wouldn't you like some breakfast first? Some ham or bacon and eggs?"

"Thank you, Captain, but I've had my breakfast."

"Would you like the mess attendant to bring you some tea?"

"No tea, but I would like some coffee. Thank you."

"Very well, then you're ready to take the conn?"

"Yessir, I am."

"All right, I'm going below to arrange some details. I'll send the mess attendant right up. Dudley, take over until I get back."

Lieutenant Commander Morton replied, "Aye, aye, Captain."

"Thank you, Captain," the pilot answered, and then to the helmsman, "What course are you steering?" He listened to Simmonetti's reply as the Captain followed by Lieutenant O'Kane went below. He nodded his head. "Steer for the church steeple up ahead until we come abreast of the white house at the bend in the river. I'll have some further instructions for you at that time."

"Aye, aye, sir," from Simmonetti.

Lieutenant Commander Morton was watching every detail with evident amusement.

"Are they rationing you people very much?" he asked the pilot.

"Oh, yes, but we're not suffering." The pilot's sharp eyes were darting in every direction. "Petrol is bad, chocolate and silk stockings are hard to get, but I guess I miss American cigarettes more than anything."

"Have you piloted many submarines into Brisbane before?" Morton asked.

"Oh, yes, it's an old story with me. Since the war started I've been piloting all sorts of odd craft up the river."

Jayson, Juan O., Filipino Mess Attendant from Catman, Cebu, called up from below, "Permission, please, to enter on bridge, sir?"

Morton answered, "Permission granted. Come on up." He reached through the hatch and took the tray that held the pilot's coffee. "When you go back down, Jayson, look in my locker and bring up a couple cartons of cigarettes, will you?"

"Yessir." Jayson ducked below.

Lieutenant Commander Morton said to the pilot, "It's rather murky weather here today, isn't it?"

"No. This is normal for this time of the year. It's summer down here, you know."

Someone was trying to get my attention on the deck below. I looked over the side and saw Bair.

"What's the name of this river, Yeo?"

"Wait a minute."

"Mr. Morton, what's the name of this here river?"

"The Brisbane River."

I turned back to Bair. "The Brisbane."

"Oh!" He hurried off.

"Sir, we've reached the white house on the bank," Simmonetti piped up.

"All right, come left slowly until you are lined up with a flagpole you will see above the trees."

"Aye, aye, sir."

Wahoo began to turn slowly with the broad curve in the stream. The trees on the left bank seemingly remained stationary, while the trees on the right bank rotated faster. *Wahoo* negotiated the turn handsomely and then straightened out in a line with a tall flagstaff, bearing the British flag, rising above the trees.

A loud shout went up from *Wahoo's* crew standing on deck. Girl whistles went trilling out and I rushed to the portside of the ship. A rectangular brick and cement wall with a wire fence around it jutted into the river. On the bank stood two beautifully shaped Australian girls in bathing suits waving at us. I waved back excitedly. In the swimming pool were several more rubber-capped beauties. Men began popping out of the deck hatches so fast I wondered if anyone was left on watch below. I became aware of "Mush" Morton standing alongside me laughing uproariously.

The pilot came over and said, "The girlies are cute, aren't they?" He added almost sadly, "There aren't many of the Aussie lads around—most of them are off to the war in North Africa."

Wahoo turned and twisted upstream for what seemed a long distance, passing many more river-adapted swimming pools and their water nymph greeters. There could be no doubting that Brisbane contained all the elements of a sailor's paradise.

Wahoo came around a curve and ahead of her spanning the river was a steel bridge. On the right bank was Brisbane proper. The sun came out briefly to show us how colorfully the tropical green of the trees could set off the dazzling white houses and their red roofs. There were clustered in a group several many-storied buildings and the church that belonged to the spire that had helped guide us in.

We pulled in past the *U.S.S. Fulton*, submarine tender, and toward the dock. Getting in close, I could hear the band playing the "Beer Barrel Polka," and then they shifted to another lively tune I had not heard before. Someone on the beach began singing, "Bless 'em all, bless 'em all, the young and the short and the tall . . ."

Several heaving lines were tossed us and *Wahoo's* bowline snaked over. She was soon moored securely to the dock. The gangway was pushed across and an avalanche of people came on board. "Secure the maneuvering watch" was the word I had been waiting for since 0400 that morning and here it was nearly noon. I put away the battle phones and went on deck. It was a peculiar sensation. My legs still wanted to roll with the ship.

There was a box of Washington Delicious apples open. I chose one and began to munch on it. Rowls was attaching a line around an ice-cream container in preparation for lowering it down the after battery hatch. Half of the *Wahoo* crew were smothering an exasperated mail clerk from the *Fulton.*

The Executive Officer found me watching them. "There you are, Yeo. Howsabout running over to the *Fulton* and arranging for our reservations at the hotel and getting transportation for us?"

I said, "Yes, sir," and went over the gangway and up the dock. Strange feeling to walk on solid ground again. My ears still rang from the roar of *Wahoo's* diesel engines. Part of the feeling, I thought, must spring from the fact that I am safe from danger—at least for two weeks to come. But I was so keyed up inside that I could hardly realize this sudden change from depth charging to peaceful surroundings. I would have to unravel slowly.

On my return, I sought out Lieutenant O'Kane topside and explained that our reservations were made at the Hotel Canberra and that a Navy bus would be alongside the dock in forty-five minutes.

"Good," he said, "I'll pass the word and you'd better hurry below and get paid. The Disbursing Officer from the *Fulton* is on board."

I went below decks into the crew's messroom and caught the paymaster before he locked his money satchel. He paid me in Australian pounds. I did not know anything about the money exchange, but I certainly had a handful of crisp brown-and-green ten and five pound notes.

Stuffing the money into my wallet, I pushed into the after battery sleeping compartment. It was filled with *Wahoo's* sailors getting ready to go ashore. I yanked off my dirty mattress cover and filled it with sweat-stained clothes from my locker. I put on clean whites, a pressed neckerchief, and a clean hat. I had only to locate my mail and I was ready to go.

I pushed shipmates aside and got pushed good-naturedly aside on my way to the office. I kept saying, "Sorry, narrow passageway."

By my typewriter was a stack of personal mail. I looked quickly through it. Three letters from Mom, Mrs. Pearl Wynn, Laredo, Texas; one from Aunt Lucy Deskin, Henryetta, Oklahoma; two from a high school girl friend, Anna Zarbock, Ordway, Colorado; and over thirty letters from Marie Henry, the petite telephone operator in Los Angeles, California. There was a postcard from the Los Angeles City Civil Service Commission telling me that I had passed their clerk-typist test and was number eleven on their list. Would I please report to the city public library for an interview for a job on Thursday at 3 p.m.?

I grabbed up a handful of blank envelopes and a half ream of onionskin paper with the *Wahoo* letterhead, wrapped a couple of rubber bands about the whole bundle, and dropped it into the mattress cover with the soiled linen. I was retying a knot in the end of the cover, getting ready to rush topside, when Lieutenant O'Kane bustled up to me. He seemed to be busy everywhere this day.

"Hold everything, Yeo. You're staying aboard ship for a while," he commanded.

I turned to him in surprise. What had I done now?

"There's going to be a Change of Command, and you'll be needed to do the correspondence," he explained.

I felt relieved and at the same time resentful. Did the Executive Officer know that I had not had any sleep for over thirty hours? I pushed the makeshift mattress-cover bag into the empty chiefs' quarters and took off my hat and neckerchief by way of reply.

"Have you ever done a Change of Command before?" he asked.

"No, sir, but the procedure is outlined in *CinCPac Instructions*, sir."

"Good, let me have the instructions."

I handed them to him and he went back to his stateroom. I pulled out a ruled pad and jotted down from recollection a letter from the CO to CinCPac, via the new CO, with carbon copies to the Squadron Commander and ComSubPac.

I doodled on the edges, thinking the text would not concern me, since that would be originated by Captain Kennedy and the endorsement by Lieutenant Commander Morton. Then I scribbled in a column. Inventories: registered publications, commissary, medical, ordnance, electronic. Wow! I thought, it will be after midnight before we get all this accomplished.

I was chewing on the end of the pencil and heard someone in the passageway behind me. I turned around and saw Ware, Norman C., Electrician First, from Jay, Florida, going by in liberty whites with a blue duffel bag in hand and a Bible under his arm. He smiled at me and said, "Better hurry, Yeo, the bus is about to leave."

"Sorry," I answered enviously, "but I've got work to do."

I looked after his retreating form and saw O'Brien approaching with a regulation coffee cup in hand. He came up, his eyes sparkling, and asked, "Wouldja like a Coke, *Forest?*"

A faint tentacle of grain alcohol tantalized the hairs in my nose. I replied eagerly, "I sure would," and after a quick gulp, "where did you get the Coke?"

He laughed wisely. "When you have been in the Navy as long as I have, you'll learn these things, *Forest*."

"Well, *Forest*," I mimicked, "what are you doing aboard?"

"There's a skeleton crew on board until the relief crew takes over at 1600."

I saw an opportunity. "I'm going to be busy with a Change of Command this afternoon. Morton is taking over. Do you think you can keep me supplied with Coke?"

He grinned and said, "Every half-hour on the half-hour." He hurried aft to tell the others that there was going to be a Change of Command.

At a snail's pace, the afternoon wore along. Work came in spasmodically. Captain Kennedy, Lieutenant Commander Morton, and Lieutenant O'Kane left the ship. Floating down the passageway from the wardroom came the lilting strains of "Artists' Life." It was soothing music to work by. Once I had to go to the wardroom to get a technicality straightened out. Lieutenant Paine was sitting at the table with numerous letters from home scattered about. A photograph of his wife and children was propped up before him and he was busily writing. The recording came to an end and he brought the needle back to the outer part of the revolving disk. "Artists' Life" began to reproduce itself. He explained the technical point to me and I returned to the office.

Five and a half Cokes later, the job as far as I was concerned ended. I leaned back in the office chair, smoking a cigarette and slowly sipping the Coca-Cola. It was just a matter of signatures until *Wahoo* would have a new master.

The officers returned down the forward torpedo escape hatch, and I could hear them shuffling around and talking indistinctly with an occasional outburst of laughing in the wardroom. In a few moments, Captain Kennedy and Lieutenant Commander Morton moved nearer to the Commanding Officer's stateroom.

I heard Lieutenant Commander Kennedy say, "Well, Dudley, she is all yours. Take good care of yourself and the ship and—the best of hunting."

Morton replied, "We will do our best. Good luck on your new assignment."

The smell of good leather reached me, and then Jayson came into view carrying several bulging pieces of tan leather luggage with gold initials MGK on them. He was followed by Lieutenant Commander Kennedy and Captain Morton. Kennedy stopped at the door and I stood up.

"It's been swell serving under you, sir," I quickly uttered. "I hope I have the pleasure of being with you again someday, sir."

He shook my hand, swallowed heavily, and said, "Thank you." Then he and Captain Morton were gone topside.

I sat down to wait for further developments. I was not certain that my duties were finished. O'Brien came in with another Coke. "This will have to be the last one," he cautioned. "I've got to start getting ready to go to the hotel."

"That's okay," I answered. "Maybe I will be able to leave with you. I'm through here now and just waiting for Morton to come back. I did a good job. It ought to tickle O'Kane to pieces. You know you can't hardly tell I been drinking now, can you? You know sum'en else? I ain't had no sleep since day before yesterday . . ."

Captain Morton's big form pushed through the hatch. He was grinning a great big happy grin.

"O'Brien," he ordered, "I've got a job for you. I want you to start in the forward torpedo room and work aft pulling down every Goddam silhouette you can find."

With a whoop of joy, O'Brien darted up the passageway.

"Yeo," the Captain added, "follow me."

We went to his stateroom where he dug around in a much-traveled valise. When he straightened up, he had a stack of glossy pictures of dancing girls, bathing beauties, movie stars and starlets, and cheesecake in every position.

"Got these at a Hollywood studio," he explained. "I thought it might be just the thing to bring along on a war patrol. Give these to somebody and have them go through and stick them up in every compartment."

"Aye, aye, sir!" I gasped. "It shall be done."

I caught Allen, James H., from Canton, Ohio, and Anders, Floyd, from Miami, Florida, both Seamen Second, doing nothing and gave them the happy job. They were only too glad to carry out the new Captain's first orders aboard the *U.S.S. Wahoo*.

When I returned to the office, Captain Morton was waiting for me. "Yeo, do you keep a Captain's Mast Book?"

I answered, "Yes sir."

"Don't deep-six it," he said, "but somehow get it lost while I am Skipper. We won't be needing it on my boat."

I stared at him popeyed.

Lieutenant O'Kane came up. "If you're finished here you can go to the hotel, Yeo," he announced.

I was free of *Wahoo*, physically at least, for two whole wonderful weeks. When I crossed her gangway, I threw her a kiss and promised, "Wait right here for me, sweetheart, I'll be back." She seemed to bobble up and down in the water to let me know that she understood every word I had said.

Chapter 5

Darkness had come upon Brisbane, and whether it was from wartime restrictions or a natural inclination of the Australians to economize, there were no lights along the pier. I felt my way along the road toward the red glow of a cigarette that glowed brightly and alternately like a beacon in the distance. Just before I came up with it, it streaked to the earth and went out suddenly. In the background, the clouds were illuminated by city lights. I groped on until a figure darker than the surroundings materialized.

"Taxi, Matey?" it invited.

I answered quickly, "You bet."

A car door squeaked open and a hand at my elbow helped me in. Another door opened and slammed shut. There was a fumbling around and lights under a dashboard came on, lighting up the front seat. The motor began to turn over, and I began to shake like an olive in a cocktail shaker. A model T Ford would have cringed in envy. Increased volume of the chugging informed me that the motor was racing. Finally the contraption got up enough steam to overcome its inertia and we began to move. Headlights flashed on and I could see the road ahead, lumber stacked on the right, Navy Yard paraphernalia on the left. They moved by in slow motion.

The taxicab driver turned halfway around so he could talk to me and see to drive, too, by looking around occasionally. I could see he wore an old-fashioned cap with visor.

"*Quo vadis?*" he asked brightly.

"Quo whatis?" I answered, puzzled.

"That means whither goest thou?" he explained.

"Oh," I replied weakly, "the Canberra Hotel."

"You must be off that sub came in today."

"Yes," I answered noncommittally.

"Howdya feel after being to sea so long?"

"Lugubrious," I answered, seeing my opportunity.

"What does that mean, Matey?"

"It means I'm thirsty and need a drink," I informed him lugubriously. "It's just the opposite to salubrious—the way I'm going to feel after I have a drink."

He turned back to driving and there was a long silence. The car came out on a lighted street and I could see houses on both sides.

"I was in World War I," he said over his shoulder.

Suddenly I knew why he was so loquacious. He wanted to feel by association that he had an important part in this war. He wanted to be a fighting man again. I said, "We sank a Japanese submarine, Matey, you should have been there."

He twisted on his seat again. "I hang around the Canberra a lot. If you need a taxi, look for me."

I sniffed. "Is something on fire? I smell wood smoke."

"It's the charcoal burner on behind," he answered. "Since petrol is rationed we operate on charcoal."

I looked over my shoulder and saw a smokestack running up the back. "My Gawd," I commented, "you Aussies do have ingenuity."

"We manage," was his answer as he pulled to the curb in front of a dark unimposing building. I could see by the light shining through the open doors that it was a hotel.

I set my soiled mattress-cover sea bag on the sidewalk and queried, "How much?"

He quoted a price in shillings or pence, which had no meaning for me.

I extracted a five pound note from my jumper pocket and looked him in the eye as I said, "I don't know your way of counting money. You'll have to make the change for me."

He took the bill and started making change. "You don't have to worry about an Australian short-changing you," he answered. "Everybody's honest down here." He placed four one pound notes and some silver in my palm.

I was skeptical but it looked like more than the amount of change I would have received from a five dollar bill. So I took what looked close to being a fifty-cent piece and tipped him. He seemed satisfied.

"Happy New Year," he called after me. I stopped and looked back. Of a sudden there was a rapport between us. I smiled and gave him a smart salute.

Inside the hotel, which was decorated in a late 1800 or early 1900 fashion, I sauntered over to the desk clerk. He was the typically bored, neatly dressed clerk that is encountered the world over. I wrote my name in the hotel register and received a key to a room on the fourth floor. He looked disdainfully but with no indication of surprise at my traveling bag.

The elevator moved so slowly that I watched a reader, half-hidden in a large leather chair, glance through a page of his paper and turn to the next page before my head was above the first floor. The lady elevator operator was fat and uninteresting. I turned to a placard that read: "This is a temperance hotel. Liquor and loose ladies are forbidden in the rooms. You will find a Gideon Bible in each room. Please . . ." I lost all interest in reading further.

Eventually the elevator arrived at the fourth floor and I got out with relief. I made a mental note to use the stairway.

My room was directly across from the elevator and I opened the door, tossed the key on the dresser and my linen in a corner. Then I took off my clothes and lay down on top of the covers, realizing for the first time how hot and sultry the air was.

I was tired and my nerves screamed for sleep. I lay in bed for a long time but drowsiness would not come. I tried to will myself to sleep. I'm getting sleepier and sleepier. I'm tired and I'm going to sleep. Finally I took to tossing. Whether I was too tired to sleep or the strangeness of a hotel bed interfered, the fact remained that I was not going to go to sleep. Below me and outside, sounds of a railroad engine bumping cars around began to penetrate and hold my consciousness. A passenger train rattled past, adding its shrill whistles to the noise. Jumping up, I turned on the light and went to the window. It was wide open and I looked down on a large railway yard. I watched the activity below for several seconds. It was too hot to close the window. Strolling back to the door, I read again the temperance poster displayed there also. Then I dug around in the mattress cover until I found the letters from home. I looked at them listlessly without opening them and finally tossed them on the dresser. Then, on an impulse, I dressed and went out the door.

O'Brien came out of the elevator bearing a whole armload of bottles wrapped in newspapers.

"Need some help?" I offered readily.

"Yeah," he answered, handing over part of his load. I followed him down the passageway to his room. I opened the door for him and we went in. He pointed to the dresser drawers and I opened them to put the bottles in. Each drawer was filled, so I set them on top. I picked one bottle at random, pulled the newsprint off, and it turned out to be a good gin.

We sat down with our glasses and kicked our shoes off.

"Here's to the *Wahoo* and 'Mush' Morton," O'Brien said.

"Here's to Griggs and his water-soaked hat," I offered next.

"Here's to the Jap submarine."

"Here's to . . ."

Someone knocked on the door. I opened it. It turned out to be Deaton, Lynwood N., from Liberty, North Carolina.

"I was next door," he said, "and . . ."

Someone else came up behind him. It was Davison. Soon the room was filled with *Wahoo* sailors.

Around midnight I went back to my room. I lay down and said, "Thank you, dear Lord, for pulling us through safely," and had no trouble at all going to sleep.

It was noon when I awoke. I showered, put on clean whites, and stuffed a couple of packs of cigarettes into my trouser pockets. Then I took the elevator down, fretting at its slow journey but not trusting my sea legs on the stairs yet. I found a restaurant off the hotel lobby that specialized in short orders. The menu did not look promising, so I played it safe by ordering a half-dozen soft-boiled eggs. Halfway through the eggs and my third cup of coffee, I felt life beginning to tingle in my bones again, and the balloon that I called my head seemed to deflate to normal size again. The prospect of adventuring in Brisbane increased by the mouthful.

Wahoo's sailors seemed to have scattered to the perimeter of the city or else they were enjoying the solitude of their rooms. Through the door I saw one or two straggle by. In the lobby, Carter found the leather chair and settled down to read a morning paper.

Breakfast finished, I strolled out on the street, stretched, looked up and down, and decided that I would live for the moment. I would let fate steer me into whatever situation her caprice might devise. Across the street, I saw a tailor shop with American Naval rating badges on display in the windows. I jaywalked across and while I waited had a second-class yeoman's "crow" sewed on.

Out on the street again, I stood at the curb waiting for the spirit to move me. I saw a shoeshine stand on the hotel side of the street and the spirit moved me. I jaywalked back and climbed up on one of the high seats. The shoeshine boy was not the talkative type, so I picked up a newspaper from an empty seat next to me and scanned it desultorily. "Defenders of Stalingrad holding off the entire German Army." Of more interest to me was, "Landing of United States and British Troops at Casablanca, Algiers, and Oran."

There was a disturbance and I looked up to see a U. S. Marine getting settled in the empty chair. I turned my attention back to the paper and noticed that "U. S. Army General, Dwight D. Eisenhower, was Commander in Chief of the landing forces." Another item said briefly that the Allies had thousands of planes over Europe and we were getting hundreds of them shot down each month. The war news was beginning to deaden my spirits. To hell with the war, I thought, I don't have to worry about it for two solid weeks. To hell with it.

Irritably I offered the paper to the Marine. "Here," I said, "want to find out how the war's going?"

He refused by shaking his head. Another bootblack was working on his shoes. The Marine's lack of emotion aroused my interest. I looked at him closer. He was young with tired haunted eyes. His was the spirit of an old man in a teen-ager's body. He was not like the proud, defiant, swashbuckling, fabricating Marines I had known before. There was a great humility about him—an air of stunned apathy.

I pulled from my jumper pocket a cigar I had been saving from the Christmas mess and I started taking off the cellophane wrapper. Turning to the Marine, I said, "Would you like a cigar?"

He just shook his head again.

I said, conversationally, "Been in Brisbane long?"

He looked at me dumbly before answering, "No, I've just been pulled out of Guadalcanal."

I said sympathetically, "Rough, huh?"

It was the wrong thing to say. He just ducked his head and did not answer me.

The bootblack was beginning to snap his cloth on the glossy front of my shoes. I had a mental struggle trying to think of something to keep the conversation going.

"Do you know where there is a jeweler around here? I think my wrist watch is magnetized."

He looked at my watch and showed some interest. "The only one I know is at the PX. That's a real nice watch." He looked at the submarine insignia on my forearm. "What's that mean?"

"It means I'm a qualified submariner," I replied, eager to keep him talking.

"You wouldn't be off that submarine that sank the Jap submarine, would you?"

"I sure am. The *U.S.S. Wahoo*. We got that Jap sub off Buna airfield."

His eyes lighted up. "I'll bet you sunk Oscar."

"Who?"

"Oscar. He's the Jap submarine that raised hell with us at night. He would come in, fire flares over our positions, and then drop shellfire on our foxholes. We couldn't get any sleep. It's awful laying there having shells drop everywhere around you and nothing to shoot back at."

"I hope it was Oscar. Up till now I've been feeling sorry for those Jap sailors. If it was Oscar, I'm glad." I gave the Marine all the details. By now we were both sure it was Oscar.

"Let me buy you a drink," the Marine said.

I was stunned by the request. I had never had a Marine buy me a drink in my entire Navy career.

"Okay," I answered, "on one condition. Howsabout you keeping this wrist watch? It's no good to me and I don't want to be bothered with hunting up a jeweler."

He looked at me as though he did not believe me.

"Take it," I insisted, handing him the watch.

He jumped down from the chair. "Come on, let's go get that drink."

"Lead on, kindly fate," I concurred.

I fell into step with him and we marched to a pub that he had noticed earlier. Surprisingly enough, it was crowded with civilians and only a few servicemen. A fog of tobacco smoke made a ceiling about a foot above our heads. The room resounded with cacophonous utterances. There were no seats, and everyone stood elbowing his neighbor, while the sawdust floor caught the beer drippings and saturated the atmosphere with barley and alcohol fumes. A wave of oncoming parch-throated patrons surrounded us, forcing us back into the middle of the room. I wondered whether someone was drinking my beer.

"I wouldn't be on a submarine for anything," the Marine shouted.

"It's better'n being in them damn foxholes with bullets whizzin' all around and nothing but K or C rations to eat," I shouted back.

"But I can't swim," the Marine answered, illogically.

"Don't forget," I hollered back, "there's no purple hearts in the sub Navy. You either come out whole or not at all. There's damn little chance of going through life all shot full of holes."

Someone came between us. I lost sight of the Marine, and not being able to find him or make my way to the bar, I took the easy course of resistance and worked my way to the outside. It had been cloudy before. Now it was sticky hot as well and I longed for a cool place to sit down.

I looked around for the church steeple, oriented myself with it, and steered for the Canberra Hotel. In a block or two I came across a line of people waiting at a ticket window for a theater to open its doors.

This is fate, I thought. Besides, it will be cool inside. I fell in at the rear of the line. Almost immediately the line started moving. I had not moved far when a musical feminine voice behind me asked, "What time do you have, Yank?"

I glanced at my wrist before I realized that I did not have the time. Turning while I was still looking down, I said, "Sorry, I don . . ." A pair of scuffed worn shoes came into view. Above the shoes were neatly turned ankles and above those a pair of well-molded bare calves. My eyes moved upward following the curves. They widened at the hips and almost crossed at the waist. When I finally reached her eyes, I found them to be a scintillating hazel and she was wearing a very provocative smile. I noticed a halo of red hair and just enough freckles to make her attractive. She laughed, then, at my facial expression and I could see she had beautiful even teeth. From what I had observed of Australian girls, so far, this was a rarity.

My voice came back to me and I said, "It's time that you and I became better acquainted. May I buy you a ticket to the movie?"

Someone behind said, "Move along, Yank."

We moved up and the girl behind said, "If you want to, Yank, it's all right with me."

At the ticket window I ordered, "Two tickets, please." Then I took the girl by the elbow and escorted her inside. We were directed by the usherette to seats halfway to the screen. The show had not started yet and the auditorium was lighted, so we sat talking. I quickly learned that her name was Maureen O'Casey and that she was a widow.

A candy butcher came down the aisle shouting, "Chocolate bars. Get your chocolate bars before the cinema begins."

Maureen grabbed my arm with both hands. "Oh, Yank! Buy me a chocolate bar. It's been ages since I've had one."

I raised my hands and by sign language let the man know I wanted six. He passed them over, made change for a pound note, and went on soliciting customers.

Maureen plopped five of them into her purse after offering me one, which I refused. "I hardly ever eat the stuff."

She said dreamily, "Six whole chocolate bars! You know, Yank, I haven't had a chocolate bar since the war began. They've been rationed, you know."

I looked at her, surprised at her enthusiasm, knowing that it was sincere. She snuggled up to me while she nibbled daintily on a bar. The warmth of her body and the feminine fragrance of her did something to me. My heart began to beat faster and I could feel a change in my blood pressure. I hoped she could not feel my body trembling. I sat quietly without moving, enjoying her nearness.

It was almost a relief when the lights dimmed and music came from the speakers playing "God Save the King." I stood up, as did everybody in the theater, and saluted the British flag on the screen. This was followed by "The Star-Spangled Banner" and the American flag. Then we sat down again, straight in our seats, and the movie began.

Whatever the movie was about, I had lost interest in it. When it finished, I said, "Howsabout a bite to eat? Steer me to a good restaurant, will you? I'm hungry."

The restaurant turned out to be three blocks away. As we walked I found out that Maureen was an easy girl to talk to. Everything was natural about her, there was no false pretense. We passed a window display of women's shoes. She paused and stared at them wistfully. On an impulse I blurted out, "Let me buy you a pair, Maureen."

She said, "I wish you could, Jim, but I don't have any shoe coupons."

"Why not?" I asked, bluntly.

She looked at me, embarrassed. "I've been giving my coupons to the neighbors who have children. They need them more than I."

I said gruffly, "Come on, let's go eat."

The restaurant turned out to be on the same conservative level as the Canberra Hotel. A hazy picture of long white tablecloths, potted palms, a quiet atmosphere with only two or three tables occupied, and old-fashioned ceiling fans that turned lazily to give the false impression that the air was being cooled.

When the waitress came to take our order, she turned out to be a verbal menu as well. Maureen ordered the roast beef dinner and I did the same, on the theory that the local citizens would know which meal was the best. While we waited, Maureen asked, "Are the restaurants in America like this, Jim?"

I looked around and nodded my head. "Just about. The only difference I can see is that in the States we have printed menus to choose from and there are napkins at the plates."

She began a tinkling laugh that seemed incongruous to the staid interior of the place. Patrons looked up from their meals, annoyed at such sacrilege.

Frowning, I said, "What's wrong with that? In fact, I think I'll ask the waitress for some napkins."

Maureen broke into another outburst of laughing. "Oh, no! Jim, that will never do."

Puzzled, I asked huffily, "And why not?"

"Because," she explained, quieting down, "the word napkin in Australia does not have the same meaning here that it does in the States. The waitress would be insulted."

I thought about that for a minute. Then I blushed and said lamely, "Well, anyway, the restaurants are about the same."

After a long wait and slow service, we finished the meal. I lit up a cigarette without thinking to offer her one. She looked at it hungrily. "Do you smoke?" I asked.

"Oh, yes! But I didn't want to ask you for one."

"I'm sorry," I said, "some days I'm a little brighter than others. What would you like to do now?"

"I haven't been to a dance in ages. Would you take me?"

I said, "Sure thing, but you'll have to lead the way. I'm a stranger in these here parts. Shall I call a taxi?"

"Oh, no, the dance hall is only twelve or fourteen blocks from here. We'll walk."

"What?" I roared, "a sailor walking when he can ride?"

"Yes," she said firmly, "we will walk." And walk we did.

The dance hall was crowded. Most of the men were in uniform and were greatly outnumbered by women. I soon found out that the competition meant nothing to Maureen. She was a popular girl and much in demand. We made a pact in which I got all the waltzes and fox trots, and the general assembly lined up for the jitterbugging. She never missed a dance.

I found a canteen in the corner that sold American canned beer and between dances I could be found there. I would see Maureen being swung out at arm's length and whirled about with spinning dress exposing her dimpled knees. When a waltz or fox trot started up, she would come running, with shining eyes, to claim me. I was asked to dance by some of the Australian female stags, but my answer was always the same, "Sorry, but I don't jitterbug."

At the intermission, a movie screen was let down at one end of the hall. Maureen had picked up a newspaper somewhere, and we sat in the center of the floor with others drinking beer. The orchestra played "The Wizard of Oz" and the lyrics were flashed on the screen. Everybody joined in singing. I felt rather foolish but gradually a spirit of unity came over the group and I sang as freely and loudly as anyone present. The orchestra went through "Give Me One Dozen Roses," "Whistle While You Work," "Somewhere Over the Rainbow," "Bless 'em All," and "Lili Marlene." They would play them over when the applause was loud enough. Then we were all dancing again.

The dance ended at midnight with "God Save the King," which, of course, was saluted instead of danced to. We left the hall with the milling crowd.

I said, "Take you home in a taxi?"

She answered, "No, it's too wonderful a night to be riding. Let's walk."

I could see nothing wonderful about the hot, humid, cloudy night, but my companion made the walk seem worthwhile, so we walked.

We walked and talked until we came to a plaza filled with magnolia and banyan trees. An Australian soldier came out of one of the walks with a long-necked bottle under each arm, singing loudly. He stopped short in front of Maureen and they both stared at each other in surprise. He turned to me and handed me the bottles, and Maureen and he went into a tight embrace with kisses and words of endearment.

I sighed, sat down on a near-by bench, and uncorked one of the bottles. It was excellent Australian beer, reminding me of some of the San Diego prohibition beer that I had drunk in the past.

They just stood there embracing and kissing and talking in an excited Australian vernacular that was entirely strange to me. Finally something that Maureen said aroused my curiosity.·

I said, "What do you mean by your 'soul turned over,' Maureen?"

They both turned to me, apparently startled by my presence.

"Oh," she laughed, "we were talking about a dance we both attended three years ago. We went to school together."

The soldier turned to me, all friendliness. "Have a drink of beer, Yank."

"I have," I answered dryly, "and very good beer it is, too."

They both looked at each other and laughed merrily.

"What gives with this 'soul turned over' business?" I inquired again, politely.

"A fight started at the dance," she explained patiently, "and I was right in the middle of it. It means I was scared nearly out of my wits."

The soldier sat down beside me and threw an arm about my shoulder. Maureen sat on the other side and we passed the bottle around.

They began to speak in English, so that I could understand them. His name turned out to be Harry something or other. Maureen explained to him that I was a submariner. He did not seem impressed. I asked him if he had seen any fighting yet.

"A little," he answered, "I'm back on furlough from Africa."

Question by question and little by little his story came out. When his battalion had landed, there were not enough guns to go around. They had marched across the desert in long, thin lines, the front line carrying all the weapons. Those without guns, but carrying ammunition, followed behind in waves. They sang "The Wizard of Oz" and kept going. When a front-line Aussie fell, a second-line Aussie would pick up his gun and carry on. They captured Tobruk and held it against the German African Army.

He gave his story so simply and modestly that I was sure he was unaware of how heroic it sounded.

I said pointedly to Maureen, "We can't stay here all night drinking up Harry's beer."

She jumped up saying, "Of course not. Harry, Jim and I will be going along now. Do look me up before you go back."

He grinned, tucked the full bottle under his arm again and went striding off. His voice came singing back, "Wonderful, wonderful Wizard of Oz." We looked after him—trousers tucked into combat boots and large sombrero-type hat with the ostrich feather—vanishing into the poorly lighted gloom of the street. I reached down and took Maureen's hand and squeezed it.

We turned and walked hand in hand the other way. It was quite a distance to the little bungalow where Maureen lived. She said, "Come on in for a drink."

The living room was comfortably furnished, and I sank into a large upholstered chair with a sigh, thinking of the difference between this and the hotel room. She busied herself in the kitchen, making tinkling sounds with glasses.

She came back and handed me a gin and soda.

I said, "I'd offer you a cigarette only I'm out."

She went to a closet and rummaged around. When she came back she tossed me an American brand package of cigarettes. "I've been saving these for a special occasion."

We drank silently, just looking at each other.

Finally I set the glass down and at the same time noticed a photograph of a sailor in a British petty officer uniform on the stand.

"Who is this?" I asked casually.

Maureen looked at the picture and answered in subdued tones, "That was my husband. He went down on the cruiser *Canberra* when she was sunk by the Japanese." She began to cry softly. I wanted to comfort her, but all of a sudden I felt like an intruder in another man's home. It was probably my imagination, but I could feel his presence strongly in the room.

I got up and went to the door. I turned with my hand on the knob and said in a small voice, "Good night, Maureen; I had better get back to my room."

She just looked at me with large appealing eyes, and I turned the knob and stepped out, closing the door quietly behind me.

Walking back toward the main part of Brisbane, it seemed oppressively hot. I stumbled along, cursing myself for a fool. At one place the street came close to the riverbank. On an impulse, I walked along the river until I came to a secluded spot. I took off all my clothes and dived in. The water was warm but had a cooling effect. I swam for perhaps a half hour before coming out.

Before I got back to the hotel, it began to rain heavy globules of warm water. My clothes were soaked through and I left a watery trail on the lobby floor. The desk clerk looked at me disapprovingly, shook his head, and went on sorting mail into the guests' key boxes.

On the way up the stairs, I kept thinking, This is a helluva way for fate to end the day.

I was awakened by a light tapping on the door. I hollered sleepily, "Wait a minute" and slipped into my damp trousers. Sunlight was streaming through the window and I judged the time to be about 8 or 9 a.m. I opened the door and was confronted with a good-looking room maid.

"Good morning," she said brightly, "I brought you your clothes back." In her arms was a large stack of my clothes, snowy white and neatly ironed.

I said, "Thank you," wonderingly, because I had not even realized the bag of soiled linen had been taken away.

She stood waiting after I took them, and I gave her my best early morning, ingratiating smile. I set them on the dresser and reached in my pocket for my wallet.

She laughed and said, "Didn't you miss anything, Yank?"

I answered, "No, I don't think so. How much do I owe you?"

Pushing out her hand, she opened it, and I stared at nearly ten pounds in change.

"So?" I inquired.

"It's yours," she said. "It was in your jumper pocket." Then hurriedly, "You don't owe anything for the laundering. It is part of the room service."

I picked up all but about three pounds. "You can keep that for your trouble."

She seemed very embarrassed. "You *Wahoo* sailors are really too generous with your money."

I said, "Look, sweetheart, money in the pockets of a man rotting in the bottom of the sea isn't going to do him a damn bit of good. We are all living for today because in a few days we may be out there getting our guts shook out with a lot of depth charges."

She blushed and hurried away.

I closed the door and thought, maybe that taxicab driver is right. Maybe they don't have anybody but honest people in Australia.

Now that I was awake, I decided to get ready for another day. I shaved, showered, and went below via the stair route. Again I stopped at the lunch counter and this time ordered sausage and eggs.

One egg and a sausage later, Pappy Rau tapped me on the shoulder. "Mind if I set down and have a cup of coffee with you?"

I said enthusiastically, "Sure thing, Pappy, pull up a seat," and to the counter waiter and fry-cook, "Bring us another cup of coffee."

Pappy laid a folded paper on the table, took out his pipe, and lighted it up. "I want to apologize for what happened the other night."

I said, "Forget it, Pappy, I have. Besides, it's a real honor to get punched by the best damn submarine sailor in the Navy."

He grinned. "I don't know what came over me—nerves, I guess."

I said, "Next time, don't telegraph your punches. I could see it coming a mile away."

Pappy laughed and answered, "You've got the hardest head on anything outside of an army mule that I ever swung into before. I nearly broke my wrist."

I nearly choked on a piece of toast. "That's no compliment," I replied gaily.

My eyes fell on the newspaper and with an exclamation I grabbed it An item boxed in for effect and in large black type announced, "WARNING! Sharks have invaded the Brisbane River as far as the city. Swimmers are warned to stay within swimming pens until . . ." My mouth dropped open as I read.

"What's the matter?" Pappy asked, concerned. "Is something wrong?"

I pointed at the item, nearly speechless. "I was swimming in the river last night for nearly an hour. Why don't people tell me these things?"

Pappy chuckled, "You don't have anything to worry about. A shark would have to be a dipsomaniac before it would tackle you, and I haven't met up with any alcoholic sharks yet."

Just as I was about to come back with a snappy retort, O'Brien came through the door and interrupted me. "Hey, Yeo, there's a good-looking babe with a swell chassis across the street. Says she wants to see you."

I was flattered but tried to conceal it. "What's she want?" I tried to appear unconcerned.

"I don't know. She stopped me and said that if I saw you to tell you she would be waiting for you across the street. Some guys sure have got it." He winked at Pappy.

"Why didn't she ask for me at the desk?"

"I don't know. Maybe she doesn't want the desk clerk to think she is a loose woman or a streetwalker or something. Anyway, if she was asking for me, I wouldn't be just sitting on my duff, I'd be across the street by now."

I answered nonchalantly, "Maybe I'd better see what she wants," and, paying the waiter, walked out.

Across the street, Maureen, more beautiful than I remembered, dressed in a colorful summer frock, was idly looking into a store window. I crossed over.

She saw me coming and a smile brightened her pretty face, which had been serious but a moment before. She met me at the curb. "Oh, Jim, I'm so glad I didn't miss you. I want to tell you that I'm sorry about last night."

I said feelingly, "Nothing to be sorry about. It just happened that way is all." Then before she could answer, "Do you know of a cocktail lounge someplace that we can go get a drink and talk?"

She hesitated. "There's a rather exclusive place near here. Their drinks are terribly expensive."

I said, "Lead on, beautiful fate," and took her arm. Thus, and accidentally, I discovered why I had seen so few *Wahoo* sailors about the hotel.

The lounge was modern, expensive-looking, and patronized by the elite of Brisbane and the *Wahoo* crew. The table alcove we chose was soon the most popular site in the lounge. A steady trickle of shipmates to our booth acknowledged my presence. The ulterior purpose, of course, was the secret hope of an introduction to my fair companion. Her easy greetings quickly made her the *Wahoo* sweetheart of Brisbane. Gratis drinks crowded the table. It was the last place a man would want to take a girl he wished to talk to privately. "Let's get to hell out of here," I growled savagely.

She picked up her purse and we left a disappointed mob of sailors behind us.

I said, "Where would you like to go?"

She thought a minute and said, "We have a lovely amusement park in Brisbane."

I answered, "Okay, let's go, but no walking." At that moment I saw a taxi cruising down the street and I stepped out on the curb and flagged him. We got in and settled down.

"*Quo vadis?*" The driver turned around, grinning at us. It was Matey.

"Take us to the amusement park and pull out all the stops," I answered.

Maureen asked, "What does he mean by *Quo vadis?*"

I said, "It's a game with us. We were shipmates on the old *Tuscarora* . . ."

Surprisingly, Matey turned in his seat and added, "The bloody old ship with a glass bottom and seven straw decks."

We both laughed while Maureen looked from one to the other, apparently deciding whether or not we were crazy.

On arriving at the park, Maureen and I got out of the taxi, climbed a slight incline past the merry-go-round, and came out into a square with carnival tents on all sides. We rode the roller coaster. It was real fun holding her in my arms and watching the full enjoyment that she extracted from the moment. We started taking in the sight-seeing shows and taking chances at each booth. At a wooden milk-bottle booth, I knocked the bottles off with a lucky throw. The attendant, dressed in a straw hat and striped shirt with sleeve garters, handed me a box of caramels. I offered them to Maureen and she pointed to a group of mannerly children following us. "Give them the caramels."

I had not paid much attention to our entourage before. I chose one freckled urchin and ordered him to divide the candies with the others. Immediately our admirers increased. I turned back to the booth attendant and handed him a pound note. "When that is gone, let me know."

Handing three baseballs to Maureen I said, "Go to work. Earn those kids some sweets."

64

We passed out six or eight boxes before our arms became tired. I said to Maureen, "We started something. How are we going to finish it?"

Her peals of laughter had been entertaining the park. Now she stopped long enough to point to the Ferris wheel. We Pied Pipered the youngsters over to the ticket booth and put them all on board, filling up all the seats. "Come on." I grabbed her hand as we fled from the park.

Shadows were getting long in the late afternoon, and we could hear the carnival music considerably subdued when we got out on the street. Matey was standing by his dilapidated vehicle, grinning. We climbed aboard and I said, "Drive us across the river and out into the country a few miles."

I pulled Maureen over to me and we just sat quietly taking in the countryside until it got too dark to see. I tapped Matey on the shoulder and ordered, "Turn around and go back. Do you know of any place to eat along here?"

He grinned and answered, "There's no eating place, Matey, but I know a farmhouse where I can get a roast chicken."

"Get three, if they have them."

"Righto," was the answer.

We turned around and now could see the reflected city lights against the clouds. The country air was cool and fragrant. After a mile or two, Matey pulled into a farmyard and stopped. I gave him money and he went over, knocked on the door, and was granted entrance.

I lighted up two cigarettes and handed Maureen one. When one or the other of us inhaled, I could see by the light that she was sitting with her legs folded under her. Presently I took a deep pull on the cigarette and at the same time reached over and pulled her dress hem above her knees. I expected she would slap my hand but she did not.

She said softly, "What did you do that for?"

I answered playfully, "I was just admiring the dimples in your knees."

She moved around so that the back of her head was on my shoulder. Then I bent over and kissed her. Her breath was warm and she reached an arm up to hold me tight. I was in a dreamworld that had no place in wartime reality. She sat up suddenly and asked, "Jim, what happened to us last night?"

There was a short pause while I groped for an answer. "I think it was my Puritan heritage that got the best of me. My conscience wouldn't let me stay in the room that belonged to your husband. When you began crying, it was the last straw. I just simply had to leave, that's all."

She said, "I won't cry tonight. I promise."

I said, "Howsabout his picture?"

"It won't be there. I put it away."

I pulled her to me in a long embrace.

Matey came back with three paper-bundled cooked chickens. The heat of them could be felt through the paper.

"Take one home to your family and eat the other. Maureen and I will share ours."

We headed back to Brisbane and Maureen's home, leaving chicken bones scattered along the road.

I saw very little of the hotel room after that. One afternoon I spent in my room answering letters I had received from home. Another afternoon I took a bottle to O'Brien's room and we had a couple of drinks, while I found out the exact date we had to report back to *Wahoo*. At the same time I learned there was to be a ship's dance in *Wahoo's* honor the night before reporting back. The rest of the time I spent with Maureen.

We went for long walks about the city, rented horses one day and bicycles a few days later. We stopped in at the cocktail lounge once or twice and then, all too soon, it was the night of the *Wahoo* dance.

I managed to get one or two dances with Maureen, but mostly the gang treated me as though I was not there. They kept tagging in on the dances and keeping Maureen laughing with pleasure the entire evening. I did pull her away long enough to introduce her to the officers at Captain Morton's table. Before long, she was dancing with Ensign Misch or Ensign Griggs, and I soon lost track of her again. When the dance broke up, we went to her home for the last time.

We talked about the war ending and where we would be. I told her that I wanted to leave without any promises between us. She only said wistfully that she hoped she could come to the States some day.

The next morning we ate breakfast downtown, and I rode back in Matey's Rube Goldberg contraption to the docks.

I was in a gloomy mood when I crossed the gangway and went below. The business of going to war again was heavily upon me.

Chapter 6

The transition from whites to dungarees was always a pleasant one, but this time there was a real tinge of regret.

I opened the door to the ship's office and pulled out the expected bags of mail. Emptying them, I stacked the mail to one side, to be opened later. I found orders and records of a Chief Boatswain's Mate, Lane, James E., from Yonkers, New York, in the action basket. While I was taking up his orders, a sailor came to the door with the records of fourteen more men, of which he, Clary, John W., Motor Machinist's Mate, First Class, from Galena, Kansas, was in charge.

I stepped to the chief's quarters. "Pappy," I called, "we got some new men come aboard."

Pappy came out, followed by a young muscular chief with a pleasant smile. Pappy said to him, "This is our yeoman. Keep your hand on your wallet when he is around," and then to me, "This is Lane. He will be Chief of the Boat after this patrol."

Surprised as I was, I acknowledged the introduction, and then turned Clary over to them. They all went aft to get the new men squared away.

I sat back down at the typewriter and was interrupted again. This time by a pleasant and slightly bewildered Ensign whose name turned out to be John S. Campbell, from Chadwicks, New York. I took his orders and he went forward to the wardroom.

Lieutenant Chandler C. Jackson II, from Kansas City, Missouri, came up and said, "Have a cigar, Yeo."

I looked at his bright new silver bars and answered, "Congratulations, sir. Did the Bureau make another mistake?"

"I ought not to give you a cigar after that crack," he retorted, "but seeing as how I'm in a good mood today, take one anyway."

"Thank you, sir."

He hurried down the passageway with his box of cigars in search of more compliments.

I lit up the cigar and turned back to the typewriter. The buzzer in the office rang twice. That meant Lieutenant O'Kane wanted me. I went to his stateroom and caught him shaving. He turned from the mirror and muttered through the lather, "There's a list of men to be transferred on my desk." Picking up the paper. I returned to the office.

Gradually, as I got involved in my work, I began to get the feel of *Wahoo* again. A different *Wahoo* this time. I could feel the stirring of a strong spirit growing in her. The officers acted differently. The men felt differently. There was more of a feeling of freedom and of being trusted to get our jobs done. A high degree of confidence in the capabilities and luck of our ship grew on us and we became a little bit cocky. It was a feeling that *Wahoo* was not only the best damn submarine in the Submarine Force but that she was capable of performing miracles.

Ensigns Misch and Griggs came to the door. "Yeo, are you busy?"

I pushed papers aside, so I could see them clearly. "Well, sir, I'm not exactly playing tiddlywinks underneath this pile of work," I growled. "I'm fouled up worse than a Wave after a ship's dance."

"We just wondered if you could help us censor some letters. We're snowed under."

"Just close your eyes, sir, and stamp and seal the envelopes. There's nothing to it."

"We can't do that. Regulations won't let us."

I said, "It should be fun reading all the scuttlebutt of what the guys did here in Brisbane."

"Oh, that part is all right. But every man in the crew is using this device to let the officers know what he thinks of us. They're even telling us how to run the ship."

"Is that bad, sir? So what is so wrong with that?"

The Executive Officer came up. "Leave the yeoman alone so he can get some work done. Yeo, have you got a sailing list made out yet?"

"My Gawd, sir, give me a chance. I haven't got these transfers and receipts done yet. I don't even know who is on board."

"Well, get on it right away." They all went to the wardroom.

I got up, craned my neck around the doorjamb, and watched them out of sight. Torpedomen drinking coffee and resting, machinist's mates in diesel-soaked dungarees looking at blueprints, and quartermasters trying to correct navigational charts filled the compartment. It was a madhouse.

Minute by minute something new came aboard. There were torpedoes, ammunition, food supplies, fuel oil, and more supplies. I wondered how much *Wahoo* could hold.

In a little while my conscience began to bother me and I went back to the office. It was 0400 when I quit. The clacking of the typewriter did not seem to disturb either the officers or the chiefs, and I could only conclude that they were conditioned sleepers. I groped my way to my green plastic-encased mattress, unzipped it, pulled a blanket over me, and went fast to sleep.

Reveille was conducted by Lane, who came in, turned on the lights in the compartment, and went around shaking sleepers. "Show a leg. Show a leg. Rise and shine. Reveille, reveille."

I poked my head over the side to let him know I was awake so he would not shake me.

"All right, Yeo, another day, another dollar. Hit the deck."

I climbed out of the bunk, got a cup of coffee, and went to the office. I did not feel up to eating breakfast.

Appel, the youngest man on the boat, came by the office. "Yeo, what does the Chief of the Boat mean when he hollers 'Show a leg'?"

"That's an old Navy tradition, Appel. In the British Navy, on the old sailing vessels, sailors were allowed to have their wives on board. When the Bos'n Mate held reveille, he used to make the person in each hammock show a leg. That way he knew whether it was a woman or a man."

"Gee," Appel commented, "I wish I was in the Navy in them days." He went aft to breakfast.

I went into the control room and grabbed the mike to the loudspeaker. "Beatty, Radioman First, report to the ship's office."

Beatty came in almost immediately. I handed him a set of orders and a large package containing records of the men being transferred. "You're in charge, Beatty. I sure wish I was staying here in Brisbane with you. Be sure and check out with the deck watch."

We shook hands and he left the office.

Wahoo went to sea that morning for trial runs and exercises. I had a sailing list to pass over to someone on the beach when the gangway was pulled in. As soon as the maneuvering watch was secured, I went down and crawled into my sack. I did not have any watches to stand until *Wahoo* left on her third war patrol and my second.

After three days, *Wahoo* came back to the same dock to top off fuel and for final preparations before leaving on patrol. Liberty was granted but I stayed on board. I had made my break with Maureen and I did not want to have to do it over again. Most of the crew went ashore except for the unlucky duty section, but as it turned out most of those got away too. Many of the men staying aboard were married and they volunteered to take the duties of the others. I took the duty for Terrell, William C., Seaman First, from Louisville, Kentucky.

In the morning, I finished up the sailing list which contained information relative to each officer and enlisted man attached to the Wahoo. It gave for each the name, rate, next of kin, and home address. The sailing list was the last thing to leave the ship before sailing, and in the event of a casualty furnished the basis for notification of next of kin.

After finishing the list, I wrote a few last letters home. I took them to the post office on the Fulton and while I was there went to the small stores and bought three-dozen white socks, six pairs of dungaree shirts and trousers, and a dozen white hats. I was preparing for a long war patrol.

On returning to the Wahoo, I ate a lunch of corned beef and cabbage and went topside to relieve Johnson, Kindred B., Torpedoman First, from Lenoir City, Tennessee, who had the deck watch.

I took the web belt and forty-five from him, checked the automatic to see that it was not loaded and the cartridge pocket for full clips. Then I went aft, noted the ship's draft, and on the way back, I carefully scrutinized the slack in the lines that secured Wahoo to the dock. After making entries in the deck log, I stood idly by the gangway returning the salutes of men going ashore or coming on board, at the same time alertly watching for strangers and checking on their business.

Things quieted down and my attention was drawn to two Australian soldiers who were unloading boxes of canned goods from a freight car on a siding near the dock. They had been working steadily, but now they stopped and I watched them as they separated one box and opened it. They took a can of pork and beans from it and proceeded to open it to sample them. In a little while, one of the Aussies came over to the edge of the dock and called down to me, "Yank, why do they call these pork and beans? I have eaten half of them and I haven't found any pork in the tin yet."

I laughed, and by way of answer replied, "Wait a minute."

I went to the after battery hatch and called down, "Hey, below decks, is Rowls down there?"

Rowls came to the bottom of the ladder and looked up. "Yeah? Whadaya want?"

"There's a couple of hungry Aussie soldiers on the dock. Think you could feed them?"

"Sure, send 'em down."

I went back to the Aussie. "Tell your buddy to come on over. Our ship's cook will give both of you a warm meal."

"Blimy now, that's bloody well good of you, Yank. Joe, come here."

When they passed over the gangway, I said, "I'll watch the boxcar for you. If anybody comes fooling around, I'll let you know." I steered them to the hatch.

"Thanks, Yank, I've never been on a submarine." They disappeared down the hatch and I heard Rowls saying, "You guys sit over there. I'll get you a hot plate in a second."

They went back to work an hour later. "Best meal we've had in days. You Yanks really have the rations."

Just astern of *Wahoo's* position, the dock began to fill with people and the *Fulton* band straggled down and waited. The indications were that another submarine was coming in off patrol. I walked back on the fantail and shouted over, "What boat is coming in?" The answer came back, "*Silversides*." I went back and shouted down the control hatch, "Below decks watch. Tell the duty officer that the *Silversides* is coming in."

In a few short minutes Lieutenant Henderson came topside. I saluted him and repeated the information. We stood on the outboard side and looked downstream. A submarine came around the bend in the river and headed directly for us. When it got in close, the band began playing "There'll Be a Hot Time in the Old Town Tonight."

Silversides had one of the best submarine records in the war, to date, and both Lieutenant Henderson and I stared enviously at her. Her Commanding officer, Lieutenant Commander Burlingame, was on the bridge, wearing an Australian soldier's hat and sporting a bushy beard that would have done Robinson Crusoe justice. I saw quite a number of bearded crew members topside. The *Silversides* tied up and I stood popeyed as they went over the gangway en masse and climbed aboard a waiting bus. It was the quickest evacuation of a submarine I had yet seen. I wondered who was left to man the ship until a relief crew came aboard.

On the 2000–2400 watch, I looked at the lighted clouds above Brisbane and suffered nostalgia. The four hours went slowly and I kept thinking of the night when Maureen and I had ridden into the country in Matey's taxi. I was glad when Anders showed up to relieve me.

With morning reveille, I bounced out of my bunk with a momentous feeling for the day's happenings. I had just finished a breakfast of hot cakes and sausage when word came over the speakers, "Fall in for quarters. Fall in for quarters."

I straggled topside with the others and stood around exchanging banter. Pappy Rau and Lane came along, and Pappy shouted, "All right, you guys, fall in like two rows of corn." We formed a two-line formation and waited. While Pappy was mustering the crew from a little black memorandum book he used to keep the duty sections straight, the officers came along and lined up in a row facing us. I tried to read the expressions on their faces. They all seemed relaxed, waiting for something. Captain Morton and Ensign Misch had the broadest smiles. Lieutenants Paine, Grider, and Henderson's faces were expressionless, while Lieutenant O'Kane's eyes seemed to be darting every which way, making many mental notes. Pappy finished mustering and saluted the Executive Officer. "All present or accounted for, sir." Lieutenant O'Kane looked at *Wahoo's* new Commanding Officer expectantly.

Captain Morton walked forward and began to address us quietly. "I am glad to have everyone of you aboard the *Wahoo*, personally. I will be brief, as what I have to say can be stated simply. *Wahoo* is expendable. We will take every reasonable precaution, but our mission is to sink enemy shipping. We are going out there on this war patrol to search for Japs. Every smoke trace on the horizon, every contact on watch will be investigated. If it turns out to be the enemy, we are going to hunt him down and kill him." He paused for effect. "Now, if anyone doesn't want to go along under these conditions, just see the yeoman. I am giving him verbal authority now to transfer anyone who is not a volunteer. This is still a volunteer service as far as I am concerned. Nothing will ever be said about your remaining in Brisbane, but I must know within half an hour who will be leaving, so that I can get replacements." He turned to Pappy and added, "That will be all. Dismiss the men from quarters."

Pappy echoed, "Dismiss from quarters," and we all fell out, milling around talking or returning to the after battery hatch.

I went below to the office and waited, meanwhile smoking and putting suction on a cup of coffee. The time ticked quietly by and Captain Morton came hustling in. "Any customers, Yeo?"

"Not a one, Captain. It looks as though I won't have to make any changes in the sailing list."

He grinned. "That's the kind of stuff I like in a crew. We're going to sink some Jap ships this trip." Then he hurried off.

I turned around, inserted the first page of the sailing list into the typewriter, and dated it January 15, 1943.

Wahoo got underway about noon, with Captain Morton and the Executive Officer on the bridge. I, of course, was handling the telephone talker's set. There was a crowd at the dock and the band was playing "Bless 'em All." There were the usual stations for getting underway and maneuvering watch while putting out to sea, the quartermasters signaling with blinker lights or semaphore flags, the tugboat and pilot, the lookouts on the periscope shears. Then a last glimpse of Brisbane's skyline, and we were running northward along the Australian coastline close inshore. Finally the welcome word to "secure the maneuvering watch" was ordered.

I went below with the strangeness of the first day at sea upon me and a deep-seated desire to look into the future. In the control room, I paused to ask Pappy, "When's my first watch?"

He looked at his notebook. "You should be on lookout now, but since you've been on maneuvering watch so long, we'll make it the 2000-2400 watch. That okay?"

I said thankfully, "Sure, Pappy, I think I'll hit the old sack."

"Need to recuperate from the recreation period?"

"Hell, yes," I growled, "but I could use a lot more of it."

I went aft and turned in.

Muffled noises of dishes being scraped by knives and forks and a monotone of voices seemingly speaking all at once, with only a louder word or two becoming distinguishable now and then, coming from the other side of the bulkhead awakened me.

I was not hungry, so I lay there smoking a cigarette and dumping the ashes into a makeshift ash tray that I had rigged up on the cot frame.

Lindhe came in and crawled into his bunk opposite me. He turned on a small reading lamp he had cumshawed from the electrician's mate.

I said in low tones so as not to disturb others who were sleeping, "Where was you in Brisbane? I don't remember seeing you around anywhere."

"Wouldn't you like to know?"

"Not particularly." I yawned. "Just being sociable."

I added, "Never was like this back in Binghamton, New York."

"Yeah, wish I was back there now."

The messroom sounds were diminishing, and I could hear the messcooks cleaning up, banging around benches, clacking dishes together, making the corn broom swish over the deck, and a hundred other familiar sounds that go with cleaning up after a meal.

"What did we have for supper?"

"Chili con carne and corn bread. Don't you ever eat?"

"Sure, between meals. Where are we going on this patrol?"

"Don't know. They haven't told us yet."

The noise stopped in the crew's messroom. "I think I'll get up." I crawled out as Lindhe rolled over and started reading a Western magazine.

I went in and sat down on one of the green plastic-cushioned benches. O'Brien came in. "Well, look who's here. If it isn't Casanova himself."

"Oh, go to hell, willya, *Forest?*"

Vidick sat down with us. I glanced over at him and said curtly, "Why don't you make a noise like a depth charge and go off?"

He looked hurt and I felt ashamed of myself.

O'Brien laughed. "Where did you hear that one?"

"Don't you guys give me any credit for originality?" I growled back at them. To Vidick, "Never mind me, my mother dropped me on my head when I was a small baby."

Vidick looked relieved. "They took me off the job of waking up the watch. You don't think Pappy or the Exec are mad at me, do you?"

"No, but I have an idea that Morton had something to do with it. He's making a lot of changes around here."

"Look, Yeo, I didn't say anything to Pappy Rau . . ."

"It's okay, Vidick, I know you didn't, and besides, Pappy and I have got that all squared away."

Krause and Hunter crowded around the table. "Speaking of changes, what's new on the bridge?"

Hunter said quickly, "Plenty. We've got two lookouts now instead of four. 'Mush' has taken the lookouts off the cigarette deck, and there's only the two on the shears, and they're rotating the watch now. An hour each on lookout, radar or sound, the helm, and the messenger duty in the control room."

"That'll be a relief," I offered. "It gets damn monotonous doing the same thing for four hours."

"That's what Morton said. And something else, too. 'Mush' says that anybody who makes a contact on watch, and we sink the ship, is automatically promoted on the spot."

Carr, sitting at the next table, came over. "Is that true, Hunter?"

"I cross my hand and hold up my heart, it's true," Hunter replied.

Carr said, "I'm going in and volunteer for extra watches," and hurried off. Rowls, who had been puttering in the galley, hollered, "Wait a minute, Carr, I'm going with you."

This was the first time I had ever known of a ship's cook volunteering for watches. The rest of us looked at each other and burst out laughing. Even Vidick chuckled a little.

"Is that really true, Hunter?" I sobered up long enough to think of some of the difficulties Captain Morton's promise would create.

"So help me," he swore, solemnly raising his right hand.

"That's sure enough true," Krause added, and that made the statement a certified fact.

I said out loud to myself, "But how in hell is he going to do it? The regulations are specific about time in service and rate, and there's a lot of ratings on board that don't have a vacancy complement. I wonder how he will do it."

Krause answered me, " 'Mush' will find a way." He was so confident that I had to believe him.

We were arguing vociferously when a quiet came over the crew's mess, leaving us shouting at each other by contrast. We looked up, startled, to find out what had caused this sudden quietude.

Captain Morton had come into the messroom, but the thing that caught our attention and made us speechless was the way he was dressed. He had on an old red bathrobe and go-ahead slippers. He also had a navigational chart under one arm and a bucket of soapy water in the other hand.

He said, "Good evening, men. Can I join you for a few minutes?"

There were some scattered "Yessirs," and then a quick movement to clear a space for him at a table. He set the pail down and proceeded to thumbtack the chart on the bulletin board. It looked to me to be a map of New Guinea. He came back, sat down on the end of a bench, pulled a soaked khaki shirt from the pail, and began to alternately douse it and knead it between his large knuckles.

He asked, "Any of you men ever operate in this area before?"

When he received all denials he said, "We're headed for Palu Island, but we have a special mission to try and locate a harbor along this coast that the Japanese seem to be using pretty heavily. Some of the army planes out of Australia have reported a lot of shipping."

"Are we supposed to reconnoiter it, sir, if we find it?" Hunter asked.

"The orders leave that up to my discretion," Captain Morton admitted. "Would you guys like to go in and look around? Maybe we will find a submarine tender with a lot of submarines alongside. I sure would like that."

I caught his enthusiasm, as a mental picture of torpedoes striking into a nest of submarines took hold of us.

"By the way. I'm forming a group of commandos. Pass the word around that, if anybody wants to volunteer for it, to come see me in my stateroom tomorrow."

He picked up the bucket. "Guess I'll go back and hang this shirt up in the engine room to dry out." He slippered along the passageway until he was out of sight. A few seconds later we heard the increased noise of the diesels beating out a piston tune and felt the air suction as he passed through into the engine room, then a loud clanging thump as he pulled the watertight door closed against the pressure.

"Rowdydow," somebody commented, and as if that was a signal, we all began to talk at once.

Lennox came in and said, "Hey, Yeo, hows to come up to the chief's quarters with me a minute?"

I said, "Okay," and got up to follow him.

O'Brien piped up, "Some guys sure do have a drag."

I gave him an exaggerated sneer as I left the crew's messroom.

Pushing aside the curtains, I found myself in the small space that quartered the chiefs. They were sitting on the lower bunks of the two rows of four-tiered bunks. A big locker in the rear contained their uniforms, and near the door was a metal washbasin that was folded up against the bulkhead. I looked around and saw Pappy Rau, Lennox, Wilcox, Lane, and Jesser.

Lennox said, "Howsabout it, Yeo? You been on the China Station with 'Mush' before. Do you think he's crazy?"

I answered stoutly, "Yeah, like a fox."

Some of the chiefs snickered.

"He's a little eccentric, maybe, but he was the best-liked officer out there." I went on prevaricating like an old salt, for I knew very little about him or his Asiatic activities outside of a slight acquaintance.

The chiefs seemed to accept my word for it. Lennox said, "Well, somebody told me that when he had his R-boat in the Caribbean Sea he used to make plans for attacking German U-boats underneath the water."

"So what's wrong with that? It can be done, can't it?"

The chiefs all laughed at my naïveness and began arguing the point among themselves.

I said, "If you guys are through with me, I'll go back to the crew's mess."

Pappy said, "Sure, Yeo," and I left.

A glance at the clock in the control room informed me that it was nearly time to go on watch. I took a pair of red goggles, donned them, and felt my way into the messroom for a last cup of coffee. In a few minutes I came back, and Lane was waiting to check off the watch standers. He sent me up to the starboard lookout station. It was an awe-inspiring night with big bright stars overhead. *Wahoo* was moving through the water at a steady clip, and the only noise to disturb me was the music of the waves created by *Wahoo's* bow pushing through the water. Not too far away was land. The air was musty with the rich fragrance of tropical underbrush and strange flower scents. It seemed altogether too peaceful for there to be a war in progress and death lurking someplace in those jungles and at sea also.

In an hour Anders climbed up on the frame and relieved me. I went down into the conning tower and relieved Appel at the wheel. The whole universe, of course, was shut out to me, but it was a pleasant change watching the indirectly lighted gyrocompass. When it would start moving in a circle jerkily to the right or left, a slight twist of the wheel and a short jerk back to check the ship's swing would bring *Wahoo* back on the course. Once during the next hour, I was ordered by Ensign Campbell to change course a few degrees in compliance with the Night Order book written by Lieutenant O'Kane, the Navigational, as well as Executive Officer.

Anders came down from lookout, relieved me on the hour, and I went below to stand in front of the radar screen while Appel lounged close by as messenger. Later I relieved him of the messenger watch, and he went topside to relieve Wach on lookout.

After I had been relieved of the watch, I went into the crew's messroom. It seemed strange to find Lucas doing the baking. I interrupted him long enough to wheedle him out of a large slice of apple pie, procured a generous portion of cheese from the night ration table, and sat down with a cup of coffee to eat.

Rowls came in, got a fork, and sat with me. He kept sampling the pie to see how good a baker the new cook was. I did not get much of it. He kept mumbling until I had to ask, "Whatinel is eating you?"

"Aw, them damn people in Brisbane kept trying to fill my cold box with mutton. Don't they realize they ain't a submarine in the fleet that will take the lousy stuff? Submariners just won't eat it."

"Tsh, tsh," I sympathized, "beggars can't be choosers."

"The hell they can't. The Navy advertises that the submarines get the best chow in the Navy, and I aim to see that *Wahoo* gets the best of that wherever we go." Then, apropos of nothing, he continued, "What's more, they didn't clean out my cold box right either. Next time I'm going to clean it out myself."

He jumped up to see if the messcooks had squared away the sink properly and said gloomily over his shoulder, "That meat's going to get moldy in the cold box before we get back, I betcha."

I shook my head and wondered if the Oakland, California, fog from whence he came had anything to do with his disposition. Anyway, *Wahoo's* crew were not going to suffer gastronomically as long as Rowls was around to champion them.

O'Brien came in, looking important.

When I did not say anything, he said, "The commandos are going to have a meeting in the crew's mess tonight."

"What about?" I asked, interested.

"Oh, guns and knives and who will guard the prisoners and who will get the code books in case we have a boarding party and that sort of thing."

"Who all volunteered?"

"Well, there's myself and Mister Misch, and Lane, Seal, Berg, Carter, and Carr, and one or two others. Oh yeah, and 'Tarzan' volunteered too." O'Brien was referring to Muller, Edward F., MM1, from San Diego, California, when he spoke of "Tarzan"—*Wahoo's* man of muscles.

At that moment Ensign Misch came into the messroom followed by Lane.

"All right, you guys, clear the messroom."

We moved over into a corner where we could hear what was going on. The meeting lasted nearly an hour during which there were many anticipatory plans for boarding the ships and capturing the prisoners. The plans were greatly enlarged on by suggestions from the gallery. I was certain that General Douglas MacArthur would have been interested in our detailed planning and methods for shortening the war.

Daybreak found me on lookout, sweeping the minutes of the clock away by scanning the changing color composition from darkness to daylight over every square mile of the port lookout station. An increase in movement below caused me to look down in time to see Hunter and Lieutenant O'Kane taking a "fix on the posit." Looking back again, I noticed the Mae West lifejacket strapped to the periscope. This rubberized flat belt could be inflated into a tube by puncturing two small vials of carbon dioxide in the belt end. This was another innovation of Captain Morton's, a safety precaution that might save somebody's life if they did not clear the bridge on diving.

Lieutenant O'Kane and Hunter went below. Ensign Misch, standing below, cupped his hands and roared, "Clear the bridge." He reached over and pushed the button to the diving siren twice. Wahoo immediately took an alarmingly sharp down-angle and the bow plunged out of sight. I did not wait to admire such efficiency. Instead, I dropped my binoculars to swing loosely from the leather thong about my neck, grabbed the handrail around the crow's-nest and swung under and out, straightening before hitting the deck ten feet below me. Bent at the knees and waist, I sprang upright and ran past Ensign Misch, waiting at the access hatch. Fast as this seemed to be, Veder, David A., S2, from Cincinnati, Ohio, the other lookout, was ahead of me, his shoulders and head moving down out of sight. I gave a little leap and was pulled by gravity toward the conning tower deck. Halfway down, I checked my fall by thrusting my feet into one of the rungs of the ladder. Ensign Misch, all two thousand pounds of him, hit me on the shoulders and rode me the rest of the way piggyback. How he managed to close the hatch after him was a trade secret—I did not have time to investigate. I staggered up from the deck, moved over, and dropped down into the control room. I stood there regaining my breath by degrees and bracing against Wahoo's dive angle. When I was finally able to speak, I said, "Damn you, Veder, I bet you don't beat me to that hatch next time."

Captain Morton was standing by the gyrocompass with a stop watch in his hand. "Attaboy, Yeo, but you'll have to get the lead out of your pants." Then he turned to the Executive Officer. "We clipped three seconds off our diving time. We'll continue these morning trim dives. We're making progress."

When Wahoo surfaced, the other duty section had taken over.

Each day brought with it a quota of changes and new surprises. Most of them could be traced back to Captain Morton's stateroom, but the initiative fever was catching and we all began to have ideas. Communication betweeen officers and men became increasingly easier. We had the best morale I had ever experienced aboard a ship since my Nautilus days before the war.

On the eighth day out of Brisbane, I came into the crew's mess bruised and battered from Ensign Misch's ride on my back down the conning tower hatch on the morning trim dive. Veder was sitting smugly before a platter of scrambled eggs. I glowered at him, ordered eggs sunny side up, and sat down at another table. When I finished, I stood up and stretched until a sore muscle pained me and I gave up in disgust. I turned in, rubbing tenderly the bruise over my eye where the binoculars had bumped me on the way down the hatch, and fell into a dreamless sleep.

I awoke with a start, feeling that something was off schedule. I lay for a while trying to figure it out. Suddenly I knew. *Wahoo* was now submerged, and we had been riding the surface. I went into the crew's mess and found Rowls and Boutzale sitting at a table. Carter was on the phones. I looked at Carter in surprise and, walking over to Rowls, raised my eyebrows in silent interrogation.

"It's the new deal," he almost whispered back. "We've been laying off an unknown harbor and looking it over. The Old Man thinks it might be Wewak Harbor—the one we've been hunting for."

"How'd he get the name of it? I thought it was uncharted."

"Keeter bought a two-bit atlas in Brisbane and it had a map in it. 'Mush' sure was tickled to get some information on it. I hear there's an island up there called Mushu [Musaau]. Ain't that something?"

"How come GQ wasn't sounded?"

"Like I said, it's the new deal. Morton is only going to sound GQ when there's an emergency. They just went around quietly waking the people up they needed. Guess you wasn't needed."

I said, "Guess not—but I bet I have a battle station submerged the next patrol. I'm getting tired of sitting in the crew's messroom doing nothing and wondering what is going on."

Drawing a cup of coffee, I sat with them.

In a short while the lights began to dim a fraction, and I could tell by the increased vibration of *Wahoo's* hull that the motors had been speeded up.

Hunter came hustling into the messroom, looked at us and grinned, drew a cup of coffee, and joined us.

"The Old Man spotted the masts of something on the other side of the peninsula. He's all excited. It might be that submarine tender he's been dreaming about. We're going in to find out."

Boutzale looked at Rowls and then at me before looking away. I could almost guess what he was thinking, but he was not going to let us know he was nervous.

I said with enthusiasm, "By gollies, I hope it *is* a tender with a whole flock of submarines alongside. Wouldn't that be something? We might even get the Croix de guerre or something out of it."

Rowls growled, "For what? Sitting on our butts in the crew's mess?"

Hunter said, "I better be getting back."

"How's things up there?" I asked wistfully.

"Different, lot's different, now that 'Mush' has taken over. Why, for one thing, he lets O'Kane handle the 'scope and he stands around directing everything. I think he does the mathematics in his head."

"I guess he's like me," I said. "I got a photographic memory, too."

"Huh?" They all looked at me skeptically.

"The only thing is my film never seems to develop." I smiled at them cherubically.

After that we just sat smoking, thinking, and waiting. The atmosphere was heavy with danger all about us. Our heightened senses were quick to interpret the slightest *Wahoo* change or noise. An outburst of excitement in the conning tower carried down to us and we listened until it subsided.

Carter reported laconically, "We're inside the harbor. 'Mush' is going to look around."

We relaxed.

The tension inside *Wahoo* was increasing to a breaking point. I fidgeted about on the bench, noticing that my sweaty palms were leaving hand marks on the green linoleum table.

A remark I had heard fourteen years before, in classroom, came to me: "Every person is the center of his own universe. If a straight line were drawn from the center of the moon to the center of the earth, it would have to pass through the person drawing the line."

I thought about that and about myself. That meant the imaginary line was passing right through me in the crew's mess on the *Wahoo*. If I were the center of the universe, then everything radiated away from me in circles. *Wahoo* was my cocoon, which, in turn, was wrapped in a body of water. I tried to visualize the water, and my picture of clear tropical waters with a sandy bottom was not reassuring. Surrounding this body of water must be beaches with straw-thatched huts and maybe Japanese installations with natives and soldiers and perhaps native boats drawn up on the beach or in the water. But what kind of Japanese warships were anchored here?

My daydreaming was interrupted by a sharp single *ping* that brought butterflies into my stomach and caused me to grimace with its unexpectedness. My previous radio training came to my rescue, and I recognized the sound as coming from a fathometer.

Carter moved and answered our unspoken questions. " 'Mush' had to find out how deep it is here. He took a chance on the fathometer."

After that we became adapted to the fathometer soundings at about two or three minute intervals.

Rowls said, "I wish to hell we was out of here."

I looked at him and said, "Amen and hallelujah."

Excitement stirred and spread rapidly through the ship.

"There's a destroyer up there. A *Fubuki* or *Asahio* class. They can't make out which. There's a white plume of smoke above his stack and he's heaving in his anchor."

Morton's voice carried down, "Get them damn outer doors open forward."

I sat there tense with pounding heart and rapid pulse. I experienced a dryness in my mouth and throat. We looked at Carter, as though he would be able to get us out of this situation.

"She's up-anchored and heading toward us, all fifteen hundred tons of her. She's beginning to zig. Musta spotted our periscope because she is firing at it. Why doesn't O'Kane pull it down?"

Wahoo's hull bucked as a torpedo shot out to try and intercept this terrible menace to her safety. Another left its tube at a slightly different angle, followed shortly afterward by a third torpedo. *Wahoo* settled down to a brief agonizing wait to learn the results. We could hear the distant reports of spasmodic gunfire and wondered how close to *Wahoo's* periscope the shells were landing, since they must be ricocheting across the water and exploding elsewhere.

Without realizing it, our eyes were glued to the second hand of the clock. A minute and a half clicked by.

"All three are misses," Carter stolidly reported. "She zigged in between them."

I had time to wonder if Carter had any nerves at all before terror gripped me. I felt an almost uncontrollable urge to urinate.

"She's still coming in, about fifteen hundred yards away."

Wahoo's shell bucked again as she spit another deadly torpedo at the Nipponese threat. "Mush" must have nerves of steel, I thought desperately. Why doesn't he let go the other two torpedoes?

"Another miss," Carter crooned.

I broke out into a cold sweat, and I was sure that my eyes must be dilated.

Explosions in the distance announced the arrival and contact of our first torpedoes with the beach. *Wahoo* was still fighting as another torpedo left the tubes. I had lost count. Was it the fourth or fifth? The fifth I guessed. How many were left? Only one left in the sixth tube. Would we have time to use it?

Suddenly I was calm with the cool certainty that I was going to die. I wondered, How can this be happening to me? It was unreal. It can't be happening to me!

"The destroyer is eight hundred yards a . . ." Carter did not get a chance to finish the sentence. A terrific explosion shook *Wahoo* and all her inhabitants.

"It's a hit! We got her amidships. She's breaking in two."

Shouts came from the conning tower and control room.

I stared dazedly about, unable to believe that the situation had changed so quickly. My hands shook as I lit up another cigarette. I felt as though I had sustained a severe blow in the solar plexus and was only now able to gasp for breath again. Aware again of Rowls and Boutzale, I noticed that their faces were blanched.

"Both parts of the hull are settling on the bottom," Carter reported, showing excitement for the first time. "Grider's going to take pictures."

The loudspeaker sprang into life. It was Captain Morton's voice excitedly giving us details, ". . . destroyer . . . amidships! . . . There must be hundreds of those slant-eyed devils in the rigging . . . anybody not on watch wanting a look get to the conning tower on the double."

"Good Lord," I prayed, "let's get to hell outa here. Make him get out of here. I'll be a minister, I'll go to church every Sunday, I'll do anything you want. Only, let's get to hell outa here."

Pounding feet announced the arrival of crew members from aft, anxious to have a look at Wahoo's latest victim. A need for action spurred me and I followed them into the control room. A line had formed at the foot of the ladder and I crowded in. Everyone was looking anxiously up at the hatch, hoping for a turn at the periscope.

My turn came and I looked quickly, seeing the blur of a broken destroyer hull and its slightly slanted deck near the water line. Black and white smoke was pouring from amidships, and the rigging was polka-dotted with white uniforms. A dark, smudgy tree-studded hill furnished a backdrop. Somebody behind yanked the periscope handles from my hands. I stepped back and saw Captain Morton with arms folded, near the TDC, grinning at our behavior. Lieutenant O'Kane was fretfully standing close by, but unable to conceal his triumphant mood.

I grinned weakly at them and edged my way back down the ladder.

Entering the crew's mess, I noticed Carter with disappointed face still on station. "I'll take over if you want a look," I said.

"Wouldja, Yeo? Thanks a million." He unstrapped the phones and jammed them into my hands.

I blew into the mouthpiece and said tentatively, "Testing, testing, conning tower, this is Yeo speaking. I've relieved Carter for a look through the 'scope."

Simmonetti's voice came back, "Okay, Yeo, gottcha."

Shipmates came through on their way back and I exchanged repartee and exclamations with them. Rowls and Boutzale straggled in.

"Why don't we get to hell outa here?" Rowls worried.

I was still fearful but calmer now. "We will, Cookie, only give the Old Man a chance, willya? We only just got here."

He glared at me and sat heavily on a bench. "This sure plays hell with gettin' out a meal. Noon chow will be all spoiled by the time anyone's ready to eat."

Carter came back with glowing eyes and relieved me. "Wasn't that something, Yeo? Wasn't it? Bet that old tub won't drop any more depth charges on submarines."

That gave me something to think about.

"You're right, by golly," and then more optimistically, "the war is one Japanese destroyer shorter."

Sounds of gunfire were much fainter now, and the full impact of Wahoo's daring was beginning to be borne in on me. I began to be ashamed of my fear a few moments before.

When the fathometer stopped pinging, I knew we were in deep water again. A sense of deep relief and a feeling of safety came over me. I began to relax slowly.

"Secure from battle stations" finally put an end to our immediate fears. The crew's messroom filled with excited talkative shipmates. There was a great deal of movement as they slapped each other's shoulders, moved from table to table, and put a strain on the coffee urn.

Hunter and Krause came in and by virtue of their prestige became the center of attention.

"Boy, you shoulda seen O'Kane," Hunter began. "He's the coolest cucumber you'd want to see in an emergency." Krause nodded agreement.

"Man, he stayed right on that periscope and looked right down their throats with that destroyer coming in plenty fast and shooting right at us. I never seen anything like it."

Krause moved over to me. " 'Mush' really knows his business. Between 'Mush' and O'Kane, they make a great team."

Hunter was saying, "I nearly started for the head when that fourth fish missed . . ."

Captain Morton came into the crew's messroom and took the show away from Hunter. He had a wet towel that he kept pressing on the back of his neck.

"Where's that damn Pharmacist's Mate? All my nerves are tied up into a knot at the back of my neck. Has anyone seen him?"

"He's still on watch in the conning tower," Krause offered. "I'll go get him, Captain."

Captain Morton said, "Did all you guys get a look at him? Boy, we sure did break his back, but I thought for a few minutes there he was going to get in on us."

Lindhe pushed his way through the door. "You wanted to see me, Captain?"

"Yuh damn right I want to see you. Howsabout passing out that depth-charge medicine and then I'd like to see you in my stateroom about getting these Goddam nerves in the back of my neck straightened out."

"Yessir," Lindhe replied enthusiastically, "I'll get right on it, sir." He dashed aft.

Captain Morton went back toward the control room.

Almost immediately Lindhe was back with a large pasteboard carton with a lid on it. "Get your depth-charge medicine here. Anybody don't want theirs, let me know."

This made me suspicious. "I'll take mine, Lindhe."

"Aw, you don't want this nasty old medicine, it'll burn your throat out. I'll keep yours."

I said stubbornly, "Give me whatever the damn stuff is."

Reluctantly he lifted the lid and I saw several dozen miniature bottles of Three Star Hennessy brandy. My eyes must have widened considerably because he said more kindly, "Maybe you need it after all, Yeo," and he handed me a ration. He had no trouble getting the rest of the crew to accept theirs. I heard Ware refuse his bottle and I watched enviously as Lindhe put it in his shirt pocket.

"Anybody else don't want their depth-charge medicine?" He started through the boat on his errand of mercy.

I sampled the brandy and it hit the spot. "Sometimes I wish I'da been a chancre mechanic," I said to Hunter as we toasted each other's health.

"This is another one of 'Mush's' ideas," Hunter commented.

Chapter 7

No land was discernible from the lookout station on the 1600–1800 watch. The watch was not wasted, however, as it produced an awe-inspiring tropical sunset. When the sun balanced itself precariously on the earth's horizon for that fraction of a second before the earth continued revolving eastward, it presented an enlarged blood-red, slightly distorted orb that could be viewed with the naked eye. The overhead sky took on chameleon changes from blue to a deep purple. In the east, a darkening band of gray widened, getting ready to push the colors out of the sky as soon as the sun would be swallowed up. A dim moon took shape, becoming a brighter silver in proportion to the evening's waning.

Gradually the sun flattened out and dissolved into nothingness. I had a tremendous struggle keeping my attention away from this awe-inspiring phenomenon and concentrating on other areas of the sea, for I knew that an enemy submarine, plane, or ship would like nothing better than to get *Wahoo* silhouetted against nature's footlights.

Wonderful, tantalizing, exotic tropical smells carried across the darkening greenish graylike ocean in an effort to seduce me into quiescence—a lassitude that *Wahoo* could ill afford, since the safety of every man aboard depended on lookout's alertness. Appel was the other lookout.

This feeling of oneness with the universe lasted until Ater relieved me from my pleasant occupation. I came below decks with a deep feeling of serenity upon me.

I had just managed to manufacture a Dagwood sandwich, several layers high with cheese, sardines, cold roast beef, pickles, and a few condiments made available by Rowls, who watched my handiwork with distaste, and was drawing a cup of coffee when Lane came in. He sat down across the table from me.

"They certainly do starve a guy on this boat," he observed sagely.

"You said it," I managed between bites. "I'm nothing but a mass of skin and bones."

"Bunch of belly-robbers," Lane added.

Rowls leaped up angrily. "If you bastards don't like the way I feed on this boat, why don'cha get yourselves transferred?" His eyes were flashing dangerously.

Lane said soothingly, "Take it easy, Cookie, we're only kidding. Besides, I've got some news you'll want to hear."

I picked up my big ears and flapped them, waiting while Rowls, now curious, calmed down to a simmer.

"Yeah, what is it?"

Lane lowered his voice and we unconsciously bunched our heads in conspiracy.

"Tomorrow we cross the equator. Now Pappy Rau has already learned that you two guys are shellbacks. We're going to have a meeting of the shellbacks in the messhall at 2000. Yeo, you go through the service records and get me a list of the qualified shellbacks, and Rowls, chase everybody out of here at 2000, okay?"

I answered eagerly, "You damn betcha I will only . . ."

"Only what?"

"Only will 'Mush' let us hold an initiation?"

"He's the one that suggested it. He told Pappy about it on your last run and gave him money to buy some shellback cards in Brisbane. We should cross the equator after noon chow sometime tomorrow, so Rowls, you get the noon mess squared as soon as you can."

Rowls was all enthusiasm now. "Boy, them guys will hardly get seated before I start yanking their plates away from them."

Lane got up and strolled away. I picked up the remnants of the sandwich, looked nonchalantly about, noticing that the card games were in their usual progress and that we had apparently not been heard, and sneaked secretively to the sink, disposed of the food in the garbage pail, set the cup down quietly on the sink, and crept secretively out.

0800 found shellbacks ensconced in the crew's messroom.

Pappy Rau said, "I crossed the equator in '22. Anybody cross before then?" He looked around at our negative head swings. "Okay, I nominate and elect myself as King Neptune by virtue of seniority." He made some notations on the list and then read them to us in a low tone.

"Lennox, you be Queen Neptune, Lane be Davy Jones. Yeo, you'll be Royal Scribe, Wilcox be Royal Prosecutor. There won't be any need for a defense counsel. Let's see—Rowls is about the fattest, so he can be the Royal Baby. Who is the youngest shellback, Yeo?"

I thought over the list. "I guess Krause is."

Rau said, "Okay, then, Krause will be the Royal Princess. Lindhe can be the Royal Physician, Hunter the Royal Barber, O'Brien the Royal Electrician, and let's see— Oh, yeah, we'll make Muller the Royal Executioner, and Carr and Vidick the Royal Masters-at-Arms." He paused, studied the list, and said to Lane, "That ought to do it." Then to me, "You'd better get started making subpoenas."

O'Brien tapped me on the shoulder when the midwatch came around and I left the typewriter to go up on lookout.

After the watch ended, I finished doing the subpoenas and turned in.

The monotonous clanging of the general alarm bell brought me upright. "Man your battle stations surface, man your battle stations surface" whipped out of the speakers as I hit the deck and slipped into my moccasins. Already dressed, I lost no time in running for the control, bumping into others as I ran. Rau was waiting with binoculars, which I grabbed as I sped by—up the two ladders onto the bridge, into dazzling sunlight, and on up to the starboard lookout platform, passing Gerlacher on his way down.

I quickly adjusted the binoculars to my eyesight after making a fast visual search. I could see nothing but water and clouds. Then bringing the horizon and distant waves into closer focus with the high-powered glasses, I began to scan the entire area closely. Now that my reflexes had stopped working, I began to wonder if this was a drill.

I took time to look below and saw men at their gunnery stations, some still moving agitatedly about. Captain Morton, Lieutenant O'Kane, and Lieutenant Paine were on the bridge. Reports came drifting up. "Twenty millimeters manned and ready, sir." "Deck gun manned and ready, sir." "All stations manned and ready, Captain."

"Very well, stand by."

I turned my attention back to my job but kept my ears tuned to what was going on below.

"There she is, Captain, two points off the port bow."

The sun was getting warm on my face and neck. I cursed myself for not stopping long enough to grab a blue-dyed hat, and made a mental note to have one handy the next time.

When it came time for me to search the ocean forward again, my curiosity got the better of my judgment, and I swung the glasses across the bow and two points the other side. I saw a long narrow native banca in the water with six men in it. Three were standing up with their arms raised above their heads. I swung the binoculars back into my allotted area of ocean and searched it thoroughly. There was still nothing on my side.

"All clear on the starboard quarter," I sang out.

Lieutenant Paine below answered automatically, "Very well."

Captain Morton's voice drifted upward, "Come left to three-two-oh."

"Left to three-two-oh, sir," the helmsman echoed.

"Steady on three-two-oh, all stop."

"All stop answered, Captain. Steadied on three-two-oh, sir."

"Very well, hold her there."

"Aye, aye, sir."

Wahoo's speed reduced and we coasted toward the banca.

"Roger, take Carr and Rau and go up on the bow. See if any of the natives speak English and find out what they're doing away out here."

"Yes sir, Captain," Lieutenant Paine's voice answered.

"If they speak English, find out if any Japanese ships have been by this way recently."

"Yes sir." Paine's voice was fainter this time.

"Control, get Manalisay and Jayson on deck immediately."

Lieutenant Henderson's voice from the bridge speaker replied, "Yes sir, Captain, right away."

"Very well, Hank."

The Captain must have turned to Lieutenant O'Kane. "When the mess-boys get here, send them down to Paine. See if they can speak these people's language, Dick!"

The Executive Officer's voice answered, "Yes sir, just as soon as they get here."

I took my eyes away from the binoculars for a quick look. *Wahoo* was moving in close to the boat, Carr, with forty-five in hand for ready use, and Carter, standing by with a Browning automatic rifle, were spaced along *Wahoo's* bow. Pappy Rau and Lieutenant Paine had their heads close together apparently talking. Rau turned, pointing the length of the boat aft and then out toward the banca.

Quickly wiping the binocular lenses with lens paper I kept in a shirt pocket, I turned my attention back to sea. Then I glanced downward at another commotion beneath my feet and saw Manalisay and Jayson tumble out on deck, still in white orderly jackets.

O'Kane said, "Hey, you two . . ." I did not catch the rest as I was peeking at the sun between the narrowed slits of my fingers to keep the rays from scorching my eyeballs while I searched in that area of the sky to make certain that no Jap Zeros were sneaking in on us with the sun behind their backs.

When I was thoroughly satisfied that there was nothing of a hostile nature in my area, I reported again, "All clear on the starboard side, sir."

Lieutenant O'Kane's voice answered quickly, "Very well, starboard lookout."

The Captain said, "Krause, go up forward and see if you can find out if they've learned anything yet."

"Yes sir, Captain." I heard Krause's running footsteps along the bridge deck.

After a little while I looked down on deck and then turned the binoculars on the banca, which was close by. The powerful glasses made it near enough to reach out and touch.

They had their arms down now and one of the three natives was making motions with his arms and hands in a sign language. I could see his mouth working. They all had strong Negroid features and had on loincloths. An old man with gray kinky hair and skinny arms, which were half raised in supplication, was staring with the blank, open-eyed fixity of a blind person. Another lay huddled in the stern of the boat taking no interest in what was going on. Still another figure sitting on his haunches got up stiffly while I was watching, and I could see that his skin was covered with scabs and sores. There were numerous spots where the dark skin had lost its pigmentation, leaving pink spaces to offset the natural color.

Having seen this much, I began searching my side of the ship again. I was not anxious to have a Jap submarine, plane, or destroyer catch us napping while *Wahoo* was dead in the water.

I heard Krause's voice as he came back on the bridge. "Mr. Paine says the messboys can't make out their dialect, but they've found out enough to know these people have been to sea for days and are out of water and food."

Captain Morton's voice replied, "Thank you, Krause. Get word below for the cooks to send up food and water. We can't stay around here too long." Shortly afterward he secured us from battle stations.

The sun was starting to blister me and my relief, the regular lookout, was late in getting topside. Finally I heard Gerlacher's voice below requesting permission to come on the bridge. I formulated a particularly scathing remark to greet him with. He pulled up alongside of me and I turned to him angrily. Whatever I had in mind I never said it, because he was dressed only in shorts, over which was thrown a blue Navy peacoat, and he was wearing leggings. A chic blue hat set the outfit off nicely. Below the peacoat he displayed bare knees and thighs, which had been anointed with tan lotion.

"Sorry, Yeo, I'd been up sooner, only Pappy made me go change into these," he said apologetically.

"A slimy no-good polliwog! Please move over to the leeward side," I answered condescendingly. "I don't care for that fishy stale smell that is polluting the air."

"Gee, Yeo . . ."

"Furthermore, don't you have some special orders? Come on, what are they?"

"I am to keep an extra sharp lookout for the equator, *sir!*"

"That's better. You can't miss it. It's a broad black belt and lays close to the surface of the water. Keep that in mind."

"Yes, sir!"

I left the lookout station and went below decks.

I picked up the subpoenas at the office and went into the crew's mess-room. Carr was there, so I handed them to him for delivery.

I went back, washed up for noon chow, and rummaged about in my locker. Finding an old mattress cover, I took it back to the office. I got out a pair of scissors and cut a hole for my head and arms. Then I remembered a spool of red tape left over from prewar days and cut off a length sufficient to make a belt. Digging around, I found a green desk blotter from which I scissored a green-leaf Roman headband. I got out some rubber bands to hold it on with and began a mental search for something to symbolize my badge of office. Remembering a rusted and useless numbering stamp machine, I pulled it out of a lower drawer and tied it onto the red-tape belt. My costume was now complete. I was ready for the afternoon's business.

Rowls, true to his word, cleared the messhall in record time. The shellbacks met in the messhall while the polliwogs were sent to the forward torpedo room to wait and contemplate their sinful living.

Pappy had on Morton's old bathrobe, and a new swab was hanging down around his ears. He had a gold cardboard crown on his head and a set of long white false whiskers that he had bought in Brisbane. He carried a wooden broom-handle trident with tips electrically charged from dry-cell batteries in a box suspended by a shoulder strap.

Lennox had on a woman's gingham dress that displayed skinny hairy legs and black socks held up with men's supporters. He had a swab hairdo also.

A black patch fitted over one of Lane's eyes, and he had a red bandanna about his head and gold earrings. Black Jack chewing gum gave him the appearance of missing teeth, and he wielded a mighty "bolivey" made of canvas and stuffed with water-soaked cotton, making a very effective, persuasive instrument.

Fat Rowls, stripped to bare skin, was wearing a gigantic diaper held together with a horse-blanket safety pin.

Krause had located a lipstick memento and painted luscious red lips on his mouth, sprayed himself liberally with a loud perfume, and was wearing an Hawaiian sarong.

Everybody had "boliveys" or paddles with holes in them except Rau, Lennox, Rowls, and myself.

When everything was ready, Pappy looked around at the eager assemblage. He had as motley a crew of bloodthirsty cutthroats as any Captain Kidd would be pleased with. "Let's go."

We single-filed into the control room and filled it with savage growls and threats. Lieutenant Henderson was the diving officer, and Jesser was handling the chief's duties.

Lieutenant Henderson called into the bridge speaker, "Captain, His Majesty King Neptune has come aboard and commands your presence in the control room."

Morton's voice came right back, "Very well, I will receive His Majesty immediately."

He came down from the bridge, followed by Lieutenant O'Kane. He saluted Pappy Rau mockingly and said, "Welcome aboard, Your Majesty. To what pleasure am I indebted for this visit?"

Davy Jones answered, "It has come to the attention of His Royal Highness that your ship is crawling with slimy, sneaky, leprous polliwogs. This is a disgrace that can only be remedied by a summons of these vermin to the Royal Court and the culprits being properly transformed into shellbacks."

Morton was shocked. "My ship crawling with stinky, low-down polliwogs? Will you ask His Majesty if it would be His Royal pleasure to hold court on the *Wahoo*?"

We all went into a huddle. When we came out, Davy Jones said, "His Royal Highness has been advised by His Court that this outrageous condition should be handled with all expediency. It is His Royal Highness' command that these—I hesitate to use the word—polliwogs be dragged out of the bilges and tried in court."

Morton answered, "I am deeply gratified that this is His Royal Highness' decision. Will he take over the ship now?"

"His Majesty will. It is his command that *Wahoo* be dived under the equator while court is in session."

"Very well, proceed with your plans."

Lane went over to the bridge speaker and spoke into it. "Officer of the Deck, His Royal Highness King Neptune orders you to dive ship."

"Very well." Then Lieutenant Paine's voice drifted down through the hatch, "Clear the bridge, clear the bridge." Two raucous blasts from the siren nearly deafened us. The duty section in the control room went into quick action. *Wahoo* tilted on her way down, and the Royal Court opened a passageway for the King and Royal Family to pass through. I heard Captain Morton laughing with loud guffaws and I looked to see what he found to be so funny. He was looking and pointing at Rowls, who waddled along behind with his thumb in his mouth.

I went with Carr, Muller, and a big portion of our piratical crew to the forward torpedo room.

"Will Polliwog Grider step forward?"

He moved away from the crowd and up the two steps to the door. Carr had a big pile of bandages waiting in the officers' pantry. He selected one and placed it over Grider's eyes. Grider's beard made a wonderful target under that and we eyed it enviously.

"Find your way to the messhall on your hands and knees," Carr ordered.

I worked my way through flailing paddles back into the crew's mess and found O'Brien, the Royal Electrician, with an ingenious electrical persuader. It was his job to help the victims through the door solicitously and then to check their vitality for run-down batteries. Laffin was on the other side of him, as Royal Traffic Cop, to direct the traffic into the crew's sleeping quarters with a handsomely made "bolivey."

Grider with half his beard and mustache missing had been through the cleansing process and was standing in the center of the messhall, still blindfolded, with Keeter and McGill holding on to his arms.

Wilcox was reading from a subpoena, "—and charged with being a polliwog and with failure to set the watch after it had run down."

"How do you plead?"

"Guilty."

Pappy Rau said, "I am inclined to be lenient with this misguided polliwog. Will you swear to be a good and faithful loyal subject for the rest of your natural-born days?"

"I do."

"Very well. Then, prove it by kissing the Royal Baby's bottom."

Lieutenant Grider was forced to his knees and his face was rubbed into Rowls' belly. He was yanked to his feet sputtering and laughing.

Pappy said, "What are you?"

Grider answered, "I am a lousy, no-good polliwog."

Paddles descended on his posterior and he waved his hands backward trying to ward them off.

Pappy repeated, "What are you?"

This time Lieutenant Grider got the idea. "I'm a full-fledged shellback."

I moved on into the sleeping quarters. Lindhe met me at the door with a shoe box filled with marble-size dough pills. "Would you like one, Yeo?"

"Hell, no." I rejected the offer. "What are they made of?"

"A little bread dough with some Tabasco sauce, red chili powder, a touch of iodine, slum, and castor oil, and I added some vinegar and a touch of soap powder for flavor."

I made a wry face and waited. Berg, Jimmie G., Fireman, from Washougal, Washington, came crawling uncertainly through the door.

Lindhe said, "This is the Royal Physician speaking. Stand up for your physical."

Berg said meekly, "Okay, Doc, *sir!*" He scrambled happily to his feet, glad to get off his hands and knees.

"Open your mouth wide, say ah-h-h, stick your tongue out, and keep your mouth open."

"A-h-h-ugh!!" Lindhe had reached over and deftly painted Berg's tongue a Mercurochrome crimson with a cotton-swathed stick.

"My, your tongue looks terrible," Lindhe commented professionally. "I prescribe one of Doctor Lindhe's cure-all pills for polliwogs. Open your mouth wider."

Berg complied and Lindhe tossed a pill into the back of his mouth. "Swallow that."

Berg gulped and screamed, "My Gawd, Doc, watcha do to me?"

Lindhe said, "You pass the physical, move along."

I watched several more get physicals and rushed to Hunter's assistance, where he was having trouble getting Davison to sit in the Royal Barber's chair. I guided Davison back into the messroom.

Wilcox was reading a summons, ". . . failure to scuttle the scuttlebutt on the scuttle deck . . ."

Steadily we changed polliwogs into shellbacks, and late in the afternoon we came to the end of the initiating ceremony.

Chapter 8

The evening meal of veal stew was seasoned with repartee.

"Hey, Yeo, howdaya get this crude oil outa your scalp afterward?"

"You don't. Just let nature take its course. You should be rid of it in three or four months. Besides, it's good for you. Grows new luxuriant hair and keeps the crabs away."

Hall said, "Old Pappy Rau appointed me Sir Diddle-de-doo, and when he touched me on the ear with that damn electrical stick, I liked tuh jumped through the overhead. Boy, did that thing sting!"

After the messroom had been cleaned, I joined O'Brien, Hunter, Carr, and Krause in a bull session in the corner.

"What gives on those natives in the boat this morning?"

"We made out there was originally nine of them. Three died. They'd evidently been trying to get away from one of the Jap-held islands. There was another real sick one laying in the boat."

I said, "I know, I saw him from lookout. Could they speak English?"

"Naw, the messboys couldn't understand but a few words. They was Polynesians or Micronesians or something like that. 'Mush' said they was Malayans. I don't know which."

Keeter, Dalton C., Machinist First, from Vickery, Texas, came over and said in a confidential tone in my ear, "Has the Old Man told yuh he rated me chief as of yesterday?"

I said, "No, it's news to me. How did this happen?" The others quieted down to listen.

"It was my Atlas I bought in Brisbane. Lieutenant Grider enlarged a photo of a map that was in it and got a good map of Wewak Harbor from it. 'Mush' was so tickled he told O'Kane to make me chief. I thought you'd know about it by now."

"Well, all right, I'll get it squared away for you first thing in the morning. I'll see O'Kane myself."

"Thanks, Yeo." He sat near me as though fearful I might get away.

Hunter was telling Carr, ". . . them Japs was really churning up the water with their gunfire around the periscope. I could hear the shells striking above and whizzing off. Whoever said them bastards can't shoot is a Goddam liar. Why, we was in such shallow water a snake couldn't a crawled between the keel and the bottom. I thought sure we was all headed for Davy Jones locker for sure . . ."

I noticed that it was time for me to get ready to go on watch. I got up to go to the control for checkoff. Hunter was still talking when I left, ". . . we didn't have no time to turn around to use our stern tubes, and when that fifth fish left the tubes . . ." I was out of ear range leaving the messhall.

Wahoo made her morning trim dive and stayed submerged. Breakfast came and went without anyone calling me for the 0800–1200 watch. My subconscious kept warning me that something was afoot. Finally, after tossing restlessly for some minutes, I awoke and got out of my bunk.

Carter, Rowls, and Boutzale were the only ones in the messhall. Without asking, I knew that Wahoo was making another approach. I plopped two slices of bread into one of the electric toasters, got a knife and butter from a locker, drew a cup of coffee just as the browned toast popped up. I sat down and started buttering my breakfast.

"What is it this time?"

"The lookout spotted a streamer of smoke on the horizon just before we dived. We got close enough to see it's a convoy."

"Howsabout escorts?" I asked, trying not to show my anxiety.

"They ain't spotted any yet. The Old Man thinks maybe this one is unescorted. They might even be rendezvousing here, waiting for the destroyer we sunk at Wewak. I sure do hope so."

"Me, too," I said fervently and stirred condensed milk and sugar into my coffee.

I turned to Carter, who was manning the battle phones. "Anything new happen?"

"Only that we're up front of them. They gotta pass over to get by. They're making ready the bow and stern tubes now, opening the outer doors."

I nibbled on the toast, thinking about the situation. The only thing I could think of was that all hell was due to break loose soon. "Have they spotted any destroyers yet?"

"No, not yet. O'Kane reports that there's a couple of good-sized freighters and another ship looks like a troop transport."

There was nothing here that seemed dangerous. I guessed that I was just edgy from the other attacks. I was leaning with my back against the forward bulkhead when I fell to wondering if a depth charge transferring its shock wave through the hull of a submarine might not be powerful enough to break a man's back. The thought made me uneasy and I moved out to the end of the bench away from the partition.

Carter moved and the three of us leaned toward him waiting. "We're laying crossways between them. They're going to pass in front of and behind our bow and stern. Boy, what a setup!"

I felt myself becoming excited. Turning to Rowls, I exclaimed, "I hope we get the whole damn shootin' kaboodle."

"Me, too," Rowls and Boutzale answered simultaneously.

I looked at the clock. It was close to 1000.

Boutzale said, "Yeo, you made a mistake on my shellback card."

I said, "Let me see it," and then, "It looks all right to me."

"Today's the twenty-sixth of January, ain't it?"

"Yeah. Oh, I see, it's dated the fifteenth. That's a typographical error. The next time you catch me in the office remind me and I'll change it. Okay?"

"Okay."

Getting in late on the approach caused me to misjudge the moment of attack. It came suddenly in a fury that left me breathless.

Wahoo began spewing out fish in such quick succession, firing them from bow and stern tubes so quickly, that I lost track of the number fired. There must have been four or five. The internal noises increased in noticeable volume. Voices and commands activated men to feverishly concentrate on their individual tasks. As time condensed into seconds, we three nonparticipants put a heavy suction on coffee cups and smoked cigarettes in two or three puffs.

Wahoo began bucking in a renewed attack, lashing torpedoes out in venomous hate.

A loud explosion was lost in the mad scramble, and Carter's words were barely audible. "We hit one of the sons-a-bitches right in the bow."

Following this came another explosion. Then still another explosion rocked *Wahoo*.

"Damn if we didn't hit another one of the ships. Yippee!"

An aftermath of comparative silence reigned while we waited for a recapitulation of results. I began thinking of Lieutenant O'Kane and wondering what he must be seeing through the periscope. Not any destroyers pushing their bows toward us, I hoped.

The voice of Morton broke out of the loudspeaker. "We've crippled one ship and a transport is sinking. We may battle-stations-surface on them after we look around a bit. All men on gun crews get ready."

I jumped up and ran back to my bunk for the blue-dyed hat under my pillow. I was not going to get caught short this time. Back in the control room I yanked a submarine jacket from a locker and picked up a pair of binoculars. Next I filled one of the pockets with lens paper and stood waiting nervously out of the way of *Wahoo* men manning diving stations. I could hear locker doors and hatches to the ammunition lockers being banged open as gun-crew members grabbed off submarine jackets, weapons, and other paraphernalia needed to fight a surface battle.

Lindhe came into the control room with his first-aid kit and stuffed a wad of cotton in my hand. I picked out strands of it, wadding them into eardrum-size pellets and pushed them into my ears. All sound became so deadened that I had to get close to hear Lindhe. Yanking out one cotton ball, I said, "What were you saying, Doc?"

He repeated excitedly, "Just before I left the conning tower, O'Kane reported that troop transport sank. It only took eight minutes for it to go down and there are hundreds of Jap soldiers in the water."

I nodded an answer, getting the mental picture. There was a buzzing of the periscope in the pump room beneath our feet. The general alarm bell began clanging, and Lieutenant O'Kane's voice came to us from the loudspeaker, "Battle stations surface, battle stations surface."

Vogeler, the other battle lookout, came alongside prepared as I was for the surfacing. Lindhe thrust a wad of cotton at him.

Gerlacher, Wesley L., Seaman, from Philadelphia, Pennsylvania, and Glinski, who had just been relieved from the stern planes, stood in the passageway leading to the messhall. They each had a container of twenty-millimeter ammunition and a gun barrel. Stooping, I looked through the oval framework of the watertight door and saw Carr moving up the ladder into the messhall access hatch. Below him stood other members of the deck-gun crew.

Captain Morton's voice vibrated the control room talker. "Surface, bring her up quick, George."

Lieutenant Grider sprang into action as the words came down. "Lookouts to the tower."

As I scrambled up the ladder, I could hear a confusion of commands around me: "Blow bow buoyancy," "Blow negative," "Bow and stern planes three degrees up-angle," "Vent inboard," "Maneuvering get ready to shift from motors to diesels," "Ninety feet, eight-nine feet, eight-eight feet."

When I got into the conning tower the commands were different. Hunter was up the ladder with his hands on the steel hatch wheel. Lieutenant O'Kane was standing with his hands on the sides of the ladder and one foot on the second rung from the bottom. Captain Morton and Lieutenant Paine were back in the far corner. I stood next to the Executive Officer and Simmonetti, the helmsman, with Vogeler behind me. Buckley was sitting at the sound gear, Krause near him, and Gerlacher and

Glinski were filling in space. On the ladder leading into the control room more of the gun crew were waiting. I glimpsed Carter with a Browning automatic at the foot of the ladder. I thought of the other wad of cotton and stuffed it quickly in my ear.

With the prospect of action upon me, I began to experience an emotional excitement. Adrenalin was pouring into my blood stream and I felt a primitive instinct to do battle.

Faintly I heard Lieutenant O'Kane shouting, "Crack the hatch." Seconds later and even with the cotton in my ears, I felt the air pressure release on my eardrums. "Open the hatch." Salt water poured into the opening, drenching Hunter and the Executive Officer, wetting my upturned face and dungaree trouser legs at the same time that air escaping from the boat helped carry me up the ladder.

Lieutenant O'Kane was leaning over the bridge coaming, looking forward, and Hunter was sliding to a stop at the end of the cigarette deck, shading his eyes, looking astern.

I slipped on the wet deck, regained my balance, and clambered up to the starboard lookout platform. I could hear footsteps running, metal striking metal, and feel the quick movements of bodies below me. A rapid hand-shaded survey showed me that there was no immediate danger in the enameled blue of the seas or the paler blue, cloudless skies on the starboard side of *Wahoo*.

"Two ships on the starboard beam," I sang out loudly. "One is crippled with a starboard list and smoking badly. The other is standing by it, sir."

Captain Morton's voice below answered, "Very well."

Vogeler, whose back was to me, shouted excitedly, "Jap troops, boats, and debris in the water off our port bow, sir."

I looked over on the portside of the ship, unable to control my curiosity. The water was filled with heads sticking up from floating kapok life jackets. They were scattered roughly within a circle a hundred yards wide. Scattered among them were several lifeboats, a motor launch with an awning, a number of rafts loaded with sitting and standing Japanese fighting men, and groups of men floating in the water where they had drifted together. Others were hanging onto planks or other items of floating wreckage. A few isolated individuals were paddling back toward the center in search of some human solidarity.

I took in as much of the scene as I could grasp in a quick look and turned my attention back to starboard. I felt a crawling sensation along my backbone at the thought of so many of the enemy at my back.

"Permission to start the turboblow." Lieutenant Grider's voice through the deck speaker.

"Permission granted," Captain Morton's reply.

"Permission to charge batteries."

"Permission granted."

The distant rattle of machine-gun fire came to my ears.

"Damn him," Morton's voice roared. "Roger, have the gun crews knock that machine gun in the motor launch out of the water."

"Aye, aye, sir," Lieutenant Paine replied.

"Commence firing on the motor launch."

This was followed by several rounds from the deck gun and the rattle of the twenty millimeters.

Whenever the deck gun went off, I flinched from the shock wave that followed. There would be a blinding flash of yellow, which I saw from the corners of my eyes against the binoculars, the shock jarring my whole body, followed by a cloud of acrid white with brownish tints and pale blue colors drifting into view on the starboard side of the ship.

A sharp explosion of a shell going off near the twenty millimeters caused me to jump. I looked down and saw the barrel pointing in the air and Gerlacher staggering dazedly away from the gun. Glinski was sitting on deck and looking stupidly at his right foot. The shoe leather was brutally torn and I could see blood spurting from a wound onto the deck. I resolutely returned to scanning the ocean.

"Pharmacist's mate to the bridge on the double," Lieutenant O'Kane yelled down the voice tube.

A yell went up from the deck-gun crew. I gathered that the motor launch had been hit.

"Cease firing, cease firing."

Wahoo's diesels were racing to pump new electrical blood into her storage batteries.

Lindhe's voice carried up to my lookout station. "Somebody bear a hand here to help me get these guys down below."

I heard a commotion and recognized Krause and Hunter's voices as they assisted Gerlacher and Glinski down the hatch.

Morton, O'Kane, and Paine moved into a huddle below me.

"What do you think? They look like Marines to me," Lieutenant O'Kane said.

"Yuh damn right they are. They're part of Hirohito's crack Imperial Marine outfit. I run into some of them before the war at Shanghai," Captain Morton replied.

"There must be close to ten thousand of them in the water," said Roger Paine's voice.

"I figure about nine thousand five hundred of the sons-a-bitches," Morton calculated. "How's our batteries, Roger?"

Lieutenant Paine answered, "Pretty low, Captain, they need charging badly."

"All right, we'll circle these bastards several times while we charge batteries and look them over."

Lieutenant O'Kane said, " 'Mush,' if those troops get rescued, we're going to lose a lot of American boys' lives digging them out of foxholes and shooting them out of palm trees."

"I know," Morton growled, "and it's a damn stinking shame to think of it when we've got them cold-turkey in the water."

"Do you think they had a chance to radio an SOS, Captain?"

"Probably, but even so there's still that oil tanker and cargo ship out there. We're going after those babies as soon as we get a battery charge."

Lieutenant O'Kane raised his voice. "Starboard lookout, are those ships still in sight?"

"Yes sir. I can still see smoke on the horizon and they are hull down."

"Very well."

Captain Morton commanded, "Secure from battle stations surface."

Lieutenant Paine picked up the word and passed it to the men on deck. "Secure from battle stations surface."

I undertook another quick look at the Japs in the water. Some had drifted in to about twenty-five yards of *Wahoo* and I could see the close-cropped skulls of those without campaign visors. They all stared without expression at *Wahoo's* hull. The situation looked about the same except that the motor launch was missing and I saw one Jap standing on a raft waving a large piece of canvas in the air.

"I didn't think the Japs ever surrendered," I said over my shoulder to Vogeler.

"Me, too," he muttered, keeping his binoculars trained on the horizon. I turned back to my own job.

Shortly after the gun crews went below, I was relieved from lookout by the regular afternoon duty section lookout.

The messroom was a shambles. Men sat around with smoke-smeared faces, drinking coffee and eating sandwiches. Empty gun cartridges filled the passageway. Carr and Kemp were dipping twenty-millimeter ammunition into buckets of petrolatum, wiping the excess off, and reloading empty cartridge containers.

"Hows to help us, Yeo?" Kemp asked.

"Sure," I said, "just as soon as I get something to eat."

Rowls had set out two large dishpans of sandwiches. I selected a sandwich, got a cup of coffee, and went back into the sleeping compartment. The lights were on and I found Lindhe fussing over his two patients.

"How are they?" I asked, looking first at Glinski who was wrapped in blankets with only his face showing. He looked terrible. His eyes were closed and he was whining softly.

"I had to operate," Lindhe said proudly. He pulled the blanket away from Glinski's feet, showing me a foot heavily bandaged in gauze and taped with adhesive strips. There was a strong smell of medication in the air. "He's under sedative now, but when I got him down here, three of his toes were hanging by skin and broken flesh."

"No fooling." I was impressed.

"Yeah, I knew they had to be amputated but I didn't have anything to operate with. So I bummed a pair of tin snips from Kohut and sterilized them and snipped his toes off."

My expression encouraged him to go on. "Well, after that I washed out the wound with antiseptic, tied off the blood vessels, and sutured the skin together. There was nothing to it."

Gerlacher was lying on his stomach in a bunk across. He was covered up to the waist and was resting his head on the backs of his hands. He grinned at me shyly.

"What happened to you?" I said gruffly. "Ain't you got no better sense than to get yourself laid up like this?" I noticed a square white piece of gauze taped with a white-cross adhesive band just under his left shoulder blade and over his heart.

"We had a hot shell, and after we changed barrels, we left it laying on deck. It went off," Gerlacher answered sheepishly.

Lindhe interrupted. "Yeah, you damn fools shoulda heaved it overboard." He pointed at the wound. "A piece of the brass cartridge went through his submarine jacket and was stuck in his skin. If it'd gone much deeper we'd a had a burial at sea. I've always wanted to see a burial at sea."

"What some gold-brickers won't do to get out of work," I remarked sagely.

Captain Morton came pushing into the sleeping quarters.

"How're the patients coming, Doc?"

"Everything's under control, sir. Here take a look at Glinski's foot." Lindhe drew back the blanket with justifiable pride.

I said, "Excuse me, sir," and edged around the Captain's big form squatting on deck to see better.

"Sure, Yeo," Captain Morton answered absently and turned to Lindhe again, "O'Kane tells me you did a magnificent job on Glinski's toes. Tell me about it."

Lindhe filled out with egoism. "Well, you see, sir, when we got Glinski down here . . ."

I moved toward the door, ". . . nothing to operate with so I got these here tin snips from Kohut and . . ."

In the messroom I sat down to help Kemp and Carr. They were handling the shells rather roughly I thought, but not being a gunner's mate I hesitated to say anything. I picked up a cartridge and dipped it gingerly into the pail of thick grease.

"Aw, grab a handful," Carr invited, "they won't bite'cha."

The recorder began to play and I looked over my shoulder to see O'Brien standing near it. "Sock 'em down, Winsocki, sock 'em down." When that record played through, there was a brief silence while he changed records and then I heard the music of an unfamiliar ballad. I turned again to ask the name of the piece when it broke into lyrics with Bing Crosby singing "I'm dreaming of a White Christmas."

O'Brien said to all the messroom assemblage, "It's a new song came out in the States. My wife sent it to me at Brisbane."

Everybody knocked off what they were doing until the song finished. We just sat there meditating in silence.

O'Brien said, "Aw, to hell with it." He changed the record back to "Sock 'em down, Winsocki, sock 'em down."

We finished with the cartridges and I helped them clean up the crew's messroom. It was going on to 1400.

Wahoo was running on the surface. Hunter came in for coffee and told us that the officers were still plotting and tracking the other two ships and that he expected *Wahoo* would catch up with them around 1800. Some of the men off watch turned into their bunks. I was too keyed up to lie down for even a little while, so I waited in the crew's mess. Rowls did not attempt to cook an evening chow. He just filled three large dishpans with more sandwiches and kept the coffee urn filled.

Keeter came in and by way of greeting said, "Got me fixed up for chief yet?"

I answered, "Will you get to hell out of here? I ain't about to lay a finger on that typewriter until this attack is over."

"You don't have to be so sarcastic about it."

"If you're so all-hell-fired to make chief, why don't you see O'Kane yourself?"

"He's busy now or I would, but he would listen to you."

"Oh, bat feces. If you'll just keep your pants on until this is over, I'll get you squared away, but if you pester me again, those papers will get lost in the mail," I added ominously.

"Okay, Yeo, I won't bother you again, but hows to get on it as soon as you can, huh?"

I just looked at him sullenly, and he turned and went aft.

The 1600–1800 watch standers came in, ate, went out again. The men they relieved drifted in, ate, and drifted out. Finally only Carter with the talker set on and myself were left in the compartment. He was preoccupied with a *Life* magazine and that left me with nothing to do except twiddle my thumbs, drink cup after cup of coffee, and smoke cigarettes.

It was getting close to the time for me to go up on lookout, and I was debating with myself whether to relieve early or not when things sprang into action again. There was a commotion topside, followed by quick movements in the control room, and the Klaxon gave warning that *Wahoo* was diving. Blasts from the horn were still echoing in the boat when

Appel, Jesse L., Seaman Second, from Evansville, Indiana, burst into the crew's messroom and looked wildly around. He still had on a submarine jacket, and the binoculars he had been using on lookout dangled heavily from the strap about his neck.

Seeing me, he scurried over and huddled up close as though he thought I might be able to protect him from some wild terror. His teeth were chattering, his face pale under a lookout's tan, and his eyes were dilated.

Wahoo was on her way down to put tons and tons of protective water around her.

I looked wonderingly toward the watertight door to see what could have scared Appel. As I looked, Tyler the other lookout came in out of breath.

"What happened?"

"Boy, did Appel ever clear that bridge!" Tyler said admiringly. "We got in too close to that Jap freighter and he started firing at us. One of the shells screamed right over us. Appel was down that hatch before Paine could push the diving button. I never saw anyone move so fast before."

Hunter came in. "Hey, Yeo, you shoulda seen Appel come down that hatch. He was just a blur when he went through the conning tower."

"All right, you guys, take it easy." I turned to Appel. He was blubbering something I could not understand. I said soothingly, "Everything's all right now, Appel. There's nothing to be afraid of. They can't reach us here."

He said a little plainer, "They was shoo-shooting right at me. I c-c-c-could hear that s-s-shell going right over my head."

I said, "Hunter, get him a cup of coffee." Then to Appel, "The guys are real proud of you the way you cleared the bridge."

He said, "Yeo, I'm scared. I don't care what anybody thinks. I'm scared." I thought he was going to cry.

Everybody stopped whatever they were doing and listened. *Wahoo* was firing torpedoes again. A terrific explosion let us know that one of them was a hit.

Appel said, "I gotta get up to the forward torpedo room, they might need me there," and he left.

Carter announced into the silence that followed, "We got that oil tanker that was standing by the freighter. That damn freighter has got away again."

Hunter said, "The Old Man's raving about the flashless gunpowder the Japs are using. You can't see their gun flashes unless they're firing right at us, then it's a little late to do much dodging. It's darker'n hell up there too. Good thing we got radar to track with."

I asked, "How big were the ships, Hunter?"

"Well, the transport was about seventy-five hundred tons, the crippled freighter up there about a ten thousand tonner, and the other freighter and oil tanker are in the vicinity of about seven thousand . . ."

Krause had stuck his head through the door. "Hey, Hunter, the Old Man wantsya."

Hunter jumped up and went out.

Pruett, Ralph R., Electrician First, from Topeka, Kansas, came into the messhall with a checkoff list and a flashlight. "Better get some red goggles and wait in the control room, Yeo. We're going to surface in about ten minutes, and you've got the port lookout."

"I know, I know," I said, "I'm coming."

Pruett grinned at me and went on to the sleeping compartment.

I got up, stretched, and lit a cigarette—it would be my last for a while—and smoked it going into and while waiting in the control room.

Everything was red with the goggles on, but they were necessary in order to adapt my sight to the dark night when I got up on lookout.

I watched idly Stevens, George V., Fireman Second, from Springfield, Illinois, on the stern planes. He sat on a swivel seat without shirt or undershirt. Sweat made the muscles on his back glisten, the highlights rippling with his shoulder blades and neck muscles whenever he turned the large wheel in his hands from right to left or back again. His concentration was entirely on the dial in front of him. Moving the indicator up or down a few degrees made the rudders rise or fall, keeping *Wahoo's* stern on an even keel and at the required depth.

His team mate, Berg, was operating the bow planes station. When either or both got off the required depth, even a foot, Lieutenant Grider was right behind them urging them to get back on depth. They would jockey the wheels quickly and then relax back on their seats waiting for a change to occur.

Pappy Rau was standing by the Christmas tree with all its green lights showing, sucking on his pipe and meditating about something probably far removed from the business at hand. Vidick was the eternal sentry, standing stolidly by the electrical switchboard.

A portable board table was placed on the master gyrocompass. This was covered with graph paper tacked down along the edges with thumbtacks. A parallel ruler, an Artgum eraser, and several sharpened pencils were neatly set in one corner. By looking close through the red goggles, I could see penciled lines that were terminated with X's and then going off on a tangent to change position at another X. Faintly penciled in by the X's would be a compass bearing, and every half inch or so were Naval chronological times. There were three separate trails of lines, one of which terminated with a circle around it.

Interpreted, this chart was showing the exact positions of three ships in a scale area of miles. One I knew was the *Wahoo*, the other the freighter we were having so much trouble with, and the line with the circle ending was where the tanker had sunk. This was a graphic picture of the late afternoon and evening battles.

Veder came in and donned red goggles. We stood quietly by nervously fingering the binoculars at the strap ends. I zippered down my submarine jacket, opened a button of my shirt, and stuffed the binoculars inside, zippering back over. This would keep salt spray off the lenses until I got them to my lookout station.

There began a stirring in the conning tower, and I noticed the watch standers in the control room tense with muscular expectation. I felt my own breathing quicken and my heart beating faster.

"Bring the masthead out of the water, George, and man the radar screen."

"Aye, aye, sir." Lieutenant Grider said to the planesman, "Bring her up to . . ." His voice was drowned out by the whine of the periscope motor. He turned to me and ordered, "Yeo, man the radar screen until we can get Cook in here to relieve you."

I moved over to the screen, flipped the toggle switch to "on," and waited for grass to appear. I could feel *Wahoo* slanting upward.

The grass came up suddenly and I spotted a constant sharper pip about two-thirds along the strip. "Pip contact at fifteen thousand yards," I sang out.

Lieutenant Grider was at the speaker mike. "Radar contact at one-five-oh-oh-oh, Captain."

"Very well. Prepare to surface."

Someone shouldered me aside. "You're relieved, Yeo." It was Cook.

"Lookouts to the conning tower."

I did not wait for Lieutenant Grider's command. Instead, I started up the ladder followed closely by Veder.

Krause said, "Lookouts in the conning tower, Captain."

Captain Morton's voice from the shadows in the corner replied, "Very well. Surface."

I followed Hunter and Lieutenant O'Kane out into a watery world, which was lighted only by the faint radiance of bright stars overhead. Water showered down from the radar mast wetting my thin hat. I jerked the binoculars to my eyes and realized for the first time that I still had the red goggles on. Yanking them off with one hand and stuffing them into my jacket pocket, I bent forward with the glasses trying to bring the horizon in closer.

"Shift to all four diesels. All ahead standard." The tinkle of the annunciators in the conning tower, *Wahoo's* four main engines roaring into being with loud blasts from the exhausts aft, sixty-four cylinders began urging the twin screws to dig in and push.

"Swing left and come to two-seven-oh."

"Swinging left to two-seven-oh, sir."

"Hunter, fix a pair of binoculars into the port TBT" (target bearing transmitter).

"Aye, aye, sir."

"All clear on the port lookout."

"Very well, keep a sharp lookout at about three-eight-oh. The target is too far away for you to see it yet."

"Aye, aye, sir."

"All clear on the starboard side, sir."

"Very well."

Wahoo pushed steadily into the night. From below, periodic reports of the lessening distance between the freighter and *Wahoo* kept coming up.

"See her yet, Yeo?"

"No, Captain, all's clear on the port bow."

"Very well. Let me know as soon as you spot her."

"Aye, aye, sir."

I strained my eyes into the darkness, willing the ship to materialize. I caught a glimpse of a darker object and waited a fractional moment to be sure my eyes were not deceiving me. Yes, it was still there.

"Ship ahoy, two points off the port bow."

"Very well."

I heard quick steps below and could just barely make out the Captain's form bent to the TBT. "Relative bearing . . ." The wind carried his voice away.

I searched hurriedly the rest of the ocean but kept coming back to the freighter. We got in close enough for me to see the dark hulk without the aid of the glasses.

My hair stood on end, and I felt an urge to drop off the lookout station and run as sharp cracks of gunfire reached me.

"He's firing off the other side," Captain Morton's reassuring voice came up.

"Probably spotted a whitecap on one of the waves. Bet the skipper is really anxious," Lieutenant O'Kane's voice replied.

"He's not taking any chances. Probably shooting at anything suspicious trying to scare us off. He's a nervy devil," Morton answered admiringly.

"Searchlight beam on the port beam," I screamed as loud as I could shout.

"Where away? I see it. It's flashing around the water."

"Whataya think, Captain? A destroyer or a cruiser?"

"That's hard to tell, he's too far away. Hey, I bet that freighter will stop zigging and head toward it for protection."

"We can't fight a warship with only two fish in the stern tubes, Captain."

"I know, but we're not going to let that freighter get away. Helmsman, come left to two-two-five. All ahead emergency."

The target moved right, past *Wahoo's* bullnose, as *Wahoo* swung left. I lost sight of the freighter as it moved into Veder's area but I had a new interest now. The searchlight was having an almost hypnotic effect on me. I could hardly pull my eyes off it for quick looks at the rest of the ocean.

Morton called below to the fire-control party for information on the distance of the track, to intercept the freighter as it swung toward the searchlight beam.

I was watching the light search the ocean and get nearer when *Wahoo* changed course again and the light moved back to the port beam. I looked carefully forward but could not see the freighter, so it must still be on the starboard side.

"Come left, full rudder."

Wahoo began a circle. The searchlight seemed to be about ready to burst over the horizon and onto us. It started moving up toward the bow as *Wahoo* circled. I wondered what the hell the Old Man was up to now and remembered that our last two torpedoes were in the stern tubes.

The light disappeared as *Wahoo's* bow swung around. Veder reported, "Searchlight on the starboard bow, sir."

"Check the rudder and steady on one-zero-zero! All stop. Back two-thirds on the starboard engines."

There were some more commands that I did not catch in my concentrated search for the freighter. I caught up with it on the port quarter.

"Ship three points abaft the port beam," I yelled.

"All stop," I heard again.

Wahoo settled down to watchful waiting.

"Fire nine!!" I jumped at the suddenness of the command. I swung around looking aft.

"Fire ten!!" *Wahoo* shuddered as number nine left the tube in a vicious hungry search for Oriental prey. *Wahoo* bucked again and number ten swished out of its tube.

I kept the binoculars glued to the freighter's silhouette. It seemed a long distance away and I wondered if the torpedoes would reach it.

"All ahead standard. We're heading for the barn." A thrill of pleasure and relief ran through me.

Wahoo stood still until her propellers caught footing in the water and then we began to move. I kept the binoculars pressed to my eyes until the metal eyepieces hurt the skin. I was just about to give up hope of a hit when a white and yellow flash spread out on the horizon like a heavy sheet of summer lightning. It grew in size and faded away.

"We got 'er, we got 'er!" officers and quartermasters on deck were shouting in jubilation.

The explosion, muffled by distance, swept by my ears as another flash lighted the ocean temporarily. "Two hits, two Goddam hits," Morton was screaming.

Still watching, I saw the searchlight beam sweep across the ocean and steady on the sinking ship. The second explosion roared by on vibration wings and was lost into history. The freighter turned slowly over and split into two dark sections before one end tilted up and then slid out of sight. The other end just faded into blackness.

The wind whistled a song of victory, using *Wahoo's* radio antenna and the signal halyards for a musical instrument.

I was still watching the angry lashing of the searchlight beam, greatly diminished by distance, when Gerlacher relieved me.

"What in hell are you doing up here?"

"I relieve you. It's nearly midnight."

"I don't mean that. Why ain't you in bed with that shoulder?"

"Oh, it feels better now. It don't hurt much and I wanted to see what was going on."

"Does Rau or Lane know you're up here?"

"Yeah, I had a heck of a time convincing them I was all right. Lindhe said a little fresh air wouldn't hurt me."

"Suppose you have to clear the bridge?"

"I'll make it all right," he said convincingly.

"Look, kid, why don't you go below? It's just a little while until the midwatch comes on anyway."

"Naw, I'm all right I tell you." Then excitedly, "There's a searchlight astern of us, I just saw it."

"You're so right. At one time we was so close I leaned over and polished the lens on it."

"You're kidding?"

"Just ask the Captain. I got news for you. We're headed for the barn."

"Gee . . ."

Ensign Misch's voice called up, "Anything wrong up there on port lookout?"

"Negative," I answered. "I've just been relieved. I'll be right down."

"Very well."

I moved to the blue-lighted hatch opening and went wearily below. The messroom was filled with jabbering idiots. I grabbed a cup of coffee and sank listlessly in the corner.

"They musta been a million Japs in the water this morning!"

"It was my torpedo tube that got that last bastard. I'm going to paint a Jap flag right on the . . ."

". . . and then Doc came runnin' up to me and said, 'Kohut, do you have something I can cut Glinski's toes off with . . .'"

"The Old Man said, 'We ought to shoot the sons-a-bitches.' Say that would make a good motto for the *Wahoo*, wouldn't . . ."

I looked up and saw Lindhe stirring a cup of coffee. "How's Glinski?"

"He's fine. I just come from there and he's sleeping like a baby. He will be all right if infection doesn't set in, but I dusted plenty of sulphate powder on the wound and . . ."

"We just wanted to know how he was doing, not his medical history."

Lindhe retorted, "I never saw a worse bunch of constipated guys in my life," and he went forward.

The group dwindled as rapidly as it grew. I found myself alone in the corner with Appel. I said, "Guess I'll turn in."

In the sleeping quarters all I could see of Glinski was a bundled form. I kicked off my moccasins and climbed into my sack. The last thing I remembered was the strong smell of antiseptic and my saying, "Thank you, dear Lord, for bringing us through safely."

At 0330 Hayes came in, laid a hand on my shoulder, and was about to squeeze softly and shake gently. My eyes came open and I raised my head. "Time to go on lookout, Yeo."

"Okay." I yawned and threw my legs over the edge of the bunk. He vanished quietly. A cup of coffee did not awaken me fully, and I groped my way sleepily into the control room.

Wilcox was checking off. "Take the first helm watch, Yeo."

"Okay," I answered sleepily and somehow crawled up the ladder to the conning tower.

"You're relieved."

Wach said, "Don't you want to know what course we're steering?"

"Oh, sure, whatsa course?"

"Zero-two-seven."

Delicious early-morning fresh air was pouring through the open hatch. Its oxygen content finally worked into the blood vessels of my brain and chased out the drowsiness. I stood in the darkness smoking and eying the gyrocompass indicator, deftly coming to course when *Wahoo* was inclined to seek a tangent. The darkness began to thin out near the open hatch. Details began to stand out on objects that were dark masses a moment before.

"Bridge," Wilcox's voice from below was saying, "we got a contact on the radar bearing three-three-oh, sir, range fifty thousand yards."

Ensign Griggs answered from above, "Very well, send a messenger to notify the Captain and Executive Officer."

"That's already been done, sir."

"Very well."

A few seconds later there was a scurrying noise at the control room hatch opening, and the Captain and Lieutenant O'Kane were beside me.

"Good morning, Yeo." It was Captain Morton's voice.

I threw him a sideways glance and said, "Good morning, sir," taking in his good-natured grin. He seemed to be always smiling or laughing about something. The Executive Officer gave me a sleepy nod, his mind apparently on the more serious business ahead.

"Captain coming on the bridge," I shouted.

"Very well."

Captain Morton trailed by the Executive Officer went topside. I could hear their footsteps moving about on the steel plating and slotted wooden decks.

Ensign Griggs' voice came down the speaker, "Control, keep the radar ranges coming. Wake up Ensign Misch and set up a plot."

"Aye, aye, sir."

"Helmsman, come left to zero-one-zero degrees."

"Coming left to zero-one-zero," I repeated. I threw the helm over two degrees left rudder and waited for Wahoo to respond. The gyro indicator jumped and began jerkily swinging to the right as Wahoo swung left. About ten degrees before it reached zero-one-zero, I eased up on the rudder, and just before it passed the mark brought the rudder three degrees right, checking Wahoo's swing and bringing the rudder back to zero. "Steady on zero-one-zero, sir."

"Very well, hold her there until further orders."

Krause came into the conning tower. We exchanged good mornings. Hunter showed up and went onto the bridge. The light streaming through the hatch announced it to be nearly daybreak. I was on the wheel an hour and a half while the contact was being investigated.

"There's two or three pips on the radar now, bridge. It looks like it might be a convoy." This was Lieutenant Jackson's voice. He was evidently checking the operation of the radar.

"Very well, Jack." There was a silence and then, "Control, call the battle stations submerged watch."

"Aye, aye, sir." Another long silence and presently I heard sounds below that informed me men were moving quietly to their stations. Lieutenant Paine came into the tower and played with the TDC.

Simmonetti came up with a cup of coffee in hand and relieved me. I went below.

Janicek and Robertson, the two messcooks, had the tables set for breakfast. They and Rowls were sitting in the corner, Rowls with a facial expression of deep disgust and disappointment. Carter was manning the battle phones. I looked over the neat arrangement of dishes, knives, forks, coffee cups, and bowls.

"What's doin' up there, Yeo?" It was Rowls inquiring.

"You got me. We spotted a convoy. Only with no fish left to fight with, I guess we'll just look 'em over and let 'em go by. Maybe radio their position to Pearl."

Carter said, "They've spotted the masts and stacks. Radar reports four ships. I wish we had some fish left."

Hunter came in full of suppressed excitement. "You know what, fellows? The Old Man's going to make an attack!"

"What?" We ejaculated in surprised unison.

"He's going stark raving maniac crazy," Janicek added.

Hunter put two slices of bread into the toaster and waited, keeping us in suspense. When the toast was ejected, he went on, " 'Mush' says we're going to get up ahead of them and submerge. When they come over, we're going to surface and fire the guns at them."

"My Gawd," I groaned and asked the inevitable question, "Howsabout escorts?"

"They haven't spotted any. Looks like this convoy is unescorted, too."

Rowls jumped up and said to the messcooks, "Better clear these tables over the ammo locker. Stack the dishes on the other tables. They'll be wantin' to get into the locker soon."

I ducked into the sleeping compartment to get an extra package of cigarettes.

Glinski looked weakly up at me. "What's going on, Yeo?"

I said, "Hiya, kid. There's another convoy out there."

Lindhe raised up in bed. "What's that? Another convoy? What's 'Mush' going to do?"

"We're going to surface in the middle of it and go to battle stations surface."

"You're kidding?"

"Wish to hell I was."

Lindhe slipped out of his bunk. "Wonder why I wasn't called?"

"We just spotted 'em a little while ago. I had the watch is the reason I'm up. We'll probably be diving shortly."

Kohut raised up, stretched, and slid out of his bunk. Two or three others got up. O'Brien in an after corner lit up a cigarette and lay smoking it. I went out as Lindhe walked over to Glinski's bunk.

Rowls handed me a heaping plate of scrambled eggs. "Anybody else want anything to eat?" I was just finishing eating when *Wahoo* dived. She leveled off and Lane came through the boat. "Any of you guys got a battle station surface better get ready for it." And he went aft.

Carr came in, pushed back the mess tables, unlocked the big brass padlock on the ammunition locker, and threw open the trap door. Members of the deck-gun crew came in, and soon there was a stack of fixed cartridges in the passageway. It was getting crowded so I moved into the control room and picked up a pair of binoculars. Veder was already there waiting.

After a long wait, we began to feel the presence of ships overhead. Excitement built up to equal the air pressure in the boat. The beat of propeller screws grew out of nothing and became loud all around *Wahoo*.

Wahoo eased up her depth controls and came to periscope depth. She poked up an artificial eye for a quick looksee, and then Morton pushed the button to the general alarm bell. The Klaxon let loose with three loud blasts. "Battle stations surface, battle stations surface"—fighting words that tightened the glands in the small of my back even as I raced out of the ship and onto the starboard lookout station.

Wahoo had burst from the depths and was rolling lazily on the surface with a great expanse of aerated salt-water bubbles to show from what part of the ocean she had erupted. Below me, voices were screaming.

"Decks are awash, sir!"

"Twenty millimeters manned and ready, sir!"

"Get that deck hatch open."

"Two ships on the portside, sir!"

"Full left rudder. All ahead standard on the diesels."

I added my voice to the others. "Two ships on the starboard side, sir. Both veering away."

"Get that ammunition on deck on the double."

"Deck gun manned and ready, sir."

"Close in on that small oil tanker. It is slower than the rest. Roger, have the men aim at the pilothouse and the rudder first."

I could see the sterns of two large ships as they headed away from *Wahoo* on divergent tangents. I almost missed the mast and stack of another ship just over the horizon. I swung the glasses back and saw smoke come boiling furiously out of its stack.

"Another ship abaft the starboard beam." I put everything I had into the shout.

Lieutenant O'Kane's voice, "Repeat that again, starboard lookout. Whereaway?"

"Another ship abaft the starboard beam, sir."

A rush of feet to the starboard side acknowledged my report.

"What is it? Dick! Can you make it out?"

"Looks like a destroyer, Captain, moving up fast."

"Gun crews secure from battle stations surface."

New noises below, stampeding feet.

"Leave your guns and ammo topside. Clear the top decks. Never mind the gun, Carr! Get your tail down below."

I kept my glasses on the destroyer. The smoke volume seemed to grow. Her superstructure was beginning to break the rim of the horizon.

I pushed the binoculars inside the jacket, grabbed the rail with both hands, and bent my knees. Looking below, I saw Captain Morton face upward cupping his hands to his mouth. At that moment I moved out into space, hit the deck with a jarring thud, regained my equilibrium, and skated on the slippery deck past the Captain. I never heard him call, "Clear the bridge."

The next thing I remember I was standing in the messhall, braced against *Wahoo's* steep down-angle dive.

Veder came in and began to shake my hand. "Congratulations, Yeo, you not only beat me down, you set a new record getting here."

Wahoo was searching frantically for the bottom, piling tons and tons of protective water over her back. "Rig for depth charge, rig for depth charge."

I felt *Wahoo's* decks level off and at that instant Pandora's box opened and all hell broke loose. Three depth charges went off in succession, seemingly right on deck over the crew's messroom. We were plunged into complete darkness, and a loose piece of metal shooting through the void struck my left ear, causing it to sting sharply. Dishes stacked on the tables were lifted and thrown about. Loose knives and forks flew about at random, their screaming lost in the blasts of the depth charges. Patches of cork showered down, followed by a ventilationless room full of choking dust.

Carter coolly turned on the blue emergency light.

I waited in terror-stricken silence holding on to the table with a death grip. It could not have been much longer than a sharp circle turn before the approaching screws warned us to brace for the next depth charges. There was a repetition of the previous inferno, and then we settled down to a long period of peaceful quiet running.

Carter was the first one to break the silence. "The sonarman reports that the screws of the DE are going away."

I sat fearfully waiting for them to come back. Five, ten, fifteen minutes went dragging by.

Carter said into the phones, "The lights are out in the galley. We got the emergency lights on. From what I can see there are no leaks in the messhall or the sleeping compartment."

I got up and walked unsteadily into the sleeping compartment and looked for leaks. I could not smell chlorine gas so I figured the batteries were all right. Glinski was asleep and I guessed that Lindhe had given him a sedative. I came back to the messroom feeling better. "Everything's okay in the sleeping compartment." Carter nodded his thanks to me. Sitting down, I felt the weight of the binoculars bump against my legs. I had forgotten completely about having them. We huddled in the messroom for nearly an hour. Finally *Wahoo* sneaked back to the surface.

"Everything is clear topside," Carter reported. "The Old Man seems to think that destroyer was only interested in keeping us down until he could collect his ships and get out of there."

"Secure from depth charge, secure from depth charge."

I got up slowly, got a cup of coffee, and sat down again. I lit a cigarette off the stub of one I had in my mouth. I wondered stupidly when I had lighted the first cigarette or was it the second or third. I could not remember.

Electricians came and replaced the light bulbs. The messroom by the brilliance of the white lights was a shambles. Rowls and the messcooks began cleaning up. The messroom began to fill with sailors and their experiences. Lindhe came through delivering a ration of "depth-charge" medicine. "You all right, Yeo? Your ear's bleeding."

I felt woodenly of my ear and stared dazedly at the slight blood smear on my hand. "It's just a scratch. I'll be okay after I drink this."

He turned away as I swallowed the contents of the bottle in two gulps.

I returned the binoculars to the control room and crawled into my bunk.

About 1630 I awoke suddenly with a guilty feeling that I was doing something wrong. I got up and went through the messroom, noting the time and the fact that the messcooks were starting to clean up after evening chow.

In the control room Pappy Rau and Lane were chuckling over something one of them had said to the other. I said, "Gee, Pappy, I'm sorry I overslept for the watch but I don't remember being called."

They looked at each other and laughed again. "Don't worry about it, Yeo. We didn't call you. The Exec left orders to take you off the watch list until we get in. They're going to start getting out the War Patrol Report."

"Gee, thanks." I went into the officers' country. The curtains were drawn on every officer's stateroom. Behind one or two I could hear gentle snores. I saw Manalisay in the pantry and asked, "What time are the officers going to eat tonight?"

He said, "Nobody eat tonight, everybody sleep but duty officer."

The action basket had some preliminary details to be rough-typed concerning the attack on the destroyer at Wewak Harbor. It hardly seemed possible that only five days had elapsed. I fell to studying the handwriting preliminary to the typing. Lieutenant O'Kane came to the door all business. "Good evening, Yeo. Ready to go to work?"

"Yes sir," I replied eagerly.

"I see you're studying those roughs. There will be more as fast as we can keep them coming."

"Yes sir."

He started to leave. "Oh, Mr. O'Kane, Keeter was telling me . . ."

I worked on into the afternoon, subconsciously interpreting the sounds around me. Sometime in the afternoon we dived. I tried to continue the work but could not. Finally I got up and went into the messroom.

I found Hunter, O'Brien, Krause, and Rowls in our reserved corner.

"What gives with the dive?"

"We're going in close to Fais Island and take some pictures through the 'scope of the phosphate works."

O'Brien said, "I hear you beat Veder off the bridge finally, Yeo."

I said hotly, "I had an incentive. I could see that destroyer coming and he couldn't. They say it was shooting at us but I didn't wait to find out."

One afternoon Captain Morton came by and drove me into the typewriter with a slap of his massive hand, and after laughing at my frustration asked, "Have you made out the papers on Keeter's rating yet?"

"Yessir."

"Good, that atlas of his was a real find. Also, I rated Hall for spotting that first convoy while on lookout."

"The papers are all made out waiting for Mr. O'Kane's signature." I handed them to him. He went through them. "Good men, all of these." Seeing Gerlacher's name, he said, "I'm making a recommendation before we get in to get Gerlacher and Glinski Purple Hearts. There will be a recommendation for a Navy Cross for O'Kane, a Silver Star for Lindhe, a Bronze Star for . . . I guess I'd better see O'Kane about this now and get something started on it." He hurried away.

The next morning found *Wahoo* approaching the island of Oahu, and it did not take much coaxing from Lane to get the crew to turn out for reveille. The blessedness of being alive was on us all, and the prospect of two weeks at the Royal Hawaiian Hotel was so motivating that we polished our shoes and had our sea bags packed before the island ever came into sight.

Krause caught me at breakfast and handed me a slip of paper. "Will you do me a favor and type up a requisition for this item? I'll get the Old Man to sign it."

I glanced at the paper. Scribbled in Krause's neat handwriting were the words, "Ten gallons of grain alcohol. Purpose: to be used for cleaning periscope lenses."

I looked up at him and he gave me a broad wink. I replied, "I'll give it number one, triple A priority."

Standing on the bridge of *Wahoo* after returning from a successful war patrol. From left, Lieutenant Richard 'Dick' O'Kane and Commander Dudley 'Mush' Morton.
Photo: *Real War Photos*

Following her Mare Island (CA.) overhaul in July of 1943, *Wahoo* takes to the sea in her new form.
Photo: *National Archives*

Seated at the desk in his cabin aboard *Wahoo* is Commander Dudley 'Mush' Morton. Note photos of Morton's wife and children at the upper left.
Photo: *National Archives*

July, 1943 near Mare Island, California; an excellent photo from
the 'wake of the *Wahoo.*'
Photo: *National Archives.*

A United States Navy band (on the right) begins to play as *Wahoo*
returns to Pearl Harbor after a successful war patrol.
Photo: *National Archives.*

Dalton Keeter (pictured) just made Chief Machinist Mate, "So we threw him over the side," said Sterling. The hand on Keeter's head belongs to Yeoman Forest Sterling.
Photo: *From the author's collection.*

As seen through the periscope of *Wahoo*, the *Nittsu Maru* takes its final plunge to the bottom of the Yellow Sea after being torpedoed on March 21, 1943.
Photo: *From the author's collection.*

In another periscope photo, *Wahoo* sinks the *Satsuki Maru* in March of 1943.
Photo: *Real War Photos.*

In *Wahoo's* conning tower, Commander Morton (nearest camera)
and Lieutenant Roger Paine work on a firing solution.
Photo: *National Archives.*

August, 1942: viewed from her stern, *Wahoo* maneuvers up to the
dock at Alameda, California.
Photo: *National Archives.*

Crewman David Veder stands watch as starboard lookout (top
center). Lt. Richard O'Kane stands on the lower left. Lt. Roger
Paine is on the bridge (on the right). Note the string of victory
flags and pennant flying from the SD radar mast and broomstick
tied to the #2 periscope signifying a "clean sweep." SJ radar and
mast have been censored.

Photo: *From the author's collection.*

After returning from their third war patrol, the crew of *Wahoo* receives their mail from home.
Photo: *From the author's collection.*

Chapter 9

Krause stood looking over my shoulder while I typed the requisition. When it was finished. I ratcheted it out of the platen and passed it over my shoulder. He took it eagerly and went to Morton's stateroom.

I leaned back in the office chair to hear better. A rapping caused by Krause's knuckles meeting the doorjamb reached me first. There was a movement and a chair scraped back followed by Captain Morton's voice. "Yes? Come in."

The sound of curtains sliding back and Krause's voice came to me. "Captain, would you sign this requisition for me, sir?"

"Why didn't you give it to Mr. O'Kane?"

"It's a special requisition, sir. Requires your signature."

I heard Captain Morton's booming laughter fill the passageway. When he laughed the whole ship seemed to vibrate in resonance. He quieted down for a second and went into another siege of hearty laughter.

"Thank you, sir."

The curtains swished again and Krause came by me waving the piece of paper triumphantly.

The Captain came out of his stateroom to my office. "Yeo, I have a job for you. Make out leave papers for Lennox, Lindhe, and Wilcox for thirty days back to Stateside."

I looked at him in amazement.

"I'm going to try to give leave to two or three of my leading petty officers at the end of each patrol."

I said quickly, "I'm a leading PO, sir."

He grinned. "You're not leading enough, yet. Besides I can't spare the best damn yeoman in the submarine Navy."

I was flattered in spite of myself. "I'll get on it right away, Captain, before the maneuvering watch is set."

"You'll have to hurry. We sighted Barber's Point some time ago." He went into the control room.

I finished the leave papers and dropped them into Lieutenant O'Kane's basket in his stateroom. Passing through the control room, I heard the Executive Officer's voice on the speakers, "Station the maneuvering watch, station the maneuvering watch." My heart beat faster in anticipation as I grabbed off a submarine jacket and changed my course to come out on the bridge.

Krause had the talker's set ready for me. I blew into the talker twice and said, "Testing, testing. All maneuvering stations make your reports to the bridge." There was a quick succession of "Stations manned and ready," beginning with the forward torpedo room and ending with the after torpedo room.

"All maneuvering watches manned and ready, Captain," I reported.

"Very well."

O'Brien's voice came over the phones. He was singing "Bless 'em all." I listened a few seconds grinning at his jubilation. "Pipe down," I growled in an undertone.

O'Brien's voice came back, "The yeoman on the *Wahoo* is . . ." The phones clicked off.

Vidick's voice said, "Where are we, Yeo? Pappy Rau wants to know."

I looked over the side. "We're passing the channel buoy. We're heading into the channel."

Something that Krause and Hunter were doing caught my eye. I watched them finish their job and then said into the phones, "Hey, fellows, the signalmen have run up eight tiny Jap flags on one of the signal halyards. They sure look pretty flapping in the wind. Two of them have the Rising Sun stripes on them for warships."

O'Kane came up and ordered, "Pass the word to secure from sea detail, on deck the coming-into-port detail."

"Aye, aye, sir." Then I repeated his order into the phones. Several yelps of joy came over the receivers in reply. When the excitement died down, I said, "You guys should see the masthead, too. 'Mush' ordered a brand-new corn-straw broom lashed to it."

I kept up a running report of our progress as *Wahoo* felt her way along the twisting channel, past the net Depot, Hickam Field, Hospital Point, Ford Island, the *U.S.S. Arizona*, the tall cranes at the Navy Yard, until the submarine base showed up dead ahead. There was a big crowd on the pier waiting our arrival.

Heaving lines made wavy arcs in the sky and landed in eager hands. Mooring lines followed and were quickly bent about bitts on the pier. The brow was pushed over while fenders were being thrown over the sides to aid the camels. Flags went down and the anchor colors broke out on signal. Everything was a confusion of shouting and movement. Finally, "Secure from maneuvering watch," and *Wahoo's* third war patrol came to a screeching halt. She had left Brisbane a comparative nonentity and returned to Pearl Harbor a celebrity.

The bridge was deserted quickly. I took off the phones and said, "Secure from maneuvering watch," into an empty line.

A Navy ambulance was on the dock, and while I watched, Lindhe came up out of the access hatch, reached down for an object. Muller quickly ran over and dropped to his knees to help Lindhe. They pulled up a Navy wire stretcher with a blanket-bundled Glinski strapped in it. He looked like an Indian papoose or an Egyptian mummy. Two pharmacist's mates in whites came out on deck and started carrying the stretcher along the deck below me.

I looked into Glinski's eyes as his upturned face went by, and he smiled. Lindhe shouted to Gerlacher, "Get your fanny up here. We ain't got all day." Gerlacher came on deck with a blue ditty bag and dressed for liberty. Lindhe and Gerlacher hurried off the ship and into the rear of the ambulance. It drove off, apparently headed for Tripler Army Hospital.

A Lieutenant Commander, Supply Corps, crossed the gangway with a money satchel and packing a forty-five. He was followed closely by two armed, rated white hats.

A chief came on board and asked, "Where's the yeoman?"

"Here," I answered. "What you want?"

"I'm the relief crew yeoman. Want to give me all the dope? I'll be doing your work while you're at the hotel."

I took the chief to the office. "There's damn little to do outside of opening the mail and answering it. The reports are all up to date."

The chief said, "I wish all the boats' work that comes in would be this easy. You should see some of them."

"The Exec took me off watch before we got in," I explained. "I understand we're getting some new men. You might have to take up their records, but the Exec says he ain't going to transfer no one in the crew until we get back."

"You'd better hurry to catch the bus. I've got all the dope I need to know."

I said, "Call me at the hotel if you run into anything you don't understand," and left the office reluctantly to another man's care.

Climbing into the bus, I was the last man. Krause shouted from the rear seat. "I got your mail for you, Yeo. Who's Marie Henry?"

"She's a cute little telephone number in LA," I answered. "Why?"

"You've got about fifty letters from her all addressed in green ink."

"Thanks," I said gratefully, "I'll get 'em from you when we get there."

I got squared away quickly at the hotel desk and in my room and then hunted up the room Krause and Hunter shared together. After knocking on their door and receiving the summons, "Come in," I threw open the door in time to see Simmonetti crawling out of the bath tub. He had all his clothes on. Hunter and Krause were laughing crazily at his discomfiture.

"What happened?" I asked curiously.

"Come here. We'll show you."

I walked over to the bathroom, felt rough hands grab hold of me, and I sailed into the tub filled with water and dirty clothes. I came up sputtering, crawled out dripping wet, and felt for my wallet.

"Damn you guys, you got my wallet all wet," I snarled angrily. "What did you want to go and do that for?"

"We're only clowning," Hunter said. "We forgot all about your wallet."

Krause said, "Gee, we're sorry, Yeo, but we had it all made up that anybody who comes to the room looking for a shot of that grain alcohol would have to pay for it first."

"Well, lift their wallets first," I growled.

Krause said, "Pitch in four bits for Coke and I'll go down to the fountain and get it."

I pulled a water-soaked dollar bill, with the wartime occupational surcharge HAWAII in large letters across the back, from my wallet and threw it at him. "I'll be back as soon as I can change into some dry dungarees," I threatened.

Ware came in with a newspaper. "I've been looking all over the hotel for somebody off the ship to show this to." He held up a late afternoon edition of the *Hawaiian Advertiser*. The headlines proclaimed WAHOO RUNNIN' JAPS A'GUNNING.

With a roar the whole crew crashed through the door, down the hallways, into the lobby, quickly buying up all the papers.

Back in Krause's room, I quickly read the story of how *Wahoo* had been the first submarine to sink an entire convoy. There were two or three paragraphs about the battle with the destroyer at Wewak, much about "Mush" Morton and O'Kane, the story of Lindhe's initiative in amputating Glinski's toes, and *Wahoo's* arrival in port with a broom at her mast. I reread the item several times. Everybody in the room had an open newspaper in front of him.

I looked hurriedly through the headlines of the rest of the paper. Franklin D. Roosevelt and Winston Churchill had met at Casablanca. The Russians had surrounded a whole German army at Stalingrad and German soldiers by the thousands were surrendering. Russia was still screaming for a second front. A communiqué from General Douglas MacArthur's headquarters in Australia announced that mopping-up operations were in progress at Guadalcanal.

I took the paper back to my room, placed it in my seabag, showered and went to bed. The sound of musical palm leaves outside my window lulled me quickly to sleep with the blessedness of knowing I was still alive and had a two-week guarantee that I would remain that way.

Songbirds outside the window awakened me to a morning of cheerful sunshine. I lay there breathing delicious fresh air wondering what time it was and not really caring to know.

As a second class petty officer, I was entitled to a room with only one other occupant. The other bed was not assigned and looked strangely out of place with its bare mattress in such an elegant room.

While I was lazily pondering on this luxury, the door swung open and Phillips walked in with his seabag and a small suitcase in hand. He threw his luggage on the other bed and strode across the room to mine.

"You old son-uv-a-gun," I exclaimed, pleased to see him. Raising on one elbow, I shook hands and then accepted a cigarette he offered. "I thought we left you in Brisbane."

"Just a nervous breakdown. I raised so much hell with them they flew me back to Pearl to rejoin the *Wahoo*."

I spied the first-class chevron on his arm. "What's this?" I asked, pointing.

"Oh! When I left *Wahoo* at Brisbane, 'Mush' went with me to the Squadron Office and asked them to rate me. He told the Squadron Commander I was the best damn baker in the submarine force. He said he wanted me on the *Wahoo* as soon as they was through with me in the sick bay."

I grinned. "He told me I was the best damn yeoman in the submarine Navy. We got a lot in common."

Phillips looked at me shyly. "Yeo, do you ever get the feeling that you're gonna die in this war?"

"Naw," I answered matter-of-factly, "I've always had a feeling that I was going to see the year two thousand. I get plenty scared at times, though, that I'm not going to make it." Then seeing the expression on Phillips' face, I asked concernedly, "Why do you ask that?"

"Oh, I don't know. Just a feeling, I guess. Yeo, I just know sometimes that I'm going to go down on the *Wahoo*. I just can't get away from the feeling."

I said, "Bull," feeling uncomfortable. "Besides, you got nothing to worry about as long as I'm attached to *Wahoo*. You heard the old saying—you can't kill a man that's born to be hanged."

He said, "Do you think you'll get transferred?"

"Hell no. Who ever heard of a yeoman getting transferred after they get on these damn pigboats. Everybody on the *Wahoo* will get rotated before I will and then I'll have to write my Congressman. When they start giving out leaves, I'll be the last person. They'll give everybody thirty days, and I'll have to beg on hands and knees for ten. When any other rate leaves the ship, there's always somebody to do his work for him, but when the yeoman or the pharmacist's mate leaves, the ship goes to pieces. If I put in for a transfer, you know what they'd do? They'd laugh right in my face and ask me where they could get a replacement. The Squadron's full of yeoman sitting on their big fat duffs, drawing submarine pay and growling because they're stuck away out here at Pearl Harbor or Brisbane and the liberties are tough." I caught my breath and saw that Phillips was chuckling at my vehemence.

"Aw, to hell with that," I said sheepishly, "have you had breakfast yet?"

Phillips said, "Yeah, the chow's lousy, but I'll come down and have a cup of coffee with you while you tell me about the last war patrol."

"Sure, sure." I dressed quickly in liberty whites and we took the elevator down to the main floor. The cafeteria was open and manned by Navy personnel. There were no set hours for any of the meals. We just procured an aluminum tray and went down the line choosing what we wanted. We went out on the patio where we could look down Waikiki Beach and at the hundreds of sun bathers and swimmers. There was a noticeable shortage of females present, so Phillips and I had a long discussion without any disturbing distractions.

O'Brien came in and greeted Phillips with, "If it ain't the prodigal son come back. Welcome aboard, you old gold-bricker, which reminds me I'd better see a dentist before I go back to sea what with all the hardtack we'll be having on board."

Phillips was not displeased at all. "Hi, O'B. Did you ever find your lost circuit? I hear you been spending all your time on somebody else's."

"Aw, you're one-eighty off. Hey, have you guys heard about the luau this afternoon?"

We shook our heads.

"The Chamber of Commerce is going to fete our feats of heroism by feeding us."

"Phooey," I added.

"No fooling. The order of the day is for all *Wahoo* sailors to show up promptly at Lau Yee Chai's restaurant at 1300 sharp."

I said, "Look, there's Gerlacher coming through the chow line."

Phillips said, "Yeah, he and I came out from the submarine base together in a taxi. He's all right, that kid."

Gerlacher started for another table. I called, "Come on over here, Gerlacher. Whatcha, antisocial?"

"Hi, fellows. I just thought you might want to be alone, is all."

O'Brien said, "And have people say we snubbed a Purple Heart holder! Hell no, my social prestige can't stand it."

I said, "When you finish, Gerlacher, I'll buy all you guys a drink. Anybody know a place close by?"

O'Brien was quick to reply, "Yeah, the Wagon Wheel or we can catch a taxi to Trader Vic's."

I said, "Let's start with the Wagon Wheel and see how far we get before 1300."

Gerlacher looked up from eating. "You guys go ahead without me. My shoulder's kinda sore. I'll catch up with you at Lau Yee Chai's."

"Okay, kid." O'Brien, Phillips, and I left by way of the ornamental façaded front of the hotel and turned left on the sidewalk toward the Wagon Wheel.

By 1300 we were in the beer garden of the Blaisdel Hotel and feeling exuberant. The potted palms, banana trees, and other tropical plants that decorated the patio had a peaceful atmosphere despite its being crowded with servicemen. We left reluctantly to find Lau Yee Chai's restaurant. It turned out to be a two-story building of Chinese-designed architecture with large gold Chinese hieroglyphics across the front.

At the door, Lane in chief whites was watching to see that only *Wahoo* sailors were admitted. He let us in with, "About time you guys showed up. I was getting ready to send the shore patrol out looking for you."

O'Brien piped up, "My, aren't we important? They'd had a heck of a time finding us in that mob of sailors that's filling the streets."

Lane laughed and thumbed us through the door. "Okay, wise guys, inside."

We took off our white hats and entered a large room with several rows of long tables covered with white tablecloths and decorated with Hawaiian flowers. The room was sweet with their fragrance and intermingled with the perfume was the smell of Chinese cooking. Two-thirds of the reserved seats were filled. Where we sat I could see into the open amphitheater of a stage. *Wahoo's* officers were already seated at the front table.

At the next table I noticed Hunter and Krause drinking Coke hi-balls. Looking around, I spotted the door leading into the bar. I said, "I'll be back in a minute, fellows, I got floating kidneys."

I was back in a matter of minutes with a hi-ball apiece for O'Brien, Phillips, and myself.

Food was placed on the tables, and there was every dish that could be imagined at a Hawaiian luau from *poi* to *huma huma nuka nuka a pua aa.* The waiters began serving drinks as well. Nothing was too good for *Wahoo* sailors that day.

We were given a welcome speech by the President of the Chamber of Commerce followed by a thank-you speech of short duration by Captain Morton. Then the entertainment began. Every child of school age who could sing, dance, or recite had a chance at us. The hula dance was performed by every nationality in the "melting pot of the Pacific." Everybody was eager to entertain us. The act that stole the show, as far as I and the comments of my shipmates indicated, was a high school troupe of teen-age chorus girls doing a patriotic theme, with a pretty little Japanese girl dressed as Uncle Sam singing "In Apple Blossom Time," while her barelegged background kicked in unsynchronized unison. Their toothy Oriental smiles helped our enthusiasm, and we jumped to our feet applauding, whistling, and shouting as though they were the Ballet Russe.

The following morning I stopped by the souvenir counter run by the Navy Exchange and saw a beautiful intricately carved jade necklace with a fine gold chain. It made me think of the telephone operator in Los Angeles. The saleslady promised to wrap and mail it for me, so I bought it.

Time was boring and yet precious. I could find nothing better to do than attach myself to the first *Wahoo* sailor or group of sailors that came out of the door and make the rounds of bars. Even drinking became dreary. I was too restless to try to read, and there were few places to go for any diversion in a city overcrowded with thousands of servicemen. I wrote letters but could not tell what I wanted to because of the censors.

The days slipped by into the second week. I came into the lobby one morning to drop into the mailbox a handful of letters saying, "I'm fine, hope you are fine," with the notation "free" in the corner of the envelope. They were unsealed so the censoring officer could read them. A Red Cross lady was recruiting submariners for a party in a private home. Carter, O'Brien, Rowls, Hunter, and myself went along and had a quiet afternoon of bridge and dart throwing.

Our time ran out and a Navy bus came to take us back to the *Wahoo*—and a beautiful sight she was—decked out in her new coat of paint. I could hardly believe she was the same girl I had fallen in love with just four months previously. On the other hand, I was just one of her seventy-seven beaux.

Chapter 10

The relief and repair crews had done right by our little *Wahoo*. As soon as I got my locker and bunk squared away, I hurried to the ship's office. A tinge of jealousy ran through me when I saw the chief yeoman at my accustomed seat. He was much neater than I. The desk top was waxed and polished. The chief had a precise place for everything. After he explained what he had done in my absence, I had to grudgingly admire his efficiency. He said, "This is a swell ship. Good officers, good crew, and good morale. You wouldn't consider a swap, would you? I'm in the squadron pool waiting for a boat."

"Hell, no," I exploded, thinking guiltily of the speech I had made Phillips.

"I didn't think you would," he said, "but I thought I'd ask."

After he left, I looked for something to do, but the chief had taken care of everything. Even the filing was neatly put away, which was something I usually let collect until necessity forced me to stuff it into the filing cabinet. I looked under P for personnel and in the P-16 folder found a list of the new men who had reported on board for duty. A Chief Motor-Machinist's Mate by the name of Record, Burrel A., from Long Beach, California, had been in charge of fourteen men reporting on board. I looked down the list and noticed that the Pharmacist's Mate who would take Lindhe's place was a First Class whose name was Kohl, Jerome T., from West Bend, Wisconsin. I wondered idly why we were getting two more ship's cooks: First Class, Dietrich, Helmut O., from Cedarburg, Wisconsin, and Idalia, Colorado, and a Third Class, Rennels, Juano L., from South Gate, California.

Lieutenant O'Kane came by the door and gave me the answer on a slip of paper. "Here's the transfer list, Yeo." I looked down the list and saw that Rowls, Lucas, and Boutzale were leaving. I hated to think of Rowls leaving but was glad for him in another way. He would have a good job at the submarine base for a while. Pappy Rau was going back to New London for new construction submarines. Hunter and Vogeler were being transferred.

While I was contemplating the list, Lieutenant George W. Grider, Long Beach, California, stopped by. "Yeo, I'm being detached. Is there any of my work hanging fire?"

I looked at him in surprise. "No, sir, everything is fine. Do you want me to make up your orders now?"

"That won't be necessary. It's all taken care of at the Squadron Office on the *Sperry*. I'll just need my service jacket, health record, and pay accounts is all."

I pulled out the drawers containing his records. "We'll miss you on the *Wahoo*, sir. Who will be the Engineering and Diving Officer in your place?"

"Mr. Henderson will take over those duties. You're not getting a replacement for me."

Smith, Donald O., Boatswain Second, from Humbolt, Nebraska, was next to come by the office. He was in greasy dungarees and had a big crescent wrench in one hand and oily waste in the other.

"Does your typewriter need fixin', Yeo?"

I exclaimed, "My Gawd, they don't care who they let out of sick bay nowadays. I thought we left you in Brisbane."

"You did, but you guys ain't about to get rid of me that easy. I got an IOU from Hunter for two dollars and fifteen cents I won in a penny ante game."

"Then you better hurry and catch him," I said. "He's being transferred to the States. Besides, I got a suspicion you turned into sick bay just to get out of being initiated on crossing the equator."

"All yeomen are suspicious of everybody." He grinned. "Try and prove it."

Lane called to him from the control room and he ducked through the watertight door. I turned back to the business of transferring shipmates to new duties.

Wahoo spent the next several days at sea drilling, testing new equipment, and getting into that split-second condition so necessary for survival in an emergency.

The last afternoon before returning to Pearl, Rennels got me in a corner. "Can I borrow twenty dollars from you, Yeo? I want to get into a poker game."

"I'm sorry," I answered, "all my money is tied up in the Brooklyn Bridge."

He looked honest. His disappointment was obvious, and it was always good policy to stay on the ship's cook's side, so I relented. "Okay," I said, "you got ninety-nine years to pay it back in."

Rennels said, "Thanks, Yeo, you'll never regret this." He hurried eagerly to the table that was dealing in pecuniary luck. Poor sucker, I thought, this *Wahoo* crew will soon make a Christian out of you.

As I was looking after him, another young sailor came to me. "Yeo, could I get an allotment increased before we go on patrol?"

"What's your name?"

"Whipp."

"Whipp, Kenneth L., Fireman First, from Springfield, Ohio?" I asked, grinning at his look of surprise at my memory. "Sure, follow me into the office."

I looked at his records. "You've got the maximum for your rate that can be made out now."

"Can't you increase it for the extra pay that I'll be getting for submarine duty?"

"Yeah, but it isn't going to leave you much for cigarette money and necessities."

"Well, it's for my twelve-year-old sister. You see, she's in an orphanage, and every cent I can send back helps to buy her clothes, and the authorities save what's left for her education. Besides, I don't smoke."

I said, "Okay, Whipp, fill out this form in the rough and I'll take it over to the pay office and get you squared away as soon as we get in."

"Thanks, Yeo."

We went back to the crew's mess. Rennels sitting in the game said, "Come here a minute, Yeo."

I went over and my eyes bulged at the sight of the money he had stacked in front of him. "Here's the twenty I owe you. I've been having a streak of luck."

McSpadden, sitting in on the game, said, "Yeo, do me a favor and transfer this guy to Timbuctoo. I think he's a professional gambler."

I answered, "It's about time you guys received a lesson. Kohut's been telling me you was a bunch of crooks."

"Wanta get in the game, Yeo?"

"Not me," I said religiously. "I have seen the light."

McSpadden answered, "There's nothing so pure as a converted whore."

"I'm just smart is all," I retorted, and turned my back on them.

Bair and Deaton were talking with the new Torpedoman Second, Neel, Percy, from Nampa, Idaho. I overheard the words "electric torpedo" and my curiosity got the upper hand.

126

"What gives with this electric fish business?" I inquired.

Deaton answered, "It's the newest thing in torpedoes since Farragut ran aground in Dewey Bay. They run on juice from storage batteries."

"Yeah, and the beauty of it is they don't leave no wake," Bair piped up.

"Boy, that is somepen," I said impressed and sat down with them. "Imagine! No torpedo wakes to give our position away."

Neel said importantly, "I been working on them at the submarine base. They're real cheesy."

Trying to impress Neel that I was an old salt, I said, "Reminds me of the time on the old *Barracuda* when we fired a fish and surfaced right after. Do you know that fish was laying fore and aft on the deck just as pretty as you please? All we had to do was slide it back down the torpedo loading hatch."

Neel said, "I heard about one that was brought in that musta been fired off an old F-boat. It was all covered with barnacles. The Navy thought it musta been stuck in the mud on the bottom and for some reason broke loose. Earthquake maybe."

I sat there a few minutes trying to think of a torpedo story to top this one. When I could not think of one, I got up to get a cup of coffee. I heard Neel say, "Boy, he ought to join the liar's club somewhere." I did not know whether to feel proud or insulted.

The next morning *Wahoo* pulled into Pearl to top-off fuel, complete the provisioning of ship, and make final preparations for getting underway on her fourth war patrol.

I made the sailing list out for the next day and dated it 23 February 1943. Then I made my way up to the submarine base where a beer canteen had been set up near the outdoor swimming pool. After two beers I did not feel like bucking the noisy line again. Giving the rest of my tickets to a man near me, I returned to an almost deserted *Wahoo* to write some last-minute letters home.

Next morning I turned the sailing list over to Lane to get off the ship and manned the phones on maneuvering watch. Watching on the starboard side, I listened to the getting underway commands: "Make preparations for getting underway for sea," "Stand by to answer bells," "Ship ready to get underway, Captain," "Very well, take her out on time," "Take in two and three," "Take in the brow," "Take in number four," "Starboard back one-third," "All stop," "Throw off number one," "Cast off."

There were corresponding sounds of bells tinkling, mooring lines slapping the water hard and being slid aboard, the gangplank rasping against metal and wood, a diesel snorting after popping several times, the quartermaster's whistle shrilling, and the ship's horn drowning all sounds out for the space of several seconds.

Wahoo backed and turned to starboard. She stopped altogether, propellers churned the waters of the harbor into a salt frenzy as she reversed. Then we slid out of Pearl Harbor along the freeway of the channel and out into the open sea. *Wahoo* turned her stern to windward, took a thirty-degree tangent away from land and continued westward.

Maneuvering watch was secured. I took a last look at Oahu Island and went below to find out what watch I would have. It turned out to be the midwatch.

After chow, O'Brien came in with his "Tell me a sea story" routine and announced his arrival with "Sock 'em down, Winsocki." I wondered what would happen if the recording was accidentally broken.

Krause dropped in for a cup of coffee and sat down.

"Where we going, Benny boy?" I asked.

"Officially the word isn't out, but for you and O'B, it's someplace around Japan."

I whistled. "How do you know?"

"Well, two things. One is I know we're going to stop off at Midway. We've got about twenty bags of mail on board for them. The other is the fact that my new navigational charts cover the Yellow Sea area and the southern coast of Japan."

The fragrance of apple sauce and doughnuts frying reminded us that Phillips was back.

Turning to Rennels, I asked, "Howdidja come out on the game yesterday?"

By way of answer he pulled out his wallet and opened it. I could see a twenty dollar bill. He thumbed around in the wallet a second and pulled out a money order stub. It was made out for $250. "I've been paying off my home in South Gate, California, with gambling money I send to my wife Lottie."

The conversation hit a snag with the dullness of the first day at sea upon us. I said, "Look, fellows, I got a mid coming up. I'm going to turn in now." I got up and walked out.

The week at sea was routine in its watch standing and daily sea duties. No one on watch growled when we passed a time zone, because there was only a three-hour watch to stand instead of the usual four as the clock was set back an hour. Soon we would lose a whole day when we crossed the International Date Line.

Wahoo pulled into sight of Midway Island at daybreak. The morning was heavy with grayness and low-hanging clouds. Two planes came out to investigate us and buzzed angrily across *Wahoo's* superstructure, so low we could see the goggled aviators staring down at us. I was on lookout. Krause pointed what looked to be a new type of shotgun with a thick barrel at them and began to blinker a code word of recognition. Satisfied, the planes began to circle us in ever-widening distance, searching the water for hostile periscopes or torpedo wakes.

A binocular view of Midway detailed the two low-lying atolls and the ocean beyond them. Hundreds of birds were gliding about in the air in a melee of graceful wings and white feathers. The islands themselves were covered with sand thrown about in glaring wind-blown piles.

Gerlacher had been made a quartermaster striker and was standing with Krause below me. I looked down and saw Krause pointing to the adjacent island. "That's Sand Island where the air base is located."

I turned the binoculars back on the island but could see nothing but sand. While I watched, a PBY lumbered slowly into the air from the edge of the ocean and began a slow circling ascent. I could not tell where it had come from.

Getting in closer to Midway, I could begin to make out low-lying huts among the sand dunes, so perfectly camouflaged that only the doors and windows gave substance to their form. A group of tall coconut palms, maybe eight or ten in number, marked a series of long, low buildings that were also camouflaged.

The maneuvering watch was stationed, and I was relieved from lookout by Anders to man the phones on the bridge deck. Captain Morton and Lieutenant O'Kane were on deck, with Morton at the conn. They were being careful of the course because the area had been well mined and there were in addition dangerous coral formations just beneath the water.

Wahoo zigged with proper respect and caution between marker buoys until she came alongside a crude pier that was the harbor at Midway. A short distance away another pier was in the throes of rapid construction. Hammers were pounding, planks being dropped on planks, truck motors racing, and thousands of protesting albatross voices were added to the sum of deafening, maddening noise.

After the maneuvering watch was secured, the Executive Officer stopped me a moment. "Get another sailing list ready, Yeo. There won't be any transfers or receipts here, so a copy of the one at Pearl will do."

"Yessir. Is there anything else?"

"No, you might have Lane pass the word that, if anybody has any letters to mail, it's their last chance before we leave on patrol. We're going to be here a few hours."

"Yessir."

He went down on deck and Krause came over. "How do you and O'Kane get along?"

"We get along fine. I always get the last word in."

"You do?"

"Yeah, I always say yes sir, and he walks away."

Krause grinned.

"Are those large albatrosses the ones they call gooney birds?"

Krause answered, "Yeah, this island was a government-protected sanctuary before the war. This is one of their breeding grounds. There's lots of bosun birds, and fairy terns, sea gulls, pelicans, and all sorts of birds here."

Wahoo was a guest for only a few hours and shoved off again pointing her nose westward. After the regular sea details were set, I went to the wardroom in search of Lieutenant O'Kane. I found him with Captain Morton playing acey-deucy in the wardroom. He looked at me, rolled the dice, and exclaimed triumphantly, "Acey-deucy," as the one and two spots turned up. He made his move and turned to me. "What do you want, Yeo?"

I said, "Sir, I'd like to request to be given a battle submerged station."

The Captain and Executive Officer both looked at me in surprise. "You don't have a station? How did we happen to overlook you?"

"I guess it's because Lindhe's been manning the station the yeoman would ordinarily have, sir."

Lieutenant O'Kane said, "We'll remedy that. On the next submerged battle stations you come up to the conn."

I said, "Thank you, sir," turning away and feeling a little foolish because I had been too proud to volunteer before.

I went back to the crew's mess and was greeted by Rennels. "The Skipper on here is a pretty good Joe, isn't he, Yeo?"

"Why?"

"He came into the messhall a little while ago and pinned up a chart of the Yellow Sea on the board. He said that's where we're going on this patrol."

I grinned. "Did he have on an old red bathrobe?"

"No." Rennels was surprised. "But he talked to us like he was one of us. He said the depth of water here was on an average about ninety feet. He said this was virgin territory for a submarine and that we ought to find plenty of shipping. He's a fire-eater, ain't he?"

I said soberly, "The best. He probably knows this country like the palm of his hand. He done duty out here before the war."

"You know what? He put his arm around my shoulders and said. 'Juano, I hope you like the *Wahoo*. I asked the squadron for the best cooks they had on the base to replace Rowls and Boutzale. I told 'em I wanted a submarine cook with some imagination and not too Goddam regulation. They sent me you and Dietrich.' How do you suppose he knew my first name? No officer ever called my by my first name before."

I said, "If he comes around and tells you you're the best damn cook in the submarine Navy, you've got it made. I think he's got a crystal ball for a brain. How he picks up and remembers details gets me. All I know is that he's the best damn officer I ever worked for, and I'd go through hell with him."

Rennels said, "I've never seen anything like him."

Several days later, *Wahoo* was rounding the southernmost part of the Japanese mainland. She had taken to diving during the day to avoid aerial patrols. I was off watch and dreaming I was back in Los Angeles with the little telephone operator and we were dancing together at the Lock. A hand was laid gently on my arm and the dream dissipated into the ventilation pipes and electrical wiring overhead. Instantly alert, I looked down at Hayes and the finger-shaded flashlight.

"Yeo, you're wanted in the conning tower. We've made a contact."

I slid out of the bunk while Hayes used the flashlight to look at the next name on his list. I went past him and on up into the conning tower.

The Captain was sitting on a swing-out stool as Lieutenant O'Kane, bent way over, peered through the periscope. In the corner, Lieutenant Paine was leaning against the TDC, which whirred softly as one or two of the handles and dials on it turned slowly. Back in the after corner Parks was quietly standing by. Buckley was listening with complete concentration to the sonar earphones. Krause was standing by the Executive Officer with his finger close to the periscope button and a stop watch in his other hand. I sat down on a swing-out stool next to Buckley and waited. A noise on my right caused me to turn my head in that direction, and while I watched, Simmonetti came through the control hatch and relieved Appel of the wheel watch. The tower was damp, almost foggy, and the air was cool on the skin.

Lieutenant O'Kane was saying, "Bearing, mark, bearing, mark," and Krause kept calling out the bearing from a compass on the periscope rim. Lieutenant Paine was feeding the information into the TDC. Morton just watched moodily.

"Down 'scope." Lieutenant O'Kane backed away from the periscope, slapping the handles against its sides. Krause pushed the black button and let up after the whining cables pulled the periscope down one-third its length. It stopped moving.

Lieutenant O'Kane said, "Smoke is pouring out of her stack and she's riding high in the water."

Morton said, "Did you notice anything new or different about it?"

"Well, it looks like a lightship, has a tall smokestack amidships, and the water line is high out of the water." He noticed me for the first time. "Yeo, look in that locker over there and get out those three identification books you'll find there."

I broke the books out. He said, "Put the one marked Warships back."

I complied.

"Now put the one marked Commercial ships, two smokestacks, back."

I complied.

"Look under the section titled lightships."

I opened the last book and saw pictures of different kinds of ships with one smokestack. I found the section marked lightships and handed the book to him. He shuffled the pages, looking at the pictures. "This one, Captain. This looks. like it." He held to book down, pointing so Morton could see. The Captain just nodded his head and looked thoughtful.

He turned to Lieutenant Paine. "Anything new on the target's course, Roger?"

"No sir, still going around in circles, Captain."

The Captain shook his head. "I don't like it."

Lieutenant O'Kane said hopefully, "She could be rendezvousing with a convoy here, Captain."

"Yeah, she could be a Q-ship, too, waiting for us to disclose our position so the entire Jap navy can drop in on us."

"Let's attack when she circles back again, Captain. It's only seventeen hundred yards to the track."

"I don't know," Captain Morton began doubtfully and then, seeing the enthusiasm in O'Kane's face, added, "Well, we will fire one torpedo. That's all she's worth if she's worth an eight-thousand-dollar torpedo." He stood up. "Up 'scope."

Krause pressed on the white button and the periscope sight came up out of the well. He stooped, waved his fingers on the handle for Krause to stop the upward thrust. Krause let loose the white button. Captain Morton swung the periscope all the way around twice and then settled in one direction. He looked for several seconds and backed away. "Take over," he ordered the Executive Officer. Lieutenant O'Kane grabbed the handles eagerly.

Captain Morton turned to Gerlacher on the phones. "Open the outer door to the tubes forward." Gerlacher pressed the button on the speaker and repeated the command into the talker.

The Captain said to Lieutenant Paine, "Get a setup to fire one fish. Set gyro for six feet."

Lieutenant Paine took over, giving commands to Gerlacher to be relayed to the torpedo room. Krause moved to a set of push buttons near the TDC.

"Outer doors open forward. Torpedoes ready for firing, Captain, gyro set at six feet."

"Very well."

Lieutenant O'Kane was calling, "Bearing, mark, bearing, mark."

"The target is at firing point, Captain," from Lieutenant Paine.

"Fire one," was echoed by Gerlacher, and I saw Krause push on one of the buttons that had a red light above it now. The light went out.

Wahoo jarred and swished out a threat of destruction aimed at the Japanese ship.

"One's fired, Captain."

"Very well." All human noise stilled in the boat while mechanical noises clamored to be heard.

Captain Morton sat back down, waiting with his head resting in his hands. O'Kane stayed glued to the periscope. He would have made a good model for a sculptor. Krause was standing facing inboard, peering at the stop watch's impersonal second hand as it ticked off the seconds. Buckley was listening to the torpedo's progress. Simmonetti twisted the steering wheel back and forth keeping on course. Parks and Lieutenant Paine were studying the TDC, gathering information from the dial gyrations that were unintelligible to me. Gerlacher was calmly waiting for the next order. Below me I could hear the interlaced mutterings of bow and stern motors working to adjust *Wahoo's* keel to an ordered depth, and one of the tanks gurgling water, flooding in weight to adjust the keel to the loss of the torpedo.

Lieutenant Paine and Krause reported together, "The torpedo should have gone off by now."

"What's she doing, Dick?" Morton had raised his head to ask Lieutenant O'Kane.

"Nothing, Captain. I couldn't see the wake of the electric torpedo and apparently the Jap ship didn't either. He's still circling and smoking. Down 'scope." He stepped back and looked at the Captain. "Let's try it again, Captain, when old *Smoki Maru* comes around again."

Captain Morton replied, "Hell no, Dick, I'm not going to waste any more shots on what might turn out to be a trap."

Lieutenant O'Kane turned purple with frustration. "Captain, we ought to sink that son-of-a-bitch. Let's don't let him get away with that."

It was the first time I had seen Morton angry. "That's enough, Dick," he answered in a cold brittle voice. "Goddamit, when you get to be a captain in your own sub you can shoot all the torpedoes you want, at whatever you want, too." He said to Lieutenant Paine, who was watching them in astonishment, "Break off the attack." To Simmonetti he growled, "Come to course two-two-five." He started down the hatch. "Secure from battle stations submerged."

I followed the Executive Officer down. In the control room he went forward while I turned the other way into the crew's messroom. Krause joined me in a cup of coffee a short time later. He said, "That's the first time I seen 'Mush' mad about anything."

Phillips sat with us and I noticed how nervous he was. "What happened?"

I answered Phillips' question. "We had a ship up there running around in circles and smoking like mad. 'Mush' thought it might be a Q-ship and we fired one fish and took off."

"Where's our patrol area, Krause?" Phillips asked.

"All over the Yellow Sea, the Old Man can go any place in there he wants to."

"Any idea where we're going first?"

"He's going to try the Nagasaki-Formosa shipping lanes first, I think."

Sometime later we surfaced. I caught the 1600–1800 watch and relieved Kirk, Eugene T., seaman, from Philadelphia, Pennsylvania. It was chilly in these latitudes and I kept the warm collar of the submarine jacket above my ears. My trouser bottoms were tucked into my socks.

Morton came up on the bridge to look around and get some fresh air.

Rennels' voice floated up, "Permission to come on deck and dump garbage?"

Ensign Misch, the duty officer's voice, replied, "Permission granted."

The watch ended. A midwatch went by. I caught the watch again on the 1200–1600. Wahoo was riding the surface in a gray world. We were someplace in the vicinity of the Yangtze River. I had been there too many times before to doubt the character of the sea with its muddy content and the decayed smell it gave off. Veder had the port lookout, I had the starboard. Suddenly I stiffened as I saw two large Chinese junks.

"Chinese junks on the starboard beam, sir."

"Chinese junks and a small ship on the port beam, sir." It was Veder shouting.

Below me Ensign Griggs ran out on the cigarette deck and swung his glasses alternately in both directions. He ran to the voice tube and shouted, "Captain to the bridge. Ship contact made."

Shortly afterward, Captain Morton and Lieutenant O'Kane were topside.

I began reporting more sampans and junks as they came into sight. Veder was finding more sampans, too.

Captain Morton's voice came up, "Damn if this isn't a regular Sampan Alley. That small collier is going to get away. He's got his stern to us and headed for land." They walked aft and conversed in low tones.

Captain Morton and Lieutenant O'Kane came back. ". . . we better get some water over us. With all these sampans around we've got about as much chance for secrecy as a burlesque actress doing her act on Times Square."

When Ensign Griggs called, "Clear the bridge, dive, dive," I beat Veder to the hatch all right, but only to have him and Ensign Griggs both ride me to the bottom.

After the watch we had fried chicken for evening chow. The crew's mess was cleaned up and I came back with a *Look* magazine to my corner. I sat for a while sulkily looking at the pictures. O'Brien came in, turned on "Sock 'em down, Winsocki." I suffered silently through it. He sat down saying, "Whatsamatter, Yeo, want to borrow my crying towel?"

I looked at him in surprise. "Do I look that bad?"

He said brightly, "Tell me a sea tale, Pappy."

Rennels came in. "What's the matter with Yeo?"

"Aw, he's got a wild hair up his . . ."

"You guys make me sick," I said grouchily.

Krause came in. "What's the matter, Yeo?"

"Damn you guys. Can't a guy feel sorry for himself without you birds interfering?"

O'Brien said sweetly, "Did we hurt your feelings, Yeo?"

I was beginning to feel better. "Did any of you guys ever read Bud Kelland's 'The Silver Spoon'?"

"Was it about submarines? I never read stories about submarines."

"You're all a bunch of illiterates," I said archly. "In this story there's a grandma, see . . ."

"A sweet little old lady?"

"Yeah, and her grandson, a truck driver, is . . ."

"I'll bet he usta beat his grandma."

"Naw, nothing like that, and then there is this rich guy who is pretending he is poor . . ."

"Did he beat the grandmother?"

"Will you guys stop that? This rich guy was sitting by the fireside thinking . . ."

"About his money?"

"Stop it, dammit. No, the grandson came in and said, 'What's eating him?'" I had their interest now, ". . . and grandma said, 'Leave him be. When a man is wrestling with his soul, he don't want no spectators.'"

"Yes, go on."

"That's it, you knuckleheads. Don't yuh get the picture? Aw, whatsa use?"

Krause said, " 'Mush' says the *Wahoo* has paid for herself now and we're all expendable."

"He gets on my nerves sometimes with that kind of talk," O'Brien observed.

"He don't mean nothing by it," I said. "It's just his way of cracking funnies. He called this Sampan Alley we're in today."

"Where are we now, Krause?" Rennels asked.

"It's called Maikotsu Suido."

O'Brien said, "I think I'll turn the radio on." He jumped up and dialed the big set. He passed several stations with Oriental speakers.

Rennels said, "Isn't that dangerous?"

O'Brien answered, "Naw, it's only sending that's dangerous." He passed a station with music and twisted back to it. The station was playing "Columbia, the Gem of the Ocean." It was a good recording and the reception was good. Everybody in the messhall quieted down to listen. The music shut off in the middle and a feminine voice came on speaking in perfect English with a Japanese accent.

"Good evening, you wonderful American boys out there. This is Tokyo Rose speaking. Did you like our nice music? Did it make you homesick? You should be home with your loved ones. Your wives and mothers and sweethearts. It is so sad that you must all die while your leaders are safe at home and the civilians who are making all the money are dating your girls.

"We know where every soldier's outfit is and where every ship and submarine is located. We Japanese do not want to kill you but because you are the invaders we will have to.

"Would you like some news from home? The longshoremen are striking for higher wages. How much are you being paid? A dollar a day? Too bad so many of you are dying each day and . . ." (click).

"I heard all that boloney I want to," O'Brien growled.

I said, "I thought she had a real sexy voice."

Krause said, "I think I'll turn in."

I said, "That's a good idea. I'm going to turn in, too."

I don't know how long I'd been sleeping when something awoke me, making my hair stand on end. "Depth charge! Depth charge!" Somebody was screaming hysterically. Everybody I could see by the dim light was raised up in his bunk.

Kohut jumped out on the other side of his bunk and turned on the compartment lights. Everybody was now standing out in the passageways. My senses told me that *Wahoo* was running on the surface, but what was happening?

"Depth charge! Depth charge! The water's coming in—plug that . . ." I, with the rest of the men, began staring at a figure that was writhing and twisting in a lower bunk. I recognized Ballman's voice now.

Berg was nearest him. He reached down and shook him vigorously. "Snap out of it, Ballman. Wake up, you're having a nightmare." Ballman awoke and sat up staring wilding around. He was shaking convulsively. Gradually he seemed to realize where he was.

Lane came rushing into the compartment in his undershirt. "What's going on here? What's the ruckus about?"

Kohut said, "Ballman's having a nightmare. He's all right now."

Lane went over to Ballman, who said, "Gee, Chief, I guess I was having a bad dream. I'm okay now."

Things settled down and the lights were turned off. I had a hard time getting back to sleep.

I was awakened for the midwatch, stood it with nothing to disturb the night's darkness, and went back to bed again. I seemed hardly to fall asleep before I was awakened again, this time by Erickson. Subconsciously I realized that *Wahoo* had submerged while I was sleeping.

"We got a ship up there. O'Kane wants you in the tower. We're making an approach."

I crawled out sleepily and stumbled up to the tower. In the conning tower there was a lot of suppressed activity. The picture was the same— the same participants, the same positions and attitudes, except that now Morton was animated. He had an eager look on his face.

O'Kane looked away from the periscope, saw me, and pointed at the locker with the books in it. I broke them out and waited.

O'Kane said, "Merchant vessel, one stack amidship, a mainmast and another mast aft, two-deck superstructure."

I put two of the books back, looked at the section marked masts in the book left, thumbed to another section indexed superstructures, and waited for more information.

"Straight bow, broken deck line, cabin over the poop deck, mast height about fifty feet, about four thousand tons." He motioned to Krause. "Stand by for a mark."

While I hunted for these descriptions in the book, O'Kane was furnishing further data to be fed into the TDC. Morton gave the orders to prepare the tubes for firing. He seemed to have mental control of the entire mathematical situation.

Krause down-scoped on command. He moved swiftly, obtaining a pencil and paper which he handed me saying, "O'Kane wants you to keep a chronological record of everything that goes on to check against later."

I nodded my head. I had found two pictures that fitted the description. O'Kane came over and I pointed them out. He studied them for several seconds and said, "Captain, I think we've got it. It's the *Nanka Maru* class, maximum speed nine to twelve knots, keel depth twenty-four feet when loaded. She's down to the water line."

Morton said, "Thanks. Dick, set torpedo gyros for ten feet. How does that click with the TDC?"

"Looks good to me, Captain. We're coming close to the firing point, range one-two-double-oh."

I wrote on the piece of paper, "0535, 09 March 1943—Approach on Japanese ship *Nanka Maru* class," with the additional descriptive information.

When the word came to fire, I wrote the time and the words, "fired one torpedo from number four tube." One minute later I added the new time and wrote, "torpedo hit amidships."

Lieutenant O'Kane looking through the periscope was keeping up a running commentary. "She's broken in two. She's sinking. My God! She's sunk."

I jotted down the time and the single word, "sunk." Two minutes and twenty-six seconds had elapsed since the torpedo struck. *Wahoo* was swishing her tail with a vengeance.

Gerlacher was echoing into the phones, ". . . O'Kane said, 'My God! She's sunk!'"

Lieutenant O'Kane turned back to the eyepiece on the periscope. "There's a rowboat up there floating around but it looks empty and just a lot of debris. That's all, Captain."

Captain Morton said, "I'll take a look," as the Executive Officer moved out of the way.

"Secure from battle stations submerged. Come to course three-one-five."

I put the book away, gave Krause the slip of paper, and went directly to my bunk.

An hour later Erickson was shaking me again. "We got another target. You're wanted in the tower."

Back in the conning tower, I sat sleepily through another approach and attack on a new freighter of the *Tottori Maru* class, six thousand tons. *Wahoo* tore a big hole in one side of her and the second torpedo struck but did not go off. The time was around 0755. The freighter got away on an off tangent and Captain Morton had to give up the chase as hopeless. I learned from the comments that this ship had been spotted by a look out. This meant that *Wahoo* had surfaced and dived again while I was sleeping after the earlier morning attack.

When battle stations submerged was secured, I went into the crew's messroom, ate breakfast, and turned in. With the way *Wahoo* was running down ships between watches, I figured I had better get all the sleep I could. I wondered when the officers got any sleep. They seemed to be always up plotting, fighting the ship, or standing watches.

With darkness *Wahoo* surfaced to charge batteries, dump the garbage, get fresh air into the boat, pump air into high-pressure and low-pressure lines and tanks.

Entering the sleeping compartment, I was startled by Ballman screaming, "Depth charge, depth charge."

Somebody said, "Shut up," and I heard a shoe thud against a bunk. Ballman either awakened or turned over because the compartment quieted down again. I could hear several men muttering in angry whispers.

The next day went by uneventfully. Shortly after coming on watch, I picked up a pip on the radar. The Duty Officer, Ensign Misch, was notified. *Wahoo* turned sniffing in that direction. The Captain and Executive Officer were called.

Morton and O'Kane showed up promptly and stared at the radar screen a few seconds. Captain Morton ordered that the plotting section be called. He and Lieutenant O'Kane went up on the bridge. They came back down to the conning tower and Ensign Misch dived the ship. The contact was nearer when it faded out with water blocking it from the radar mast. I reached up, flipped the switch off. Veder was manning the sonar gear. Terrell was on the helm and Appel was on the bow planes. With nothing to do for the moment, I went into the crew's mess and drew a cup of coffee.

Rennels, Wach, and Witting had been getting the mess ready for breakfast. Now they were sitting at the table smoking and drinking coffee. "What's going on?"

"I got a target on radar. I hope we sink it. I sure could use first class."

Collins, Harry, Motor Machinist Second, from Fallon, Nevada, came in from the control room. "Yeo, I gotta wake up Buckley, Krause, Simmonetti, Parks, Gerlacher, and you're all ready up for the conning tower. Do you know where they sleep? I'm new on here."

I went with him to the sleeping compartment and helped wake them up. Each man slipped out of bed without protest and started for the conning tower. I went with them.

I got a pad of paper, a pencil, and the identification books out and waited. At 0755 I made a notation that on 21 March 1943 *Wahoo* had fired three torpedoes at a *Seiwai Maru* class freighter, 7,000 tons, and she had been hit amidships with the third torpedo, sinking in four minutes. There were thirty-three survivors in the water by Lieutenant O'Kane's count.

When the attack ended, *Wahoo* stayed submerged, moving away from the scene.

I barely got to sleep before I was awakened to go to the conning tower again. Another contact had been made.

This time the penciled scribblings said that *Wahoo* on her fifth attack, fourth war patrol, had on 21 March 1943 at 0930 sunk a 6,500-ton freighter of the *Nitu Maru* class. Three torpedoes from the stern tubes made two hits. The Japanese ship sank vertically by the bow in three minutes and ten seconds. Four survivors on a raft were floating in the center of flotsam and debris.

When Lieutenant O'Kane described the survivors in the water, Captain Morton said, "I'd like to see that." He took the periscope and stared through it. "It's colder'n hell up there. Those poor devils are really shivering." He swiveled the periscope about and came back to them. "Look at that. Those Japs are taking off their wet clothes." He paused watching. He whistled and began laughing. "That Jap must have a happy home. They're wringing the water out of their clothes. That's smart."

Morton moved the periscope back and forth a few inches. "I see a life ring and what appear to be flags in the water." He studied them several seconds, twisted the handle, and swung the periscope around slowly three times. "I don't see anything up there." He threw up the handles and commanded, "Down 'scope."

"Next thing I know they'll be calling me 'Mush' Morton and his widow makers." He called below, "Richie, bring her up slowly and man the radar. We're going to take a look around."

Wahoo eased to the surface and wagged her antenna about.

"Battle lookouts to the conning tower." I slipped down to control for binoculars and jacket and came back up. Veder joined me.

"Commandos stand by to come on deck. Surface."

Wahoo surfaced. Veder and I came spewing out onto the deck and into the crow's-nest. We became her lookout eyes.

"All clear on port."

"Debris and raft one point on the starboard bow."

I saw pieces of planks, oil rags, and a raft with three naked Japanese sailors on it. They stared at us some seconds as we came closer. Then they turned their backs to us, finished wringing out their clothes, and put them back on. They did not turn around, they stood with their backs to us.

Captain Morton began shouting and I looked down. He had a megaphone in hand. "Come aboard as our prisoners." The Japanese either did not understand English or chose to ignore the command. He turned to the voice tube. "Richie, have Lane send two or three men topside with a boat hook."

A few seconds later, Smith, Wach, and Hall came up the hatch.

"Get down on deck and see if you can drag that life ring and those flags on board."

Krause said, "Isn't that a book floating in the water there?"

Captain Morton answered, "Yes, it is. It might be a code book. Get that on board, too."

Smith, Wach, and Hall went down to the ship's rails and began fishing for the desired articles, while Captain Morton kept up steady helm and engine change orders to bring *Wahoo* closer.

I kept searching the gray horizon and overcast sky anxiously while this operation was in progress. Whenever I looked at the Japanese merchant sailors, they had their backs to us.

Presently Smith shouted up, "We've got 'em, Captain. Anything else you want?"

Captain Morton shouted back, "No, bring them up here."

There was scrambling about below me, and when I looked down again, the bridge was clear of everyone but Ensign Misch and Krause.

Wahoo began turning away on all four engines in a southerly direction. A short while later I was relieved by Tyler. Before going below I pointed out the Japanese raft and three men standing with their backs to us.

In the control room I stopped to examine the big commercial steamer house flag spread out on the gyrocompass, which had a large white "O" on it with red and white colors. The life ring was painted white and had the letters *NITU MARU TARMUI* painted in black around its cylindrical surface. A book lay open on the flag with its water-wrinkled rice-paper pages stuck together. There were pictures of a moon in its different phases and astronomical data written in Japanese block hieroglyphics.

I looked at the navigational chart on the bulletin board. Krause had been penciling in *Wahoo's* position and putting a red X where ships were sunk. There were three red X's, and I noticed the last attacks had occurred near Chosen Kan Point. Krause came in and stood looking at the chart with me.

"*Wahoo* gets around, doesn't she?" He was referring to the crisscross paths of *Wahoo's* progress on the chart.

Wahoo stayed submerged all day. On the 1600–1800 watch I had the sonar. Captain Morton came to the tower to look around. He had a few words with Lieutenant Paine and then, pulling out the swivel stool next to me, sat down.

"How's things going, Yeo? All clear on the sound gear?"

"Yes sir, it's sure a relief to get away from all them tropical fish. A guy can hear something here without wondering whether it's a torpedo or a fish."

He laughed. "We're in your old stomping grounds. We're just outside of Chinwangtao. Ever go up to Shanhaikwan, to the Great Wall, from here?"

"Yes sir, I rode them Mongolian ponies."

Captain Morton chuckled and went below. Just before the watch ended, a contact was made on a small freighter. The first indication I had was when Captain Morton and Lieutenant O'Kane passed through the conning tower on their way to the bridge. The course and speed changed and after several minutes *Wahoo* dived. Simmonetti relieved me for the approach and I turned attention to the identification procedure.

At 0410, 23 March 1943, I recorded a single torpedo shot and a hit on a 2,500-ton freighter of the *Katyosan Maru* class. The torpedo struck just under the bridge.

Lieutenant O'Kane on the periscope exclaimed, "She must have been a coal collier. A dark cloud sprang up out of her and is obscuring everything."

Captain Morton said, "Move over, I'm going to take a looksee." He peered intently for several seconds. "Get Jack up here with the photo equipment. We'll take some pictures of that."

Krause leaped to the open hatch and conveyed the word below to Lieutenant Henderson. Lieutenant Jackson must have been waiting below with the camera because he showed up in the conning tower almost immediately.

He played around with the equipment, twisted the periscope eyepiece every which way, helped along by asinine suggestions from Morton, O'Kane, and Paine. At last he meticulously adjusted the shutter on the camera and while Krause steadied the periscope snapped several pictures. He stepped back and Krause took a quick look. "Sir, she's starting to sink by the bow."

Lieutenant O'Kane grabbed the handles. "Her bow must be resting on the bottom and her stern is raising vertically out of the water."

Lieutenant Jackson said, "That would make a swell picture." The Executive Officer relinquished the periscope to him and Jackson took several more pictures.

I recorded that the *Katyosan Maru* sank in thirteen minutes.

I had sausage and eggs for breakfast. Kohl was sitting across from me. He said, "After breakfast, I'd like to see you, Yeo."

"What about? There's nothing wrong with me that thirty days leave in the States wouldn't cure."

"I want to give you a sun bath and some vitamin pills."

"What?" I stared at him incredulously. "A sun bath! How in hell are you going to accomplish that?"

"Oh, I got an infrared sun lamp. Most of the crew has been taken care of. You're one of the few left that's not had one."

I snorted, "That's for the birds. You can skip me. I get plenty of sunshine on lookout when we're surfaced and the sun is out."

He said doubtfully, "Well, if you say so. At least you can take the vitamin pills."

"I'll try them but I don't like pills in any shape or form. I'm not guaranteeing I'll keep it up."

He seemed hurt. We went into the sleeping compartment and he opened the medical cabinet. I stared curiously at the bottles with neat labels and sniffed at the strange odors. He handed me a bottle full of reddish-brown pellets. The label said they contained vitamins A, B, C, and several others.

I said, "I need something with lots of vitamin E in it and a bottle of brandy to wash it down with."

He grinned and shook his head. "These will do you more good."

I stuffed the vitamins in my shirt pocket and crawled into my sack. Kohl walked away, shaking his head bewilderedly.

The next day passed smoothly. Everybody caught up on their sleep. I came off the first dogwatch and settled down in the messhall corner to swap yarns.

Lieutenant Henderson stuck his head in the door. "Hey, Yeo, you and Krause are wanted in the tower on the double. We're making an approach."

Krause and I both leaped up and followed the lieutenant back to the control room.

I grabbed out the books in time to hear Lieutenant O'Kane say, "Two masts, a foremast near the bow, and the mainmast near the stern. One stack near the stern. Foc'sle is near the bow. Deck line low in the water. About nine or ten thousand tons, making about seven or eight knots. It's a loaded oil tanker. Down 'scope." He turned to Captain Morton standing eagerly by. "Captain, she's got a radio antenna. The moon is starting to come up and I can see her clearly."

The Captain turned to Lieutenant Paine. "Roger, get three tubes ready. We will aim at the radio shack."

Lieutenant O'Kane turned to me. I pointed out several pictures.

"It looks like this one, Captain, the *Syoyo Maru*." The lieutenant handed the book to Captain Morton, who studied the description under the picture.

"Torpedo tubes ready forward, Captain."

"Very well."

Lieutenant O'Kane was at the periscope again. "Up 'scope. Angle on the bow, eighty degrees starboard. Stand by to mark the range. Mark."

Krause said, "Two-eight-oh-oh."

Captain Morton commanded, "Come right two degrees." There was a slight tilting of the deck as *Wahoo* responded. The TDC wheels began to whirl as Lieutenant Paine readjusted them. More commands followed.

"Torpedoes ready for firing, Captain."

"Very well." A pause, followed by a quick recheck of the situation.

"Fire one. Stand by two."

"Number one fired, standing by two."

Wahoo spawned three torpedoes and they went out into the waters of the night toward their destination. Two explosions returned early to knock vibrantly on the hull.

"Damnation," Lieutenant O'Kane swore, "two prematures and a miss."

Captain Morton shouted, "Reload the forward tubes. Stand by to fire four. Fire four!"

"Four's away, sir."

Another wait, seconds speeding by, another explosion.

"Damn it, Captain, that one went off ahead of the tanker. She's going to get away."

"Torpedo tubes reloaded forward, Captain."

"Very well. Roger, get a new setup."

More commands flew thickly within the confines of the conning tower.

"Fire!" And *Wahoo* jarred three times.

Another minute's wait and Krause was reporting, "Looks like the first torpedo is a miss, sir." Lieutenant O'Kane shouting, "Amidships, we got 'er amidships." This was followed by the sound of a terrific explosion.

"That's better," Captain Morton's voice bellowing, "but she's had time to get off an SOS."

"Captain, she's firing our way with deck guns. I can see gun flashes."

Captain Morton said, "Let me see," and took the periscope. "It's all right, she won't be firing long. She's sinking rapidly."

A few minutes later I wrote on the pad, "*Syoyo Maru* sank in four minutes and twenty-five seconds."

Lieutenant O'Kane was saying, "There's a big oil slick up there. That's all I can see to mark the spot she went down."

"Well, we'd better be getting to hell out of here. The whole Jap Empire knows we're here now. Let's get the lookouts to the tower and surface." Then a few seconds later, "Secure from battle stations submerged."

Wahoo surfaced and turned her stern to the latest victim in an effort to put miles of water between herself and that very busy spot to be.

I went into the messhall and watched Krause add more penciled lines and another red X to the bulletin board chart.

The midwatch turned up a beautiful bright moon that made the hour on lookout a chore of pleasure. I came off watch and turned in only to be routed out fifteen minutes later by Holmes. "You're wanted in the tower."

I drew a cup of coffee and took it with me. *Wahoo* had submerged in the brief time I had come off watch. I got out the books and dated the pad 25 March 1943 and sat sipping the coffee.

Lieutenant O'Kane was saying, "I couldn't believe it when John reported that it had its red and green running lights on. He said he could see a cigarette glowing amidships too."

"The Japs are fatalists," Captain Morton answered. "Besides we're supposed to be clear across the sea."

Lieutenant O'Kane raised the periscope. "I can see the green running light as pretty as you please. Are we in a war or not?"

"Well, we'll soon put it out for him. In the meantime we can thank the skipper for letting us know he's up there."

Lieutenant O'Kane began the description. "One king post forward . . ." When he finished, I showed him a picture of a 2,500-ton ship with the caption *Sinsei Maru*.

Wahoo came into position and hissed a threat of death at the·ship. A minute and a half later I wrote two premature explosions on the pad.

"Goddamit, it isn't hardly worthwhile to risk our necks bringing these Goddam failures all the way out here for nothing." Captain Morton raged.

"She's going to get away, Captain."

"Like hell she is. Pass the word battle stations surface."

A few minutes later I found myself on the starboard lookout in the brightness of a full moon, which was beginning to lose its luster to a lightening eastern sky.

"All clear on the starboard lookout, sir."

"Ship turning away two points on the port bow."

"Very well."

"Gun crews manned and ready, Captain."

"Are we making all ahead emergency on all main engines?"

"Aye, aye, sir."

"Roger, we're going to come up on the portside of her. Train the gun to starboard and start firing as soon as we get into range. See if the deck-gun crew can't knock out her rudder. As soon as we get in close, train the twenty millimeters on the pilothouse. Let's get her dead in the water."

"Aye, aye, Captain."

I searched the ocean systematically. Scattered heavy clouds made a good place for airplanes to hide. Cold air was chilling the sweat produced by a warmer temperature while I was inside the submarine.

"Ship coming into sight on the starboard bow, sir."

"All clear on the port lookout," Veder shouted.

I kept searching all around and coming back to the ship ahead. *Wahoo* was rapidly overtaking the slower ship. Its running lights were out now. It looked like any one of a hundred small tramp steamers I had seen. White letters on her stern spelled *SINSEI MARU*, and there were some Japanese letters probably meaning the same thing. A Japanese white flag with the orange ball in its center floated from the flagstaff on the aftermast.

Wahoo was closing in.

"Commence firing."

A shock wave shook me off balance and I grabbed the handrail. A yellow blinding flash hurt my eyes before I could close them. This was followed by a heat wave and a white twisting, enveloping cloud of smoke with a burnt gunpowder smell. My ears rang and were suddenly numb despite the protective cotton thrust into them.

I managed to brace myself before the next blast came. Frantic, I thought, How in hell am I expected to see anything through all this confusion?

Looking down on deck I saw the breech of the gun open and an empty brass cartridge ejected onto the deck. Zimmerman, Charles A., Seaman, from Erie, Pennsylvania, kicked it aside. Carr, as gun captain, was blowing compressed air into the barrel, making it ready for the next cartridge, which was being carried from the messroom hatch along the deck by Seal. Keeter was sitting on one side of the gun, pointing it, and Phillips was on the other side training the setter. Both were twisting a wheel they had in their hands while concentrating on looking through a telescope fixed to the gun mount. One man was controlling the barrel of the gun vertically while the other was lining it up horizontally. When the crosswires of their individual telescopes centered on the target, a button would be pressed and another shell would be on its way.

I turned my face away looking at the target before another shot was fired. If they hunted for two more nervous members in *Wahoo's* crew, they could not have found anyone that would beat Phillips and Keeter, I thought. The gun went off and I stared at the Japanese ship through the binoculars. The shell hit the stern and tore the rudder away. I thought, now I will believe anything. A cheering went up from everybody topside praising the two men's marksmanship.

Wahoo pulled in closer and slowed down. The twenty millimeters went into action with a chattering, deafening overture.

The order went down to the gun crew to fire at the water line. I saw shells skip across the water and holes appear in the side of the Japanese ship near the red and black water line. A fire broke out in the charthouse with smoke pouring out the broken windows. Tracer bullets left a curved smoke line in the air and white flashes where they struck. Often the trails from different guns crossed in their flight across the fifty or hundred yards of open water.

It was impossible for me to search anything but the skies overhead and that only between bursts of gunfire. *Wahoo* kept circling the doomed ship, and it stayed in the center of my starboard lookout position. The brunt of the lookout duties had to be on Veder.

Lieutenant Jackson came on deck and took pictures.

The *Sinsei Maru* was beginning to settle heavily and visibly into the water. I had not seen a single member of her crew on deck. I wondered how many were killed or wounded and thought of the terror they must feel.

"Cease firing." Everything quieted down. The officers were lining the after handrail looking astern through their binoculars. I turned my glasses in the same direction and saw the masts of a ship. It was enough to let me know it was not a destroyer.

"Gun crews, stand by your guns. Full left rudder. All ahead standard."

The *Sinsei Maru* fell astern and went out of my range of view as *Wahoo* swung in a circle and headed for the new arrival.

Wahoo came right down on her before the Japanese captain realized that he was being attacked by an American submarine. He started evasive tactics, turning and twisting to avoid, but it was too late. *Wahoo's* first few shots knocked out her rudder and set fire to the bridge. She became a sitting duck, and as *Wahoo* circled firing at her water line, I took in the details of a neat new diesel-driven oil tanker, freshly painted gray. The name on her stern proclaimed to any viewer that she was the *Hadachi Maru*. She looked to be about 2,500 tons.

A Japanese sailor in the foretop began waving his arms. Carter, on deck, threw a burst of Browning machine-gun fire in his direction. The Jap reached out, grabbed a guy wire, slid swiftly to the deck, and scampered out of sight.

"Did you ever see a monkey move faster?" Captain Morton roared below me.

Veder shouted, "The *Sinsei Maru* is sinking, sir."

Everybody looked in time to see the ship settle into the ocean and the water close over her. Firing continued, aimed at the *Hadachi Maru*.

I had been keeping my eyes on the skies, not attempting to use the binoculars. The sun was swelling up on the horizon like an angry pimple, its rays lighting the ocean about us, emphasizing the Japanese flag flying aboard the *Hadachi Maru*, and making the job of lookout considerably easier.

A flash of light in the sky caught my eye and I turned the binoculars to it. I saw the tiny unmistakable wingspread and pontoons of a floatplane.

"Plane at zero-four-five degrees, second elevation," I shouted, my voice becoming shrill with emotion.

"Secure from battle stations surface." Feet pounded to the hatches and chopped at the rungs of ladders on their way into *Wahoo's* depths.

"Clear the bridge, dive, dive."

I was below decks. My timing was getting better.

Wahoo took a down-by-the-bow slant and water gurgled up the sides of the superstructure to meet again above the bridge. She could not go very deep without ramming the bottom. *Wahoo's* periscope eye kept us informed that the plane was circling the area but apparently had not sighted us. There was nothing to do but wriggle along the bottom of the Yellow Sea like an eel and rig for depth charge.

"Rig for depth charge, rig for depth charge."

I got through the watertight door into the messroom before Rennels closed it. I could hear doors throughout the ship being slammed shut and the dogs being battened down.

Phillips was securing the ventilation and Dietrich was closing a hand valve on the portside of the ship. Phillips looked deathly pale and he was shivering all over. He stopped by Carter to report, "Messhall secured for depth charge" and hurried through the door into the sleeping compartment. Carter looked after Phillips, made the report into the phones, and turned his attention to inspecting the Browning machine gun on a mess table.

I got a cup of coffee and sat down with Rennels and Dietrich. They began asking me questions about the gun attacks. I tried to describe what I had seen and how I felt. I was not very successful.

Rennels asked, looking around at the overhead, "Do you think we'll get depth-charged?"

"I don't know. The best friend you guys got right now is Carter. He's getting all the dope." I turned to Carter. "Hey, Carter, what's goin' on now?"

He moved an earphone up on his ear and answered, "There's a brand-new Japanese destroyer echo-ranging. That plane is still circling around. Just when the Old Man thinks it is gone, it comes back again."

"What does he mean by echo-ranging?" Dietrich asked.

"It's a sort of sound gear used in countermeasures," I replied. "The radioman on the destroyer hits a key and a sonic sound wave comes down into the water. If it doesn't strike anything, it just goes *ping-g-g-g*, but if it hits an object like a submarine, it goes *ping-g-g poing-g-g*, and the destroyer picks up the echo. Then they got you located."

We were quiet for several seconds thinking of the possibilities.

The dogs on the engine-room watertight door scraped open, followed by the sound of the heavy metal door squeaking open. It slammed shut with a loud bang, and the dogs clanked as they were being locked. It irritated me that anyone could be so careless. Heavy footfalls came our way, *clop, clack, clop, clack.* They took on an added volume in the quietness of *Wahoo's* silent running.

Witting came through the door and my eyes went to his feet. He had on heavy army combat boots. *Clop, clack, clop, clack,* he went to the sink, banged several cups until he found one he wanted, ran hot water from the faucet over it, rattled a spoon around it, and turned to the coffee urn. By this time the bristles on the back of my neck stood straight out and chills were playing tag up and down my spine. Rennels beat me to it. "Goddam you, Witting. If you don't take them shoes off and quit making so much racket, I'm going to punch you in the snot-box."

Witting looked at him in injured surprise.

I said hotly, "And when he gets through, you're going to take another beating from me."

"Whatsamatter with you guys? I ain't doing nothing."

Rennels and I both started for him. He sat down suddenly and began taking off his boots. "I don't know what's the matter with you guys. The little bit of noise I make ain't going to hurt nothing."

I said angrily, "You try standing sound watches sometimes. You'll learn to walk around pussyfoot."

As though to verify my assertions, we began to hear the *ping, ping* of the destroyer echo-ranging through the hull.

I said, "He's getting closer. Sound carries a long way underwater, so you be quiet. When you go through that engine-room door, you better be damn silent about it."

Witting went aft with his coffee in one hand and his boots in the other. He was so quiet going through the door that we wondered if he went through at all.

"Him and his clodhoppers," Rennels snorted.

Something was happening. The destroyer's echo-ranging was getting results. It was going *ping-pong, ping-pong.*

Rennels and Dietrich both looked at me with scared faces. I said, "I don't know what it is, but they ain't *pinging* on us. You'd know it if they was."

Carter said, " 'Mush' thinks that destroyer is *pinging* one of the ships we sunk this morning. He's changed course to get away."

I could feel *Wahoo's* hull vibrating with the increased speed put on the motors.

I heard the *pinging* start up again as the destroyer evidently started his run on the submerged object.

Wham, wham, wham, followed by three explosions. Distance gave them a hollow sound.

Relief flooded through me. Now if *Wahoo* would just keep moving. She was. I turned to Rennels, buoyant once again. "Well? How do your first depth charges sound?"

He grinned. "I wouldn't want 'em any closer." From that moment we became the best of friends.

It was after 1600 before "Rig from depth charge" was secured. By that time the 1200–1600 watch was ended, and I was free until 2000, the next watch.

Sometime around 1900 *Wahoo* surfaced and ran.

I had another peaceful moonlit night on lookout to be thankful that *Wahoo* was still in action. It contrasted strangely with the day's happenings. Everyone, including myself, was too tired to have a bull session that night.

The following day the Japanese stayed clear of *Wahoo*, but in the afternoon a day later, I was brought out of my bunk on the run by the clarion call of the loudspeakers. "Battle stations surface, battle stations surface." In seconds I was on the starboard lookout platform. My side of the ship was clear. It was on Veder's side that the firing would happen.

Wahoo ran along the water, belching gunfire as she went. She made a circle and headed back again. This time I could see the target. It was a 500-ton trawler. The first round of gunfire had incapacitated the ship and there was no movement on board. Smoke was escaping from a hatch amidships, and she boasted a single small cabin. The deck was canted at a thirty-degree angle. A radio antenna ran between the masts.

"Cease firing. On deck the commandos," Morton shouted.

Ensign Misch, O'Brien, Carter, Seal, Muller, Berg, and Kirk grouped on deck. Lane came hurrying up to join them.

Wahoo kept maneuvering to get alongside but heavy swells moved the ship out of reach. Disappointedly they began tossing explosive into the open hatches. It would not sink. *Wahoo* tried to ram but it bobbled out of the way. At last Captain Morton secured the gun crews and then the commandos. *Wahoo* turned away. The trawler was still drifting in the water when I was relieved from lookout.

I headed for the crew's messroom to exchange experiences with its occupants. The commandos were sitting at a table with their dungaree trouser legs tucked into their socks, web belts with forty-fives, and jungle knives in scabbards. I walked over to the table and listened to their excited talk.

I broke in on them. "Was them hand grenades you guys was throwing on board?"

They turned their faces in a group toward me. Ensign Misch answered. "Those were Molotov cocktails. The Marines at Midway made them up for us. They're easy to make. The Russians used them at Stalingrad."

Krause came in to add to the chart. I moved over to his side to watch him. Krause finished his handiwork and began criticizing it objectively. I looked at the red X for the trawler and noticed that *Wahoo* was near the entrance to the Yellow Sea.

"How much longer before this patrol ends?" I asked.

"We only got a couple of fish left. One more attack, I guess."

I said, "I'm ready to go back now. Where are we headed for?"

Krause pointed a finger along the chart. "The Shimonoseki-Formosa shipping lane. 'Mush' hopes to get a big one along there."

"Any idea where we're going for the rest period? I hope it's back to Brisbane."

"Naw, Pearl probably, but I don't think the Old Man himself knows until we pull out of area and then SubPac will give him the word."

About 1000 the next morning I was awakened by vocal waves emanating from the loudspeaker. "Battle lookouts on the bridge. On deck the commandos."

I dropped out of bed and ran forward, grabbing my equipment on the run and scurrying up to the starboard lookout station. The ocean seemed to be literally filled with fishing boats.

"A whole ocean full of sampans on the starboard side," I yelled.

This was followed quickly with Veder's report, "All I can see is sampans on the portside, sir."

Captain Morton below us looked up grinning. "Those are *Fishi Marus*." To Lieutenant O'Kane he added, "I've been hankering for some fresh fish, and these sampans are loaded to the gunwales with fish." He turned to Ensign Campbell. "Pass the word, on deck the gun crews. We're going to have fresh fish for dinner tonight."

The crew's messroom hatch ·flew open, and the gun crew led by Carr stampeded onto the deck. Through the bridge hatch the twenty-millimeter crews came surging, with Kemp supervising their actions.

Wahoo approached a sampan and left it a smoking wreck. She turned on another sampan and demolished it. After that the rest of the sampans were disappearing over the horizon in tiny specks.

Stations were secured and on my way down I overheard Captain Morton speaking seriously to Ensign Campbell. "Every time we sink a sampan, we help shorten the war. We cut down on the Japanese supply of food and they get that much hungrier."

It was after midnight when Ware came in to wake me up. "We got a contact, Yeo. You're wanted in the tower."

A short time later I was on station with a cup of coffee, pencil, scratch pad, and the identification books ready. If all went well, *Wahoo* would probably be heading in after this attack. I hoped it would be successful and not too long an attack. I felt wearily exhausted, both mentally and physically, and a glance at everyone's face in the conning tower told me that they were feeling the strain also. Captain Morton looked tired but he had lost none of his combat vitality. He was happily planning the destruction of another Japanese ship.

When Lieutenant O'Kane began the description, only the masts and stack were showing with the ship's hull below the horizon. As *Wahoo* closed the distance he described the bow and stern.

Meanwhile Lieutenant Paine was feeding vital information into the TDC while the torpedomen in the after torpedo room were feverishly completing final preparations and pinning their hopes on favorite tubes.

Krause was busily fussing around Lieutenant O'Kane, anticipating his moves with clocklike precision.

Captain Morton was coordinating all the data into activity. His brain cells, directing the teamwork, were calling the signals, double-checking on their accuracy.

I sat quietly making historical notations under the date of 29 March 1943, which would eventually get filed away as cold statistical figures in some forgotten Naval archive. The most important stimulus in my mind, however, was, Let's get these Goddam fish on their way and get out of here.

Lieutenant O'Kane established the enemy ship's identity as a 5,000-ton freighter of the *Kimishima Maru* class.

Wahoo took an hour and twenty minutes to maneuver into a shooting position. Spitting madly, she sent her last two torpedoes out of the tubes, and her crew settled down with bated breath to wait the results. Two minutes and thirty-six seconds later, an explosion was preceded by Lieutenant O'Kane observing, "Man, that whole ship lifted out of the water. She just raised out of the water and disintegrated."

Captain Morton grabbed the periscope. "Let me see. There's nothing up there to see. She musta been carrying ammunition."

In the quietness of *Wahoo* that came upon us, I began to hear sounds of minor explosions and rending, tearing sounds.

Buckley exclaimed from the sonar gear, "Sounds like she's breaking up and her compartments are collapsing on the way down, Captain."

Captain Morton pushed back from the periscope, breathing heavily. "Down 'scope. Control, man the radar screen and broach the mast. Helmsman, come right twenty degrees. Steady on zero-nine-zero. We're going to get the hell out of here. We're heading for the barn." He turned about beaming at each of us.

A short while later *Wahoo* was skimming the surface, headed on the zero-nine-zero course on all four main engines, while I stood in the messroom drinking a cup of coffee and watching the happy antics of *Wahoo's* crew as we raced for safety and a well-earned rest period.

On the morning watch the weather was beginning to get bad topside. Waves were choppy, rain clouds swept in low streamers under a solid cloud overhead. Once, the radar picked up a plane contact and *Wahoo* dived. When the watch was relieved, I ate and crept back into my sack. *Wahoo* was beginning to buck head seas and to roll. It was getting rough topside.

At 1800 I relieved Krebs on lookout. I was wearing a hooded oilskin coat and had difficulty keeping the salt spray cleaned from the binocular lenses. Clouds were low on the water and visibility was narrowed to a few hundred yards. It was still light with a yellowish grayness that was deceiving to the eyesight. Rain squalls swept across the ocean surface in bursts, causing me to turn my back to the wind for a breathing spell before shading my eyes to scan the rough seas about us. Water was breaking heavily over the boat, sweeping along *Wahoo's* slotted decks to smash against the superstructure. Spray carried across the bridge coaming, nearly drenching Mr. Misch, the Deck Duty officer.

An extra heavy swell moved out of the fog ahead and bore down on *Wahoo*. Her bow began rising to ride the wave but it overwhelmed her buoyancy. It submerged the deck from sight and struck high up on the bridge. Tons of water cascaded over onto the bridge deck.

Looking anxiously down from my perch, I saw the water pass on, and saw Misch holding onto the guard railing close to the hatch. He came up sputtering and slammed the hatch closed. A great quantity of water had spilled into the conning tower.

A loud banging noise near the after end of the cigarette deck meant that something was loose and likely to carry away. *Wahoo's* main engine exhaust popped and crackled several times and the white exhaust fumes stopped coming out.

Indistinct voices shouting commands came out of the bridge speaker, and I could tell by their tone and by the look on Mr. Misch's face that something had happened below decks.

Below me the hatch swung open and I could see Lieutenant Paine's bare head sticking out. He and Misch shouted at each other. The wind carried their words away from me. Paine, apparently satisfied, ducked below again.

Black smoke began to pour out of the fair-weather main ventilation duct.

Ater came up on lookout and relieved me. I hurried down into the messroom and found cooks and messcooks working feverishly swabbing water from the deck. I ran on into the sleeping compartment and found water sloshing about on that deck.

Kohl had Pruett over by the medical locker administering first aid. Pruett was coughing badly and water was streaming from his eyes. We were the only ones in the compartment. Pruett saw me and tried to push Kohl aside. He was pointing at the hatch that led to the big battery cells underneath. He was trying to tell me something but was too choked up to make intelligible speech. Then it burst upon me what he was trying to say. He wanted me to do something to keep the salt water from seeping down into the batteries. I looked around, saw the two blankets on the foot of my bunk, and I leaped to get them. Throwing them over the hatch, I ran back into the messhall. "Forget the water in here and get into the sleeping compartment. We gotta keep the water out of the batteries." I grabbed a swab and led the way.

With the water cleared out, I noticed acrid smoke coming out of the inboard ventilators. Since everybody seemed to have gone aft, I headed back that way.

In the forward engine room, I met Davison and Goss, Richard P., Motor's Machinist Second from Rye, New Hampshire. They had Ware between them and he was strangling from near suffocation. Goss had a smoke mask hanging about his neck. I leaned back on the cover of one of the diesel engines, which was idle but still warm from recent use, to allow them room to get by on the narrow catwalk between the engines. I went into the after engine room, a duplicate of the one I had just been through, and found a dozen or more sailors on the catwalk.

Holman was closest, so I asked, "What happened? What's going on?"

"Water flooded the main induction and stopped all main propulsion. It came out through an opening in the ventilation and shorted out the battery switches in the maneuvering room. Pruett, Ware, and Vidick were in there. The wiring caught on fire. Pruett got a bad dose of smoke and had to get out. Ware and Vidick stayed to fight the fire. It's under control now. The Skipper and O'Kane both went in there with smoke masks on."

While I watched, the watertight door swung open and Vidick came out. His eyes were watering but apparently he was not too affected by the smoke. He was followed by Lieutenant O'Kane and then Captain Morton.

Captain Morton stopped to ask Record a question. "Do you think we can go ahead on two main engines now?"

"I think so, Captain."

"We'll try it then. The electricians have got a mess to square away in the maneuvering room."

Fifteen minutes later, *Wahoo* was feeling her way heavily and slowly through heavy seas on two main engines.

By the next day *Wahoo* had outridden the storm. I caught the afternoon watch and the only thing to occur was a plane contact on radar. I got a glimpse of a heavy big plane, not too far above the water, before clearing the bridge. *Wahoo* stayed submerged about an hour, before surfacing to continue her eastward course.

When I came off watch, I was met at the foot of the ladder by Lane. "I'm taking you off the watch list, Yeo. The Exec wants to start getting out the War Patrol Report."

That evening in the messroom Young came in to thumbtack a dispatch to the bulletin board. It read:

> From: COMSUBPAC
> To: CO USS WAHOO
>
> CONGRATULATIONS ON A JOB WELL DONE X
> JAPANESE THINK A SUBMARINE WOLFPACK
> OPERATING IN YELLOW SEA X ALL SHIPPING
> TIED UP

Krause came in with some more news. "Hey, fellows, guess where we're going."

"Where?"

"Midway Island."

I looked around and could see my own disappointment mirrored in everyone's eyes. "Dammit to hell. We could at least gone to a decent liberty port to rest up in."

Chapter 11

*W*ahoo pulled into Midway with the flood tide on the 6th of April 1943 with hardly any fanfare at all. She was met by line handlers who seemed glad to see any ship from the outside world.

Moored to the recently completed pier was the *U.S.S. Sperry* with several submarines alongside.

A small knot of officers and men comprised the greeting party including the paymaster and a mail clerk. I wondered if they noticed *Wahoo* had seventeen small Japanese flags floating from the halyards and the *Nitu Maru* life ring with the commercial ship flag hooked to the masthead. I decided that they were so used to successful submarines coming in off war patrols that *Wahoo* was just another break in their humdrum life on the island. One thing I did notice was that there were hundreds of more personnel in evidence and many more camouflaged barracks than last time. A single well-beaten coral road led to the center of Midway, which was hardly distinguishable in the bright glare of the sun, except for the figures of men walking in both directions like ants. Everywhere were gooney birds.

As soon as *Wahoo's* lines were doubled up and secured to the dock, a Second-Class Yeoman came aboard to relieve me of my duties. The name on his white hat identified him as W. T. White.

After getting paid and mail from home, I was given instructions by the Executive Officer to take a copy of the sailing list and proceed with the *Wahoo* crew to the Gooney Bird Hotel and make our reservations. I led off in the vanguard with sixty-some-odd dungaree-clad *Wahoo* sailors straggling along behind me.

The Gooney Bird Hotel was a long camouflaged building with an adjoining messhall that had a water tank on its roof and one or two small bungalows near by.

We went into the lobby, and while the men clustered in groups talking, I made arrangements with the Master-at-Arms in charge of the rooms.

I gave the chiefs the first room and then assigned six men to a room by rate, the seamen and firemen at the farther end of the building. When I went to my room, I found myself in company with O'Brien, Parks, Smith, Vidick, and Seal, who had been rated Torpedoman Second on the way into port.

It was cool inside the building compared to the outside. I flopped down on a bed near the window and the act made it my possession. Outside the window I could see thousands of gooney birds.

Looking around at the others in the room, I thought, Well, what is there to do now?

O'Brien came in last, saw the empty bunk next to mine, and sat down on it. "Hello, *Forest*, welcome to the Gooney Bird Hotel."

I said, "Fancy meeting you here, *Forest*. Every place I go, I run into you. You certainly get around and take nothing but the best." I sat up and offered him a sea-stores cigarette, which he took.

He asked, "What's this I hear about you getting Ballman transferred?"

Smith, Vidick, and Parks came over to hear the answer. Seal had gone out.

"Yes, it's true," I said half-apologetically. "I had some papers for Morton to sign yesterday and while he was signing them I asked him to transfer Ballman."

O'Brien said, "I'm hungry. Let's go find out where we eat around here."

I jumped out of bed. "Let's go."

The messhall proved to be where I thought it was. The cooks stationed on the island had a lot of time to use their imagination, and the food was excellently prepared. Coming out after eating, I looked around.

Deaton, Jasa, and Shattuck were bouncing a volleyball back and forth across a high net. Gooney birds were continuously getting in the way and being chased off the court. Anders and Young were halfheartedly passing and kicking a football in the sand. Zimmerman, Witting, Appel, Whipp, and Ater had baseball gloves and were tossing a baseball between them.

I saw a tub of iced canned beer in the shade against the messhall building. While I watched, Rennels walked over and fished out a can. He opened it with an opener attached to a cord on the side of the building. O'Brien and I looked at each other and invited ourselves over.

"They're free," Rennels informed us. "Compliments of SubForce to her combatant pigboat sailors."

Several gooney birds came over to join us and stare at us cockeyed through great artificial eyes.

Anders got a can of beer and ran one of the gooney birds down. He struggled with it until he got the bird's beak open and then poured the whole can of beer down its throat.

Coming back, he threw himself down on the sand with the rest of us, and we waited to see what would happen next. The bird stood moving the muscles of its throat in ripples until all the beer drained into its huge body. It cocked its head over to one side, gave us a dirty reproachful look, and began to flap its wings. Staggering around, it took a few tentative running steps for an intended take-off. Gooney lost his balance and did a tail spin, ending up in a flurry of ruffled feathers. He got up, stared indignantly at his appreciative audience, and tried again. Once, he got into the air eight or ten feet before going into a nose dive. We finally lost him in the gooney bird crowd.

Rennels said, "I think I'll see if a poker game is going someplace."

"Wait a minute and I'll go with you," was O'Brien's answer.

Together they drifted around the end of the building. Anders opened three cans of beer for himself, Krause, and myself. We relaxed back into the shadow of the building and looked moodily out across the sand.

Anders took a couple of drinks from the can and said, "I think I'll go to a movie. They got a noon show going on around here someplace." He shoved off.

Looking around for something diverting, I saw the hotel building. "Got any idea how these buildings got here, Krause?"

He looked around curiously. "They were built before the war by Pan American Airways. Midway was a stopping-off place to the Orient. They planted the palms, too."

We watched one of the Master-at-Arms bring out a case of beer and empty the cans in the tub. He took one, opened it, and went away drinking out of the can. I went over and opened two more cans.

It began to get cooler as the sun moved toward the horizon.

Zimmerman came by. "Hey, you guys, you gonna eat? It's chow time." We finished our beer and walked unsteadily into the messhall.

Coming out of the nearly empty messhall, we walked through the eastern wing of the building. Doors to rooms were spaced on both sides of the passageway. All were open. Men in different stages of undress were moving about or lying on their beds sleeping. I noticed two or three writing letters. One man was studying the front end of a Kodak. I supposed he had just bought it at the Navy Exchange since a wartime directive forbade anyone having a camera on board ship. There were several bull sessions going with many beer cans in evidence as we passed. In the lobby several tables of poker players were charging the space with intense suppressed emotion. More tubs of beer lined the bulkheads, and a bored Master-at-Arms leaned on the hotel desk with both elbows, smoking a cigarette and watching the action.

Krause wandered off. I took a can of beer and went to my room. Parks was lying on his stomach on his bed writing letters. Vidick was studying a *First-Class and Chief Electrician's Naval Handbook*. Seal was sleeping and snoring gently with his mouth open.

I pointed at Seal. "He eat yet?"

Parks shook his head and Vidick said, "No."

I shook Seal lightly and he came wide awake. "Chow's down. You hungry?"

"Thanks, Yeo." He got up and went out.

I sat down on the edge of the bed watching the sunset and sipping on the beer. Someone jumped on my back, burying my head in the pillow. I had a hard time trying not to spill the beer. After I had nearly suffocated, the pressure let up and I raised angrily. "What the hell . . ."

Lindhe, in new dungarees and chief's hat, was standing over me grinning maliciously.

"Why, you old son-uv-a-gun, when did you get back? How's things in the States? Let me get you a beer." I ran out of the room and came back with two fresh dripping cans.

He said, "You ought to see the Stateside stuff running around loose. Why, I nearly got raped in San Francisco."

"Yeah! Knowing you, that was no problem for the girls. Hey, I got something for you." I reached in my shirt pocket and handed him the unopened bottle of vitamin pills.

He looked at the bottle puzzled for a moment and then broke out laughing. "I take it you don't like vitamin pills."

"They give me a bellyache."

Lindhe said, "I hardly ever give them to a guy unless he looks run-down. Then I suspect something else is wrong with him."

"How's things in the States?"

"Well, they had a big Naval battle in the Bismarck Sea and . . ."

Ten minutes later we were up and running like banshees for the *Wahoo*. Sirens were screaming and wailing, while searchlights were crisscrossing wildly through the sky.

Reaching *Wahoo's* bridge deck out of breath, I fumbled with the telephone set. Krause arrived and Lieutenant O'Kane appeared on deck. The Captain followed seconds later, puffing up the side ladder. Reports began to come in over the phone. "Maneuvering room manned and ready."

I turned to the Captain. "All stations manned and ready, sir."

"Very well."

The sirens changed their tune to a steady drone and then stopped. The searchlights went out one by one.

Captain Morton growled, "Secure from air-raid alarm."

I passed the word. Then I went to my locker and got a bar of soap, tooth powder, brush, and a towel.

Cursing, we straggled back to the Gooney Bird Hotel. The Master-at-Arms met us at the door. "It was a false alarm. One of our own planes didn't know the identification code password. It happens all the time."

After breakfast I wandered outside. A soft-ball game was in the process of getting organized so I entered my application.

There was a big tub of canned beer near home plate and by the eighth inning no one cared which side was winning. I was in left field. Lane hit a hard liner toward me. I raised a can of beer to my lips and flung out my gloved hand. The ball smacked into the glove, nearly yanking my shoulder out of place. Looking sideways in surprise I saw that it had stuck in the mitt. The whole gang let out a howl and started for me. I threw the ball and glove at them and turned to run. Someone tackled me before I got five or six steps and my nose dug into the sand. They hoisted me to their shoulders and carried me like a hero into the lobby of the hotel yelling like a band of *Wahoo* Indians.

Most of the following days were like that. Some of the fellows took to sun bathing. Others spent a great deal of time swimming and running along the beach. It was a rare night indeed that did not find us aboard the *Wahoo* securing from an air-raid alarm.

About the middle of the second week, I was sitting in the noonday shade of the hotel indulging in my favorite pastime. Rennels sauntered up. "Yeo, if you don't get up from there you're going to take root."

"What would you suggest?"

"Let's go over to Sand Island and bum a ride in one of the airplanes."

I thought it over. "How come you're not in a game?"

"My luck was turning sour. I thought I'd like to give it a rest. Howsabout an airplane ride."

I said, "If dog don't walk, it no get bone."

"What's that? You drunk or something?"

"Naw, just talking. Let's go."

We crossed the island and caught a motor launch to Sand Island. A long low building had a flag in front. We went in and found a Navy lieutenant sitting at a desk reading an old newspaper. There was no formality.

"What can I do for you, boys?"

"Well, sir, we're off the submarine *Wahoo* and here for a rest period. We was wondering if you could fix us up for a plane ride or something to break the monotony."

He answered jovially, "I sure can, but it will have to be in the morning. Will you be missed if you stay here tonight?"

Rennels looked at me. I shrugged my shoulders. "I don't think so unless there's an air-raid alarm. Half of the guys don't show up on the boat for that any more."

The lieutenant said, "Fine, fine, then it's all settled. You can stay here tonight." He buzzed for a messenger and directed him to put us up for the night.

"Thank you, sir." He just grinned at us as the messenger led us outside. We ended up in a dugout, and the messenger pointed out two bunks that had been slept in. "Those are yours." He went out.

The dugout was dark, damp, and cool. Rennels and I lay down and were soon fast asleep. No one called us for evening chow, and we slept on into the night.

Someone came into the dugout flashing a light. I came to my feet fully awake. The beam caught me full in the face. "You the guys that want a air ride?"

"Yeah," I answered into the darkness behind the light.

"Okay, follow me." Rennels stirred and got up. We followed our guide out into the night. It was so dark that our only sense of direction came from the crunching of his shoes on the gravel. He stopped and we almost bumped into him. There was a rustle of heavy curtains, and Rennels and I came through them into the brilliance of artificial light. We were in a steam-heavy messhall. Our guide was a white hat in dungarees, aviation jacket, and combat boots.

We grabbed trays and started down the feeding line. I passed a cook with a chef's hat on and no shirt. His skivvy shirt was greasy with food stains and sweat. A tattoo on a hairy arm proclaimed to the world that he loved his mother, and a tattoo on the other arm had two hearts joined together with an arrow and the name "Susie" under it. He dipped a big ladleful of beans cooked in catsup onto the platter and I moved along. The next server measured out three prunes, and farther along I got one slice of bacon and a small square of corn bread. Looking down at the tray, I noticed the time on my new wrist watch. It was 0335 in the morning. I almost dropped the tray in surprise.

"Move along, you."

I got seated at a table with Rennels and the guide. He ate hastily and greedily and so did we. The coffee was tasteless from many boilings and stuck to my teeth. Rennels refused to drink his.

Our guide hurried us out of the building and now we could see a little better from the light reflected in a dawning day. We moved around and about several bunkers and planes with crews working oin them. A morning breeze sprang up, awakening the island's aviary and they took to the air with rested lungs.

We stopped short at a PBY. The crew was clambering aboard and Rennels and I were entrusted to their care. We crawled up a short ladder into the fuselage and into a corner out of the way but where we could see out of the gunner's canopy.

The PBY's motors began to roar so loudly that I could hear Rennels only when he shouted. Vibration took over the plane and I wondered if there would be anything left to get off the ground. Presently and surprisingly we began to move. I saw sand dunes and men moving past the wings. We came to rest in the center of a broad strip of paving. The PBY just sat there shaking until my teeth began to chatter too. Whatever the pilot was waiting for eventually came to pass, and what I had thought of as noise before faded into insignificance as he gunned the motors. I could feel the body of the plane strain forward before it began to move. Slowly at first, then faster, it gained momentum. We rolled for what seemed like miles down the mile-long runway. Just when I thought we were going into the drink, the plane took wing and we had a parting with terra firma.

Our sky mare rose with the sun, and the propellers fought off luckless gooney birds, leaving a trail of feathers, bones, and viscera behind to litter the beach.

A bird's-eye view of the two islands was not very impressive except to emphasize how small they were in comparison with the rest of the Pacific Ocean. It did not take long to lose them from sight as the plane bore off on a northwesterly course.

The Navigational Officer came back and sat down. "How you fellows like it?"

"It's wonderful," I lied. "When do we go back and land?"

"Oh, we'll be back around 1700 tonight." He saw the expressions on Rennels' face and mine. "Is anything wrong?"

Rennels answered, "No, only we thought we were just going up for a short hop. I think we been tooken."

The Navigational Officer said, "That damn Operations Officer is always playing pranks on somebody." He left us, smirking at some secret joke.

I looked down at the blue patches of ocean seen between clouds below us and turned to Rennels. "I didn't fully realize how a submarine's silhouette might show up in the water until now."

I got up, stretched, and walked forward to where the officers were. They evidently had the plane on "iron mike" or automatic gyro control and were sitting smoking and talking with occasional glances at the multitude of meter indicators. They looked around at me and raised their eyebrows in silent interrogation.

"Nothing, sir. Just looking around."

The Navigational Officer made a calculation on an open navigational chart, got up, stretched, and said, "I think I'll turn in."

Noticing the copilot looking at me, I asked, "How far from Wake Island will we come?"

"About seven hundred fifty miles."

"Why, that's half the distance between Midway and Wake."

"That's right." He seemed unconcerned.

"Don't the Japs still occupy Wake?"

"Yeah, but they don't bother us and we don't bother them."

"What would you do if you ran into a Jap Zero out here?"

The pilot answered, "Nothing. We'd turn tail and go back and he would do the same."

Back by the machine gun, I sat down again. Rennels took a turn forward. He came back shaking his head.

When my watch showed it to be 1200, one of the crew members came back with a tiny paper cup of cold coffee, another paper cup containing two halves of peaches, and two soda crackers. "Lunch," he said, leaving us.

I sat looking down at the clouds and at an occasional postage-stamp view of the ocean. The continuous roaring of the plane numbed my senses. Below us the tiny shadow of the plane kept pace.

Aeons later the sun dipped to the horizon and I began anxiously to worry about seeing Midway. After all, such a tiny speck in all this vast expanse of water could easily be lost. When my watch hands pointed out 1630 on the dial, I saw a minute break in the horizon line. Fifteen minutes later, I could make out the islands and the black gnats that could be nothing else but gooney birds. The islands looked deserted except for a landing strip on one and a toy ship at the other. Our PBY landed and rolled to a stop thirteen minutes after 1700.

Rennels and I climbed stiffly out of the plane and left. We did not even look back.

Next day I was almost back to battery again. I ate a hearty breakfast and found a comfortable place in the sand near the beer tub. It was the first day of my sojourn at Midway that I felt completely relaxed.

Krause, Lindhe, Carr, and, to my surprise, Vidick were having a beer and listening to my detailed and embroidered tale of the great aerial saga. To my further surprise, Ensigns Misch and Griggs with Lieutenant Jackson joined the circle and listened with enthusiasm until I finished.

There was the usual repartee of cynicism, and then Lieutenant Jackson said almost casually, "There's going to be an honor review for the *Wahoo* crew by the Midway garrisons at 1300. You will all be expected to be there."

The first answer that came to mind was, "But Mr. Jackson, all my whites are down on the boat."

He replied, "That won't be necessary. All of you come just as you are."

I looked down at my old ragged clothes and out-of-shape moccasins and then at the others. Carr was the only one that looked at all presentable. I felt my three days' growth of bristles. "Are you sure, sir? We look like a bunch of beachcombers."

Ensign Misch added, "Don't worry, fellows. 'Mush' said you men were all heroes any place you went, and he would personally guarantee that there would be no spit and polish."

After the noon meal we straggled down to a large cement square, called a "grinder," and fell into formation at a place that Lieutenant Commander O'Kane designated. I nudged Krause next to me. "Look at that. He's wearing brand-new Lieutenant Commander's gold leaves."

A white uniformed band took up a position at one end of the field. They struck up a martial air that pulled back my slumping energy. Without realizing it, I straightened into a military stance with face front and chin up. A glance from the corner of my eyes showed me that every single *Wahoo* sailor was rigid with shoulders squared. I forgot all about the noonday heat.

Columns of Marines and Seabee battalions maneuvered into position and began a unified march. Color guards appeared from someplace and led the whole military consolidation into rows facing us.

High-ranking officers came forward and stood between us and the others. It seemed that everybody on Midway Island was there to honor us. The one man who was most responsible for *Wahoo's* success was absent. Lieutenant Commander O'Kane took the honors in his place.

Medals were presented to the officers, several of the chiefs, and one or two enlisted men. A speech was made by Midway's Commandant praising the exploits of *Wahoo's* recent war patrols. Then the band began to play and the formations marched abreast of us. They were given the command to eyes-right, thus giving us the greatest military honor that marching men can give to another military group.

We were dismissed after nearly two hours of standing at attention. I had to pick up some things at the boat, so I turned off and went in that direction. I picked up a change of clothes and went to the ship's office for some stationery.

White was there busily working away at the typewriter.

"Howya coming?" I inquired.

"It's a racket on this boat. Say, you wouldn't want to swap, would you?"

I grinned at him. "Hell no, I know when I'm well off." Then, curious, I added, "You've got a good job on the Squadron. Why would you want to give it up and go on patrol to get the daylights scared out of you?"

He replied seriously, "I have my reasons. I'd like to be able to tell my grandchildren that I was on a fighting submarine in this war. I like to gamble, too, and *Wahoo* has some of the biggest games of any of the submarines. You guys have the reputation of being on a happy boat."

I said proudly, "We got the best damn crew and the best damn skipper in the whole Submarine Navy. That's why I wouldn't consider a transfer for anything until I've made at least five war patrols."

Captain Morton's voice came from his stateroom, "Thanks, Yeo, will you step in here a minute?"

I was so surprised to discover that he was on board that I nearly lost my speech. I pulled the curtains to his cabin aside and looked in. He had evidently been lying on his bunk and was now sitting up. His face looked haggard.

"You wanted me, sir?"

"Yes, come in and sit in that chair. Thanks for what you just said about me and the crew."

I was pleased. "I didn't know you were aboard, sir, or you wouldn't have heard. I missed you at the review. Is anything wrong?"

"My damn kidneys bother me every now and then, and I get some bad headaches. I didn't feel up to the review today, but you lads are the ones that deserve all the honors anyway."

I felt embarrassed because no officer had talked to me like this before. "Are you doing something about it?" I asked, thinking of the coming patrol and what it would be like without 'Mush' at the conn.

"Yes, that's why I asked you to step in here. When you go back tell Lindhe to come down to the boat. He's a better doctor than most of the Medical Officers I know."

I said, "Aye, aye, sir," and stood up. His face lighted up with its old boyish grin. "We're going to get a whole slew of Jap ships if we can find them on the next run."

I caught his enthusiasm. "Yes, *sir*."

Lindhe was in a poker game when I got back. I scribbled the Captain's instructions on a slip of paper and handed it to him. He threw in his cards and picked up his money. "There's a vacant chair here, anybody want it?"

Going to one side Lindhe asked, "Where's Kohl? I'll need to get the keys to the medical locker from him."

I pointed out the room and he left immediately. Looking over at the tubs of cold beer, I decided against it and instead went to my room and its six-men private shower, feeling that it was about time I took a shave.

In bed that night, I heard bugle taps from the Marine barracks. It sounded far away and eerie and sad as though the bugler lamented all the good things in life that were past. A feeling of melancholy came over me and I had trouble getting to sleep.

Chapter 12

Our orders were to be back aboard the *Wahoo* by 1200.

We went on board, put our gear away, and parted going in different directions. A mental picture of my locker stuffed with dirty clothes haunted me. I decided that I would make a trip to the *Sperry* and get stocked up on a new supply before leaving Midway and throw the dirty ones away.

The office was vacant. White had left it shipshape with all the work caught up. I sat down restlessly wondering where to begin and not too eager to go to work. A recent *Bureau of Personnel Circular Letter* was lying open on the desk. White had underlined some of the sentences with red pencil. The subject was Stenography School, convening date, 1 November 1943. I wondered idly if he had left it as a hint for me. Scanning through it quickly, I noticed that the school was for yeomen second and first class to train them to meet the shorthand qualifications for first class and chief. The school was to convene at the U. S. Naval Training Center, San Diego, California.

I started to push the letter aside, but it had fastened its tentacles on my imagination. Picking up the letter, I went into the messroom, drew a cup of coffee, and sat smoking in my favorite corner while I pondered the letter's contents.

If I stayed aboard the *Wahoo*, I would be on board indefinitely. Only Squadron yeomen were getting new construction boats. There was a long waiting list of those whose personal contacts were far better than my own. I knew that, if I swapped with a yeoman in the Squadron, I would be unhappy with the comparative inactivity compared to that of a submarine. Besides, the *Wahoo* was the best damn submarine in the fleet and I might be assigned to another I did not like so well. Then, too, there was Dudley Walker Morton. I would have a hell of a time finding another officer that could command my Rebel loyalty as he did.

I was about to forget it when Phillips and O'Brien joined me.

"Whatcha reading, Yeo?" O'Brien asked. "Something that will get us all leave back to the States?"

"Naw, it's just a letter telling about a stenography class convening in November for yeomen."

Phillips said, "You're not putting in for it, are you? Are you eligible?"

"Yeah, I'm eligible but my request would stand about as much chance getting approved as a snowball in hell."

"If you put in for a transfer, I'm going to put in for one, too," Phillips said, concerned.

I was surprised at how seriously Phillips had taken my impromptu speech at the Royal Hawaiian Hotel. "Aw, don't believe all the malarkey I hand out," I answered pointedly. "The old *Wahoo* is due to end up in a razor-blade factory in Philadelphia someplace. They ain't nothing that can stop 'Mush' when he gets going."

"What's he talking about?" O'Brien asked Phillips.

"Yeo said nothing would happen to the *Wahoo* as long as he was on it."

O'Brien said seriously, "You know I think Yeo's right. I've had a feeling for some time that the Japs have got *Wahoo's* number. It's just a question of when. Yeo, you're our lucky-piece. You can't leave the *Wahoo*."

Phillips pleaded, "You're not going to put in a request, are you, Yeo?"

A sadistic urge came over me to torture them. "Yeah, I'm gonna prove to you guys that there ain't nothing to all that bunk. There isn't one chance in a thousand of its getting approved. I bet every second- and first-class yeoman in the Pacific Ocean is typing up a request right now. I'm just going to ask O'Kane to put 'Forwarded' on mine. You guys will see."

Phillips said, "Don't do it, Yeo."

"Aw, you guys are nuts. I'm going right up to the office and make this request out, right now." I left them in the messroom exchanging glances.

When I finished the request, it filled half a sheet of paper with the barest required facts. As a first endorsement on the same page, I put merely, "Forwarded for consideration." I took it to the wardroom and found Lieutenant Commander O'Kane. He was sitting at the table with his back to me reading official mail.

Without raising his head, he said, "Yes, what is it?"

I placed the request on top of the other mail along with the Bureau's directive. "Sir, I'm making a request for Steno School."

The Executive Officer did not turn around or raise his head. He sat there reading my request. I waited for him to initial the green file copy as his approval for the Commanding Officer's signature.

"What the hell? Don't you like the officers on the *Wahoo*?" he snarled.

I was a little startled. "No, sir, it ain't that. I just want my chance at Stateside like the rest of the crew gets rotated."

"I'm not going to initial this. The Captain won't sign it anyway."

"But, sir, I don't stand a Chinaman's chance of getting it. I just want to try . . ."

"What won't the Captain sign?" It was Captain Morton's voice at my shoulder.

Lieutenant Commander O'Kane stood up and turned around sullenly.

My mouth must have dropped open, and I was certain that I was rudely staring. The Executive Officer had one of the most beautiful black eyes on the portside that I had seen since my one-time appearance in the boxing ring at the Naval Recruit Training Center. He explained, "Yeo's submitting a request for Steno School, convening 1 November at San Diego."

"Why not?" Captain Morton responded heartily. "He's the best damn yeoman in the SubForce and I think he's chief material. He's entitled to a chance. I'll sign it. What kind of endorsement do you want, Yeo? I'll make up one like they never saw before. It will knock their eyes out."

Gratified, I said meekly, "I don't want anything special, Captain. Just 'forwarded,' that's all."

Captain Morton seemed surprised. He took the letter from the Executive Officer and glanced at it. "You sure you don't want a good recommendation?" He seemed disappointed.

"No sir, just your signature. That's good enough for me."

The Captain took my proffered fountain pen, laid the request on the corner of the wardroom table, and signed it above his typed-in name with a flourish.

"Thank you, sir," I glanced at Lieutenant Commander O'Kane's black eye. It was sparkling dangerously. Hurrying back to the office, I typed an address on an official envelope, placed the request inside, and sealed it. Then I grabbed several more letters that White had left to be mailed and left *Wahoo* to go aboard the *Sperry* and mail them. After that I put the request entirely out of mind.

Returning to *Wahoo*, I was met by every man in the crew, all of them wanting to know how the Executive Officer got his black eye. It turned out to be the best-guarded secret the Navy ever had.

I settled down to the business at hand and in the next few days transferred Ensigns Griggs and Campbell, Appel, Ballman, Clary, Cook, Hall, Holmes, Janecek, Kohl, Kohut, Parks, Veder, and Young.

Wahoo received a new Ensign E. E. Fiedler from Brooklyn, New York.

A Motor Machinist's Mate First Class, MacGowen, Thomas J. H., from Glendale, California, reported on board with eleven men in his charge.

I took a look at MacGowen's full name, whistled, and read it aloud, "Thomas Jamieson Harrison MacGowen, Junior. Boy, that's a mouthful!"

Lieutenant Commander O'Kane's voice grated through the office partition. "Who is this man? What does he want here?" MacGowen stepped back and the Executive Officer came into view.

"This is MacGowen, sir, he's in charge of the new men come aboard."

Lieutenant Commander O'Kane glared at me and said, "Let me have their records," and to MacGowen, "Follow me into the wardroom." He accepted the records and brusquely turned away.

MacGowen raised his eyebrows before he too stepped out of view. He was silently asking me, "What gives with the black eye?" I grinned to myself, got up, and went into the messroom. Noticing Gerlacher and Whipp excited about something they had spread out on a corner table, I walked over. They had about a hundred pebbles on the table examining them.

I said, "Whatcha got there?"

They looked up at me. Whipp said, "They're cat's-eyes."

I picked several up and looked at them. They appeared to be beach-scarred sea shells with a greenish and brownish spot on them about the size of an eye lens. I twisted them about curiously in my fingers. "What are they good for?"

Whipp said, "I'm going to polish 'em up. When they're polished they look like cat's-eyes. We plan on selling them in Honolulu. They make 'em into necklaces and jewelry and things like that."

Gerlacher said, "We spent all our time on the beach swimming and hunting for cat's-eyes."

"That's swell, fellas. I hope you make a fortune."

There were two or three days of getting ready for operational readiness. Then on the morning of April 25, *Wahoo* left Midway Island on her fifth war patrol and my fourth. Captain Morton was at the conn with his big happy grin. Lieutenant Commander O'Kane was everywhere on the bridge seeing that Morton's orders were being carried out. It seemed strange to see two lieutenant commanders on the bridge, and I suspected that the Executive Officer would soon be leaving *Wahoo* or else taking command and Captain Morton would be leaving.

Looking at the plodding humanity on Midway, I felt sorry for the men who would have to do eighteen or twenty-four months duty on the island. I was not, however, sorry to be leaving our gooney bird friends behind. Judging by the send-off they gave us, they were glad to see us leave.

It was no secret that *Wahoo* was headed for some cold country. The odds below decks were ten to one it would be in the vicinity of Alaska.

The heavy winter clothing brought on board was not there for extra ballast.

When maneuvering watch secured, I went on lookout and relieved Kirk, taking the binoculars he had been using. Our gooney-bird and sea-gull escort was thinning out when Krebs came up to relieve me and I went down to relieve Terrell on the wheel. Most of the morning had passed with the maneuvering watch and I was keeping *Wahoo* on a three-one-five degree course when Tyler relieved me for noon chow.

In the messroom I met with an aroma of stewed chicken and dumplings. There were a good many comments about the diminishing gooney-bird population and requests of, "Pass the gooney bird."

Dietrich went placidly about the business of ladling out steaming food, but Rennels came out into the crew's mess with flashing eyes. "Any of you guys don't like this chow, just come on back into the sleeping compartment . . ."

The messroom became so quiet that a feather landing on the deck would have sounded like a snow slide. Rennels glared around and started back for the galley. Someone in the corner said, "Pass the sea gull."

Rennels swung around, "Who said that?"

Everybody in the messhall began pointing at somebody else. Rennels said, "Aw, to hell with you guys," and stamped angrily back to the galley, followed by the taunting laughter of everyone present.

Coming off the 1800–2000 watch that evening, I found our old corner occupied by several new men who had reported on board. After each war patrol, many familiar faces were missing, and I had to get accustomed to the new ones. This slight irritation would disappear by the third or fourth day at sea, so I accepted it and found another seat. Krause, Carr, and O'Brien showed up, however, and Rennels a short time later. Ware was at another table with his Bible open in front of him, underlining certain passages with a red lead pencil.

O'Brien said, "Yeo, you're slipping. Here it is the first day at sea and you don't have a new cartoon to replace my old one."

"I'll get around to it, don't worry."

Hayes stuck his head in the door. "Hey, Krause, the Old Man wants yuh."

Krause left us and was back in a few minutes. He thumbtacked a chart to the bulletin board and sat down again. The pinochle players and Ware got up to look at it.

"Morton wanted me to let everybody know we're headed for Paramushiro. We're going to reconnoiter the Kurile Islands and then reach area off the eastern coast of Japan proper."

Phillips said, "I wonder why we're going up into that God-forsaken country. It's colder'n hell up there."

Carr answered him. "With the Japs moving in on Attu they might be getting ready to invade Alaska."

Krause said, "If they are, there's sure to be a lot of traffic up that way. Transports and cargo ships and . . ."

". . . escorts," I finished sourly.

"Don't worry, 'Mush' will know how to handle them," Rennels said, knowingly and confidently.

By this time we had a good-sized audience of *Wahoo* sailors standing around the table. Ater in the group said, "O'B, do you think we'll board any *Fishi Marus* this trip?"

O'Brien said, "I'd sure like to. I'd like to get some souvenirs to send home."

I said, "If they got a load of fish, you'll probably be bringing them on board. The Old Man said in his last war patrol that he was a 'carnivorous sailor.' "

Carr asked, "Did they mention my name in the last report?"

"Naw, they hardly ever mention any of the enlisted men's names. They don't even hardly mention an officer's name unless he done something outstanding. I'm not supposed to talk about the war patrols. Let's change the subject."

"Okay, Yeo, but we know what's in 'em anyway."

"Sure, I bet you could write a better one than they do."

Krause said, "Maybe not so technical, but I'll bet it would be more interesting."

I said, "Hell, I got to get some shut-eye. I got a four-to-eight coming up." I got up, rummaged around in the canned-goods locker until I found a can of kidney beans, and ate them before going to bed. The bull session was still going strong.

Each day at sea the weather became cooler. Each day, like a Chinaman, I added another piece of clothing to go up on lookout. On May the second, I came off lookout on the midwatch, shivering, teeth chattering, and my nose and ears so cold I was afraid to touch them for fear they would shatter into crystallized fragments. It had begun to sleet and snow, and I had stood helplessly trying to peer into a darkness that was not penetrable with the human eye. The binoculars were a useless ornamentation. Ensign Fiedler, using his initiative, had ordered Kirk and myself down to the cigarette deck where we were greatly sheltered from the wind, and we stood staring out at the sheets of icy water, unable to see more than a few feet.

When it came time to go on the midwatch again, I had on a blue Navy stocking cap drawn down over my ears, a sweat shirt and three dungaree shirts, and over these a peacoat. Wool-knit Navy gloves covered my hands, and I wore three pairs of dungaree trousers, the bottoms tucked into the outer pair of four pairs of socks. I had to wear my moccasins to fit over them.

I had difficulty negotiating the ladders leading to the bridge. I came out of the hatch face to face with Captain Morton. He stared at me in surprise for a moment and burst out laughing. "What the hell, Yeo? If we have to dive, you'll never make it down the hatch. The other men seem to get along all right without so much clothing."

"I know, Captain, but I guess I got more Rebel blood in me than they have."

"Very well." He turned away laughing.

I had rotated to the messenger duty when Tyler on the radar sang out, "Land contact on the radar screen, sir."

Chief Lennox, on duty, sent me to the wardroom to tell the Captain and the Executive Officer. They were not surprised, as they were expecting it. On the way past me, Captain Morton said, "Rebel, you're dressed for topside, would you bring a cup of coffee up to Mr. Misch on the bridge?"

"Yes sir."

I walked to the officers' pantry and found Jayson on duty.

"You gotcha cupa coffee for boss man on bridge?"

He grinned and prepared a cup from the officers' coffee urn.

I took the coffee into the conning tower and requested permission to come on the bridge. The request was granted, and I found Ensign Misch with the Captain and the Executive Officer looking through binoculars ahead on the port bow. Ensign Misch took his coffee and thanked me. I stretched my shoulders and neck to see what they were looking at. A beautiful snow-capped mountaintop rose into the wintry gray sky just above the horizon.

I said, "Gee, that's pretty."

Ensign Misch said, "That's Onnekotan Island."

I took the cup and saucer and went below decks.

Coming off watch, I poked my head into the radio shack. Carter was on watch and had been copying press. He was looking over his copy for mistakes.

"What's new on the outside world?" I asked.

He looked up at me. "Nothing much. A Japanese Admiral by the name of Yamamoto got himself killed in a plane crash. He was on a routine inspection flight to China."

At 0200 Erickson awoke me with the glad tidings, "Yeo, you're wanted in the tower."

I got up sleepily, drew a cup of coffee, and made my way somnolently to *Wahoo's* main center which was preparing for an attack. Nothing here had changed except that, instead of Parks helping Lieutenant Paine, Mills, the Radio Technician was standing by.

Sipping on the hot coffee and biting my tongue to stay awake, I somehow got the books, pencil, and pad ready. I envied Lindhe who must be sleeping in the chiefs' quarters.

Lieutenant Commander O'Kane had been peering steadily through the periscope and now he muttered something about "Four airplane hangars." The words seeped past my eardrums and echoed about in a nerve-deadened void before hitting a live nerve. Then they exploded my whole body into a tense, alive, and vibrant organism, with all defense mechanisms ready to spring into action.

Airplane hangars, I thought. That means airplanes. Where there's airplanes, there's an airfield, and where there's an airfield, there's bombs. Oh, brother, let's not stay around here long.

The Executive Officer said, "There's a large ship close inshore but there's something fishy about it. It doesn't look right."

Captain Morton took a turn at the periscope and relinquished it to stand back, thoughtfully considering what he had seen.

Lieutenant Commander O'Kane began describing the ship to me and I hunted for the descriptions. He stopped and said, "Captain, it looks like there's a large hole in her side. I'll bet she's been beached."

Captain Morton snapped his fingers. "That's it, another submarine beat us to her. There was no activity on board. That's what made her seem so strange. Do you see any other ships or any unusual activity around the base?"

Lieutenant Commander O'Kane studied the situation. "No, Captain, everything seems to be quiet up there."

Captain Morton said musingly, "We could surface and shell those hangars."

The Executive Officer swung around enthusiastically. "Howsabout it, Captain? We could set those hangars on fire."

The hair crawled on my scalp and my Adam's apple began to twitch. I noticed everyone looking at the Captain, waiting his decision.

"It's too big a job for the armament we have on board. If we surface, an incoming plane might catch us before we could damage the planes on the ground."

Lieutenant Commander O'Kane said, "This is a secret air base that SubPac doesn't know anything about, Captain."

Captain Morton answered, "That's true, but a submarine's secrecy is one of its biggest weapons. We haven't reached station yet. We'll pull out and send the location in to Pearl by radio. It will be their baby then."

There were more observations made, and it appeared that the base had a radio station and several smaller buildings that apparently were shops and living quarters. The rocky hillsides were barren of everything but drifted snow.

Wahoo ducked underwater and moved away from the island.

I turned my notes in dated 3 May 1943, and Krause added the words Matsuwa Island to the memoranda. The approach party was dismissed and I went back to my warm blankets. A short time later I was awakened. I ate a hearty breakfast of hot cakes and ham and eggs, and bundled up heavily for another foray on the icy bridge.

After relieving the lookout on the cigarette deck, I looked out across a changed world. There was no ocean to be seen but instead a vast thin ice plain. Jagged rock islands pierced this ice at irregular intervals. Looking forward to *Wahoo's* stem was a fascinating interlude. *Wahoo's* nose was clearing a pathway through the six or eight inches of ice so smoothly that the surface seemed to part at her approach. It gave the illusion that *Wahoo* was standing still and the ice was moving. I looked toward the stern and saw a neat straight path perhaps forty or fifty feet wide with small ice floes and chopped-up ice floating in a canal of dark blue water. I wondered what an airplane flying across this marked path might deduce from it. Ensign Campbell, the Deck Officer, did not seem overly worried, so I guessed that *Wahoo* would not go far before the ice either closed in or the water froze over again.

The rest of the day went smoothly by with *Wahoo* operating as an icebreaker. Below decks the crew had settled into a routine of daily habits and everybody waited. So far we were disappointed in not finding a steady flow of sea traffic going toward Alaska. Everyone was trying to solve the problem of what the Japs were up to at Attu.

From 4 May through 12 May 1943, *Wahoo* crippled a seaplane tender, the *Kamikawa Maru*, and sank another, *Yuki Maru*. She sank a large freighter of the *Huzisan Maru* class and a freighter of the *Hawaii Maru* class. She also got a hit on a freighter of the *Myoken Maru* class and a hit on another freighter of the *Anyo Maru* class. After that her torpedoes were expended.

That evening Krause brought the news. We were going back to Gooney Bird Island.

The Japanese had different plans for where they would like *Wahoo* to go. They sent out three modern *Fubukis* to find us and send us there.

Wahoo became boxed in, and we spent most of the night submerged. The destroyers knew their business, and *Wahoo* soon found her way blocked to the open sea. She wiggled desperately in every direction under Captain Morton's skillful guidance in an effort to escape the net of echoranging countermeasures all around her.

The clocks informed us that it was daylight on the surface, but *Wahoo* was hugging the bottom and was rigged for depth charge. I spent the entire four hours of the 0400–0800 watch on the sonar gear. I had no trouble keeping alert while listening to the pinging of the echo-rangers and screws of the destroyers at three different points on the compass. When one of the destroyers would become louder, I reported it. Captain Morton would quietly direct the helmsman to a different course. It was hot and stuffy in the conning tower.

On being relieved by Buckley, I went to the crew's mess and ate breakfast. Sleep was impossible, so I sat in the compartment with Rennels and Robertson who was manning the battle phones.

Lane came in for coffee and, seeing me, sat down for a word or two "Most of the watch standers are pooped out and the radiomen are dead on their feet. Would you mind relieving Buckley on the sound gear for an hour or two so he can get some sleep?"

"I don't mind. I'll get a cup of coffee and go up there now."

"Thanks, Yeo." Lane went forward again.

I went into the connng tower. Captain Morton was still up and sitting on a swivel stool with his head between his hands. He looked up at me, grinned, and put his head down again.

Buckley pointed out the location of the destroyers and turned the sonar gear over to my care.

Wach was on the helm devoting all his attention to *Wahoo's* course.

I reported the destroyers' positions to make sure they had not changed while Buckley and I had exchanged places.

Captain Morton raised his head and said, "Let's let the crew hear the echo-ranging. Throw the switch from the earphones to the speaker and turn up the volume."

I flipped over the toggle switch and turned up the rheostat. *Ping, ping, ping, ping-g-g-g.* I changed the dial to another destroyer and the resulting sound was the same. I was sure it could be heard all through the ship.

Captain Morton said, "That's enough. I don't want to scare them out of their wits but just enough to keep everybody alert."

I threw the switch and adjusted the volume.

After a little while the Captain said, "Anybody that wants a smoke can light up. The smoking lamp is lit for one cigarette."

I took out a pack and offered the Captain one.

"Thanks, Yeo, I don't smoke."

Wach lit a cigarette and a light flared in the corner as Ensign Misch or Mills lighted up. I had hardly noticed them. They were sitting quietly by the TDC.

Krause poked his head through the hatch and said, "Anybody want a cup of coffee? I'll get it."

Receiving negative answers, he asked Wach, "Want me to spell you a few minutes on the wheel?" Wach shook his head and-Krause said, "I'll be in the messhall if you need me, Captain."

Captain Morton answered, "All right, Krause."

Krause ducked down out of sight.

We sat there quietly through the dragging silence. Only an occasional noise from the control would let us know that men were working to keep *Wahoo* on an even keel and depth.

I had to say something. I turned and said, "Captain, the seventeenth is my birthday. Do you think I'll get to celebrate my thirty-second birthday?"

He looked up grinning, with some of the old fire back in his eyes. "Hell yes, Yeo. I personally guarantee it. This is a dog-eat-dog proposition. Yesterday we were biting, today they're trying to get a bite out of us."

"Too bad we ain't got any fish. At least we'd have something to fight with if they cornered us, Captain."

"I'd like nothing better. I'd send those Goddam destroyers packing or know the reason why." His eyes flashed.

I turned back to the sound gear puzzled by a new sound.

Captain Morton was instantly on his feet and standing with his big hand on my shoulder. "What is it? What do you hear?"

I said, "I can't make it out but I never heard anything like this on the sound gear before."

"Describe it to me."

I searched mentally for a simile. "Sorta like something bubbling, like hot water bubbling somewheres on the starboard bow."

Captain Morton grabbed the phones and twisted the sound handle while I leaned backward out of the way. "That's it. It's hot water bubbling or gases escaping from an underseas volcano fissure." Captain Morton was jubilant. "Helmsman, come right five degrees rudder. Steady on." He released the handle.

I listened to the new sound and switched from that to the destroyers Soon the bubbling noise was all around *Wahoo*. Our excitement grapevined through the ship. Lieutenant Commander O'Kane popped into the conning tower. Movements and sounds below us increased. Buckley and Lieutenant Jackson came to the conning tower to listen and Buckley relieved me. I went below.

The regular watch relieved at noon, and *Wahoo* gradually took on its normal regularity. The air was getting heavy, and it was getting a little difficult to find oxygen. Increased air pressure was an inconvenience that veteran submariners hardly notice.

Sandwiches were on the noonday menu. After eating I went to the office. The lights were all low in the officers' country and I turned my desk light on. The typewriter looked neglected, I used it so seldom. I decided against using it now until *Wahoo* was out of danger. Instead, I sat studying the rough reports that had to be made up.

Ensign Misch came to the door looking strangely stern. "What have you done now, Yeo?"

I wondered what he meant. "I don't know. I ain't done nothing that I know of. Why?"

"Well, the Captain's mad as a wet hen. He wants to see you right away."

"All right," I answered rebelliously. I wondered if I had said something to the Captain in the conning tower to merit his displeasure. Getting up, I ducked through the watertight door into the control room and turned toward the ladder.

"Not up there," Ensign Misch said behind me. "The Captain is in the messhall."

I swung back and went into the messroom. I was inside before I realized that the messroom was in complete darkness. Bewildered, I came to a stop. The lights sprang on suddenly, revealing the compartment filled with shipmates with Captain Morton in the middle of them. I stared unbelievingly and uncomprehendingly at them.

"Happy birthday to you. Happy birthday to you-u-u. Happy birthday, dear Yeoman. Happy birthday to you." Their voices would have sounded better in an anvil chorus.

I just stood there like a stupid ass, unable to say anything.

Captain Morton stepped forward with a saucer in his hand. It contained a cupcake with a candle in the center. He lit the candlewick with a match and presented the saucer to me. "Happy birthday on your thirty-second birthday," he said, and then, "Blow out the candle and make a wish."

Tears welled up in my eyes and rolled down my cheeks. I had no control over them. I blew out the candle and said as gruffly as my emotion-packed voice box would allow me, "I wish that we get to hell outa here."

Captain Morton said, "Your wish is granted. We have shaken the destroyers and are on our way home."

"Howsabout a piece of your birthday cake, Yeo?"

I began to pinch off small crumbs and pass them out as long as the cupcake lasted. When I looked up again, Captain Morton was gone from the messroom.

The next day *Wahoo* was riding the surface, diving at the least provocation, surfacing shortly afterward, and putting knots between her stern and the Japanese mainland. Inside *Wahoo* the tension was dissolving proportionately with the widening distance. Gaiety and then boisterousness returned to my shipmates. On-the-cuff poker games sprang up to replace pinochle, a good indication that we were coming down with "landitis."

Wahoo pulled into Midway without fanfare. The band was on hand to dutifully greet us but aside from that our welcome was different than before. There was no fresh fruit waiting and no paymaster. A mail clerk came aboard, handed the mail sack to Krause, and stood back indifferently waiting for it to be emptied.

The Captain and Executive Officer both left the ship, riding in a jeep toward the *Sperry*. Without any instructions, the only thing left for the crew to do was to stay aboard and marvel at the increase of personnel on Midway. The gooney birds flew around just as scoldingly. Disgusted, I went below for a cup of coffee and returned topside to sit and enjoy the fresh air under a cloudy overhead and to read my letters from home. The little girl in Los Angeles had not failed me, and I had a letter for every day that had gone by since our departure.

Davison came by. "When are we going to the hotel, Yeo?"

I went on reading. "I ain't got no orders."

Waldron came up. "Think we'll get paid, Yeo?"

"Damn if I know, I ain't the paymaster. We always do get paid. Uncle Sam has never failed me yet."

Rennels stopped by. "Whadaya think, Yeo?"

"Beats me, but I'm so glad to be off the war patrol that I don't give a damn."

"Me neither, but I don't know whether to get chow or not."

"Why don't you ask Lieutenant Henderson? He's got the duty."

"I think I will."

I got interested in the struggles the little girl was having with her ration coupons and how crowded the streetcars were getting in Los Angeles. The letters were so absorbing that I did not notice Lieutenant Commander O'Kane standing near me.

"Got an extra sailing list, Yeo?"

"Yeah."

Then I became aware of tan shoes and khaki trouser legs. Getting quickly to my feet, I said, "Yes sir. I've learned to keep extra copies. They come in handy for all sorta things."

His eyes were sparkling and he was smiling. "Well, get it ready. *Wahoo* is going on to Pearl Harbor."

"Yes *sir!*" I surprised him with a salute and made a dash for the messroom hatch, pushing the letters inside my shirt as I ran.

Chapter 13

When I came off the bridge from maneuvering watch, Midway Island was seeking obscurity beneath the horizon. The crew in the messroom were grumbling happily about the poor liberty in Honolulu, but only to hide their relief at the reprieve from a two-week interment on Midway Island.

I felt an eagerness to get back to my typewriter. Fortifying myself with two sardine sandwiches and a cup of hot tea, I went to the office. There was little to do, so I occupied myself with catching up on loose ends.

An avalanche landed on my shoulder blades. I extricated myself from the typewriter keys, donned an angry expression, and whirled on the Captain. "Listen, you big lug, if you don . . ."

Captain Morton was enjoying our little drama. "How's things going, Yeo?"

"Fair to middling," I complained, "if a certain person would have more respect for my tender back. I bruise so easily that I am nothing but a mass of black-and-blue bruises."

"I've got just the remedy. Don't tell anybody, but we just might be going back to the States from Pearl."

"What?"

"I said, we just *might* go back to the States after we leave Pearl. *Wahoo's* batteries need overhauling, and Mare Island is the best place to get it done. I'll have to speak to Admiral Lockwood."

"Gollies, Captain, that couldn't happen to us. My luck isn't that good."

Captain Morton started to leave but turned back with another thought. "I want to rate Carr to chief gunner's mate."

"We don't have any authority to do that, Captain. There's no allowance for a chief gunner's mate on a submarine. The only way I know it can be done is to transfer him to the Squadron with a recommendation and a request to get him back after he's been rated."

"Go ahead and make out the papers. Leave the space for authority blank, and after I see Admiral Lockwood, I'll have an authority for you. This business of transferring men to the Squadron to get them rated is the bunk. When I decide I want a man rated, I'm going to rate him."

"Aye, aye, sir," I answered dubiously, "but I'm afraid the Bureau will frown on it. They won't like it."

"To hell with the Bureau and their antique methods. We're fighting this war, and I'm going to reward my men when they deserve it."

He left for the wardroom, and I made a beeline for the messroom. "Hey, Rennels, guess what the Captain just told me . . ."

It seemed that all Honolulu knew of *Wahoo's* arrival and turned out to greet us. *Wahoo* had become a famous ship, outstanding in the performance of wartime duties among top outstanding sister ships.

Captain Morton made the trip to Commander Submarine Force Headquarters to see Rear Admiral Lockwood.

When he got out of the jeep on his return, his smile telegraphed the good news of approval for *Wahoo* to be scheduled to return to the United States. This would follow a three-day layover in Pearl for a material and personnel inspection, but no one seemed to mind except envious shipmates on neighboring submarines.

Thursday and Friday were utilized by *Wahoo's* crew in holding field day in preparation for Saturday morning's inspection. It did not take long for me to to get the office ready. Then I turned my attention to clerical duties.

Carr stopped at the office. I looked up to see him smiling proudly under a new chief petty officer's hat.

"Got my papers fixed up for chief, Yeo?"

"You bet. They're made up and signed. All I have to do is type in the authority."

"Did the Captain get an authority?" Carr had a small can of paint in his hand, which he began stirring anxiously with a brush.

"Yep. I'm to fill in that you were rated by reason of meritorious conduct on *Wahoo's* fifth war patrol."

"Really?" Carr filled with pride.

"That's right. I'll never doubt 'Mush' when he says he's gonna do a thing again. If he says he's gonna pull a rabbit from a hat, I'm gonna start looking for a carrot."

We just stared at each other for a moment in an understanding silence.

"Howsabout borrowing your paint?" I broke the silence. "I've got a few holidays that need touching up."

"Sure, Yeo." He handed me the paint and went into the chiefs' quarters.

Saturday morning came and the crew drifted topside in clean whites and polished shoes. I watched curiously as a portable microphone was set up in the middle of the deck. A number of photographers were moving restlessly about, aiming their camera sights for anticipated angles and snapping off flash bulbs to make certain that their batteries were charged.

Lane had us "fall in for inspection," and the officers, with the exception of the Captain and Lieutenant Commander O'Kane, lined up across the deck facing us. Roll call was made and the report was made to Lieutenant Paine. He went forward on deck while the rest of us were put "at ease."

I had my back to the pier but twisting on one foot, I looked behind me. There were several full captains and the SubPac band on the dock. While I watched, an admiral's car approached and his chauffeur stopped the car, jumped out, and ran to the door to open it. He saluted as the Admiral stepped out.

The band went into action playing ruffles and flourishes. It was the first time I had heard them and it added excitement to the occasion. More Admirals came aboard, and each was afforded the same military courtesy. I learned to distinguish their rank by the concluding notes.

A procession formed on the quarter-deck and moved down the portside. In the lead was Admiral Chester W. Nimitz, Commander in Chief, Pacific Forces. I felt a strong urge to step out of line and say, "Admiral, do you remember me?" Instead, my military training kept me rooted to my designated spot. The Admiral's hair was somewhat whiter, and he carried more gold braid on his epaulets, but otherwise he looked as I remembered him ten years earlier.

Admiral Nimitz stepped to the microphone and began his speech: "We are proud to be present this morning in this ship, which in the first few months of her seagoing . . . reputation that inspires every officer and man in the fleet . . ."

Everything became blurred with feeling as I thought of the hours spent on dull lookouts in all kinds of weather—of the torpedomen, the machinist's mates, the electricians whose lives depended on their skills in their chosen ratings, and of the daily humdrum existence punctured by fear of the enemy, also the bull sessions, card games, and two-week recreation periods. Here was a man who understood all these things. Here was a man who understood that it is the cogs in the wheel that make the success of his own job possible. Here was a man to be respected.

". . . my pleasure to confer upon the U.S.S. Wahoo and her crew members the Presidential Unit Citation . . . third war patrol . . ."

Admiral Nimitz began pinning medals on officers and enlisted men. I watched as Lieutenant Commander Donaho received a second Gold Star in lieu of another Navy Cross. Captain Morton received three awards including a Navy Cross. Silver Stars were attached to the blouses of Commander Fenno and Lieutenant Commander O'Kane, and a lieutenant I did not know, a chief motor-machinist's mate, and a torpedoman first class from other submarines.

The ceremony over, the strangers on board left the ship, and once more *Wahoo* was peopled by her own crew. Below decks inspection began at once in the forward torpedo room.

Little Japanese flags were painted on torpedo tubes that had fired a successful torpedo. It was hard to tell which had been the most successful, although my favorite was the number six tube that carried the "setting sun" flag of the destroyer sunk at Wewak.

I stayed close to Lieutenant Commander O'Kane as he kept up a rapid-fire dissertation on *Wahoo's* minor faults. The shorthand pad began to fill rapidly with potential repair jobs. Deaton, the old pro, kept getting between us while he explained that he had already found these discrepancies and had already made notes to have them corrected.

We moved rapidly through the ship. In the control room, I squeezed into the pump room with the Captain, O'Kane, Henderson, Record, and Lemert. I hardly reached the bottom of the ladder before we were coming out again.

In the messroom the cooks, wise to inspections, were standing by. Dietrich had a ham on the oven door, beautifully crisscrossed with cloves and decorated with pineapple rings. He was ladling sauce over it, presumably browning the already brown skin, ostentatiously impressing the officers with the cooks' culinary skills. Phillips was finishing a pan of doughnuts, which was surprising for the time of day, while Rennels was standing by the open canned-goods and cold-box lockers, which were immaculately straightened up. Someone had fried a slice or two of onion on the grill just previous to our arrival and then cleaned it off. The smell of onion added pleasantly to our inspection chores.

The inspection party reached the after battery sleeping compartment. It had been scrubbed and cleaned, and the smell of dirty socks cleared away with a fumigant from Lindhe's medical cabinet.

Seeing Lindhe standing by the medical cabinet, Morton inspected the wiring and ventilation system above the cabinet and stopped for a few jovial words with him. Lieutenant Commander O'Kane came up from behind quickly, looking at the strapped-up bunks and ordering Vidick to open the battery hatch. Vidick complied bringing into view the great storage batteries with their heavy anodes and cathodes showing on top. Lieutenant Commander O'Kane lowered himself to the catwalk two and a half or three feet below the deck. He got down on hands and knees and crawled out of sight. Vidick followed him.

I looked toward Captain Morton in time to see him step away from Lindhe with his flashlight turned up at the overhead and his gaze following the beam. Before I could shout a warning, the captain stepped into the open hatch. One leg went straight down until it contacted the catwalk. The other leg doubled under him and his chest and stomach brought up heavily against the hatch edge and the deck. The suddenness of the fall rattled him considerably.

"Who left this Goddam hatch open?" he roared.

Almost timidly in the face of his wrath, I replied, "The Exec, sir. He's inspecting the batteries down below. Are you hurt, sir?"

Lindhe and I both helped him out of the battery well. Others had turned to see what was happening.

He shook his heavy frame. "I'm all right but a man could kill himself on these Goddam old inspections. When Dick comes up, tell him the inspection is secured." He stalked angrily out of the compartment.

Lieutenant Commander O'Kane popped his head up out of the battery well. "What's wrong? What's going on up here?"

I said, "Sir, the Captain fell into the battery well. He's called off the inspection."

Lieutenant Commander O'Kane, looking surprised, left the after battery, hurriedly going forward.

I stopped by the messroom for a cup of coffee and found myself surrounded by half the ship's company wanting to know what happened.

Sunday morning, Wahoo turned her nose to the east and everybody was so busy making plans that they had no time for card playing.

My clerical work was caught up so I requested permission to go back on the watch list and had no trouble getting it approved. The day before arriving in San Francisco, I was taken off watch again to make up thirty-day leave papers for whoever wanted leave. Everybody wanted leave. Lieutenant Commander O'Kane settled it by making up two lists. The first list contained the names of men who had been on Wahoo the longest period of time. These men would go on leave first. Personnel on the second list would go on leave after the first leave party returned.

My name was on the first list but with reservations. I would have to wait around a few days until everything was squared away at the Mare Island Navy Yard. I was not disappointed. Just to be back in the United States was good enough for me. I thought of the other men who were still fighting the war and considered myself to be a very lucky man indeed.

The maneuvering watch was set outside the Golden Gate, and I stood topside on the bridge inhaling the wonderful beach odors and admiring in detail the beauty of the Golden Gate Bridge, San Francisco sky line, harbor traffic, and buildings on the beaches. Even Alcatraz on its island pinnacle was a picturesque sight. If my duty performance was mechanical, the officers on the bridge did not seem to notice because they too were enchanted by the magic of the U.S.A. Deck hatches opened and every man not needed below decks came on deck to watch.

When *Wahoo* came around the bend in the river and we could see the long water front ahead, there were only a few people watching. But as *Wahoo* approached the Mare Island Navy Yard, the workers passed the word and people left their jobs and came down to see us. By the time *Wahoo* was tied up, there was such a great number on the dock that their cheering and shouting drowned out the music of the band. What I could hear sounded like "California, Here I Come."

There was no need to pass the word, "Secure from manuevering stations." It was secured. Relief overwhelmed me, and after the bridge cleared I stood in a corner and wiped tears from my eyes. I went below decks but there was nothing to do. The men who had leave papers had left the ship. Most of the officers went ashore to meet their families. I guessed that they had fairly good codes of their own. Only the men whose leaves would come later were on board, and those who did not have the duty were getting ready to go ashore.

Rennels was getting into his liberty blues. "Come on, Yeo, let's go ashore and get drunk."

I said, "Hell yes, I got a telephone call to make anyway."

An hour later we were in Jim's Place on Georgia Street in Vallejo. The bar was packed with people, mostly Navy Yard workmen. *Wahoo* sailors drifted in, and soon we had a table loaded with drinks, in a corner.

I said, "Excuse me, fellows, but I have a long-distance phone call to make."

I got up and asked the bartender for change and went to an enclosed telephone booth. Dialing the long-distance operator, I asked for Marie Henry at the Los Angeles main telephone office. While I waited, I wondered if she would be on duty. The call went through quickly, and I heard her remembered voice.

"This is Jim."

"Oh, Jim, are you in Vallejo?"

"Yes, hon. Look, I got something I want to say to you."

"Yes, what is it?"

"I love you. Will you come to Vallejo and let's get married?"

"Will I? I'll catch the next plane up."

I said, "Do me a favor, hon. Call my mother and tell her I'm back and we're going to get married. Will you, hon?"

Marie answered, "Oh, yes. She's in Yuma, Arizona, and I have her telephone number. I went over to see her. We're old buddies, you know. Asa, your stepfather, is real nice, too."

I said, "I can hardly wait to see you. When do you think you'll be here?"

"I don't know yet but it will be soon."

An operator said, "Your three minutes are up."

I heard Marie say, "It's all right, operator. Please reverse the charges to this number."

After making the call, I felt a little groggy from the tremendous decision I had made and extremely happy that my proposal had been accepted. I bought a round of drinks and carried them to the table. Setting the drinks down, I said, "Listen, fellows, I just proposed to a dream girl on the telephone and she accepted me. I'm going to get married."

Marie arrived with Lottie Rennels two days later. Mother had come up from Yuma and was with them. Jack's mother, Lu Vana, had also come along. Three days later Marie and I were married in the First Baptist Church of Vallejo.

The next day I brought Marie aboard the *Wahoo*, and she met Captain Morton and Lieutenant Commander O'Kane. We received hurried congratulations from the Captain as he was getting ready to go on leave. Lieutenant Commander O'Kane would stay on board as Acting Commanding Officer.

Before we left the ship, Lieutenant Commander O'Kane called me to one side. He was in a pleasant mood. "Yeo, if you want to make out your leave papers now, I'll sign them."

"It won't take me five minutes, sir."

He added, "If you want to take the time, you can make out the papers rating you to first class. Let's call it a wedding present."

"Yes sir."

I left Marie with Hood, who had the deck watch, while I carried out these pleasant chores. When I came topside again I was a first-class petty officer with thirty days' leave. That added to a pretty wife summed up my universe for the moment.

Thirty days' leave seemed like a long time when it commenced, but twenty-nine days later I was wondering where the time had gone so fast. The next day I reported back on board a greatly rejuvenated *Wahoo*, and Marie was plugging away at her switchboard.

Captain Morton had not reported back from leave from his home in Los Angeles. The next item of importance I learned was that Lieutenant Commander O'Kane was being detached from *Wahoo* and ordered to report as the prospective Commanding Officer for the *U.S.S. Tang*, which was nearing completion at Mare Island Navy Yard. This was a break for Lieutenant Commander O'Kane, whose home was at San Rafael not far away. I was quick to congratulate him. The new Executive Officer would report aboard within a few days.

There were not many transfers to be made. *Wahoo* lost Ater, Dietrich, Gilbert, Hood, Krause, La Vine, Pruett, and Shattuck.

I hated to see Krause go, but he was going to new construction submarines, the *U.S.S. Escolar* at the Philadelphia Navy Yard near his home. He had returned from leave a married man.

Lieutenant (jg) Griggs reported aboard for duty again and was proudly wearing the one-and-a-half stripe denoting his rank.

Another week of stepped-up activity went by. *Wahoo* was reaching her prime again. I stayed aboard day and night keeping pace with the tempo. The older crew members had returned from leave, and the more recent ones had gone on leave.

Wahoo had to be taken to San Francisco for degaussing. It was a twenty-four-hour move, down one morning and back to the Navy Yard the following morning. With half the crew on board and Acting Captain O'Kane at the conn, *Wahoo* arrived and was tied up at the degaussing and fumigation pier in San Francisco. I had not planned on going ashore, but there was nothing else to do until 2000 when the fumigation fumes would be cleared from the ship.

While I was getting ready to go ashore, Jacobs stopped by my bunk. "I feel like going over and getting rotten, stinking, dirty drunk. Want to join me, Yeo?"

I was surprised because I had not seen Jacobs drink before. I knew, too, that his wife was expecting a baby. "Aw, I'm broke. I'm a married man now, you know. I just planned on getting some chow at a restaurant and taking in a movie."

"I've got plenty of money for both of us," he answered seriously. "I want to get pie-eyed drunk, and I don't like to do it alone. Howsabout it, Yeo?"

I said, "Well, if you'll lend me twenty bucks, I'll join you."

"That's a bargain." He handed me the money and we went ashore.

At 0200 we closed the bars. Neither one of us felt our liquor very strongly. We bought a fifth of black-market whisky and found an all-night restaurant. Finding a secluded booth, we sat drinking coffee royals, trying to hold back the hours.

"What made you want to get drunk, Jake?"

"It's hard to explain, Yeo, but I don't think I'm going to live long enough to see my baby."

"Aw, you and O'Brien and Phillips give me the willies. Sure you'll come out of this okay."

"Do they feel the way I do?"

"That's what they keep telling me, but hell man, we all get nervous. The odds is mostly in our favor, I think. Anyway, if that's what's bothering you, forget it. I don't get these crazy feelings, and I'm riding right along with you guys."

"I wish I could, Yeo, but something inside me keeps telling me I'm not gonna get to see my kid."

When I noticed the time, it was nearly 0700, and liberty was up at 0700 on board. We left the eating place in a hurry and called a taxi.

Wahoo arrived back at Mare Island, and the next morning Lieutenant

Commander O'Kane left the ship to take over the supervising duties of preparing a crew and organization for his new command, the *Tang*. I sat in the office listlessly typing.

Someone came through the watertight door, dropped a heavy object on the deck, and a second later Captain Morton's hand was driving me toward the typewriter. "Did you have a good leave, Yeo? How's married life?"

It was cheering to have the Old Man back again. We talked for about fifteen minutes while I attempted to rub my sore back, then he picked up his old black valise and went to his stateroom.

That afternoon a draft of men reported in from Submarine Administration, Mare Island. In charge of the men was Torpedoman Second, Johnson, Donald O., from Pasco, Washington.

Johnson said, "I hear you guys got the fightingest submarine in the fleet."

"We've done all right. Twenty-one ships in five war patrols ain't to be sneezed at." I looked through the men's records and jotted down their names and addresses in the rough on the sailing list.

A tall, thin Lieutenant Commander with a little gray in his hair stopped behind Johnson without interrupting us.

I said to Johnson, "See Lane, the Chief of the Boat. He will fix you guys up for bunks and lockers."

The officer stepped forward and thrust out his hand. A friendly smile lit up his face. "I am Lieutenant Commander V. L. Skijonsby, your new Executive Officer. We'll be working a lot together from now on. The Captain tells me you're the best damn yeoman in the Submarine Force. Would you like to come to the wardroom and have a cup of coffee while you give me a run-down on the ship's company?"

I was flattered, but if the crew found out about it—and they would—I would never be able to live it down.

"Thank you, sir." I shook hands with him. "But if you don't mind I would rather talk about it here."

He seemed to understand my predicament.

"Well, maybe we can do that after we get underway. I see you're busy anyway. By the way, here is my home address for the sailing list." He handed me a slip of paper and went forward, looking about him with the satisfied expression of an officer who has been on shore duty for some time and just returned to a boat.

I looked at the slip. He was from Hickson, North Dakota.

In the evening I went to the movie at the Mare Island Navy Yard. A newsreel showed scenes of Attu being retaken and how Kiska looked after the Japs abandoned it. British RAF planes were shown making night raids over Germany. Tracer trails in the darkness, searchlight beams sweeping the dark skies, and explosions as bombs landed on targets below kept the screen flashing. Another scene showed the USAAF planes in the day-

186

time. Bombs were seen leaving the big bombers by the hundreds. Below on a checkerboard map, mushrooms of dust indicated their explosions. A German plane was seen going down in flames, spiraling as it fell. An American bomber disintegrated in the air as it received a direct burst of flak. Bombs fell on tiny trains in railroad yards. I had seen enough. When the newsreel ended, I got up and walked out. I was too nervous to sit through the war picture that was coming next.

At *Wahoo* gangway, I met Muller, Neel, Smith, and Stevens going ashore. They asked me to come along with them, but I decided against it. Tomorrow would be Saturday, and I remembered that Marie would be in Vallejo for the week end.

After several days preparing for operational readiness, *Wahoo* was ready for sea and combat again. I dated the sailing list 11 July 1943 before giving it to Lindhe to pass over the gangway.

Chapter 14

The trip from San Francisco went smoothly with drills to break the monotony. Lieutenant Commander Skijonsby proved himself a fine Executive Officer. The only change he made in the administrative part of his many jobs was to have "Battle Bills" posted.

My first evening in the messroom was a disappointment because I kept expecting Krause to show up. However, O'Brien was there playing "Sock 'em down, Winsocki." Rennels and I were becoming good buddies. Carr was evidently making himself at home in the chiefs' quarters as was Lindhe, but the old spontaneity was missing. I soon hit the sack.

At Pearl Harbor, *Wahoo* stayed but a few days before heading farther westward. Lieutenant Paine had an attack of appendicitis and was detached to the hospital to be operated on. Lindhe was transferred to the Submarine Base sick bay for duty, and MacAlman, Stuart E., Pharmacist's Mate, First Class, from Auburn, New Hampshire, was received on board. We received Seaman, August, John F., from Arvada, Colorado, and *Wahoo* was ready for sea again.

The first day out, I wandered into the sleeping compartment and found Ware in one corner with the ship's portable sewing machine. He looked up at me from studying a dress pattern instruction. "Hi, Yeo."

"Whatcha doing? Going into the dressmaking business?" I asked curiously.

"I thought it would give me something to do on this trip. Sorta keep my mind off things."

"That looks like silk. Is it?"

"It sure is. I bought it in Honolulu at a Chinese dry-goods store." He was beginning to warm up to his subject. "Look at this pattern. It's a ballroom dress. I thought I would surprise my wife with it when I get off war patrol. It's real pretty, isn't it?"

"Yeah. If I tried it, it sure would be a surprise. How do you know the size she wears?"

He grinned. "I got a tape measure and took her measurements before I left the States. She thought I was doing it for fun. It was fun, too."

With a watch coming up, I crawled into my bunk. MacAlman had inherited Lindhe's old bunk. He was lying there smoking a cigarette and watching me.

I said, "How ya doin', Doc?"

"I'm all right. Where are we going on patrol?"

"Your guess is as good as mine. My contacts aren't so good anymore. They keep transferring my spies as fast as I train them. My ouija board is broken and my crystal ball is cracked."

"Can't you guess?"

"Well, we're headed for Gooney Bird Island and that usually means we will end up around Japan somewheres. We've got mail bags on board."

He took three slow puffs on his cigarette, apparently thinking of what I had just said.

Curious, I asked, "You're from Auburn, New Hampshire? *Wahoo* doesn't get many men from that state. How do you Yankees ever manage to live through all that sleet and snow and ice?"

"It's easy. We eat a lot of sea food."

"What's that got to do with it?"

"It keeps you masculine. You get so warm-blooded you don't notice the cold."

"That's a new one. Now I've heard everything."

"It's true. Why, we eat so much sea food in New Hampshire that our stomachs come in and go out with the tide."

"Oh, brother!" I turned my back to him and pulled the covers over my head. He was still chuckling audibly when I fell asleep.

The next afternoon, I pulled into the messroom, looked disinterestedly at the card games going, drew a cup of coffee, and sat down at the table where Emmons was peeling potatoes. There was another paring knife in the dishpan, so I took it and began to help. "What happened to the messcooks?"

"They're sleeping. I didn't want to bother them. I haven't got anything else to do right now anyway."

I pared a couple of potatoes, then asked, "What submarine was you on before?"

"I was on the *Sail 36* for two runs."

"Wasn't she sunk or something? Seems to me like I heard something about her."

"We run aground in Makassar Strait and couldn't get off. A Dutch ship picked us up, and the Old Man scuttled *Sail 36*."

"Did you get any ships?"

"We got a freighter on our first run."

The potatoes were peeled, and Emmons went into the galley to check on some roasts in the oven.

Wahoo reached Midway, topped off with fuel, and left again after only a few hours in port.

The days that followed were routine surface running and watch standing. Simmonetti had put a chart on the bulletin board and our destination was the Japanese Inland Sea. This was virgin territory for an American submarine, Morton told someone, who told somebody else. I got the word from Rennels.

Coming close to the Japanese mainland, *Wahoo* began submerging during the day and running on the surface at night.

I had the 2000–2400 watch going through the La Perouse Strait. Before going on starboard lookout, Lane briefed me that the Strait was hardly more than ten miles from land on the north side, which we were following. Captain Morton had decided to transit the narrow strip of water on the surface, making one-third speed. His plan was to deceive the Japanese into thinking that *Wahoo* was one of the hundreds of fishing sampans in these waters if they picked us up on their radar. Lane cautioned me to be extra watchful for anything out of the ordinary and to be prepared to clear the bridge in a hurry if *Wahoo* dived because she would be going down fast.

When I moved through the conning tower, all lights had been reduced to the barest minimum. I had to feel my way along. The idea, I realized, was to have as little reflected light as possible come through the hatch in case an airplane should patrol above us.

Even though my eyes had been adapted to the darkness with the use of red goggles prior to coming on lookout, it was such a dark night that I had to strain my eyes through the binoculars to see the horizon. Captain Morton, Lieutenant Commander Skijonsby, and Lieutenant (jg) Campbell, the Duty Officer, were on the bridge. I could hear them moving softly about below and talking in monosyllables in low tones, but I could not hear what they were saying. Once I heard Captain Morton at the bridge mike say, "Keep the ranges coming."

Wahoo moved almost noiselessly through the water. Her diesels made a low hum, while murmuring water sounded at the bow and again made small swishing noises as the water slid along her steel sides. The radar mast made movement sounds as it revolved, which were more vibrations than audio.

In a low tense voice I reported, "Captain, the Japs are signaling us on the starboard beam."

"Very well, I have it. Keep your eyes peeled for any other activity that might be going on either on the bow or quarter."

"Aye, aye, sir."

I swung around looking forward and then aft. "All clear elsewhere, sir."

"Very well."

House reported, "All clear on the portside, sir."

"Very well."

Lieutenant Junior Grade Campbell said, "Should we try signaling back, Captain?"

"Hell, no, that would bring them down on us. If we just keep going on a straight course, maybe they will think we're a *Fishi Maru.*"

The blinker light on the beach moved with us. I could make out some of the international code letters but none of the words. I had never learned to read blinker well anyway. Suddenly the blinker went out, and the darkness seemed even more frightening than before. I pictured eight- and ten-inch guns being trained in our direction.

Wahoo did not change her speed but continued moving along, occasionally changing course to meet the requirements of the channel. I was surprised when Kirk came up to relieve me. It did not seem possible that it was time for the watch to change.

In the conning tower, I made out Gerlacher at the wheel. "Are we through the Strait yet?"

"Yeah, 'Mush' says we got nothing but good hunting from here on in."

I went into the messroom for a sandwich and coffee. Rennels was nervously playing a game of solitaire. Phillips was watching him. They both looked up. "How does it look, Yeo?"

"Well, we got through all right. Them Japs was signaling like all get out, but I guess they think we're some dumb fishermen or something."

Rennels said, "What scares me is getting out again. We're trapped in here now. Especially after we get to sinking ships. They'll close us off tighter'n a drum."

I said, "I got a lot of faith in 'Mush' and SubPac. I don't think they'da sent us in here unless they had a way figured of getting us out."

Phillips said, "I'm getting sick in the stomach. Will you finish my baking for me, Jack? I don't feel so good. I think I'll turn into my sack."

"Sure," Rennels replied. "Go ahead. You got most of it done anyway."

Phillips got up apologetically and walked out. I looked at Rennels and there was sympathy in his eyes.

"He ought to go back to the States," said Rennels.

"He's too good a baker. 'Mush' will never let him go while he's skipper on here. Good cooks and bakers are the best morale factor a ship can have and Morton knows it. You're going to be on here a long time, too."

"Have you noticed a change in the boat, Yeo? The guys seem gloomier than when I first came on. There's something missing."

"Yeah," I growled. "It's fun and exciting at first, but after a few depth charges, you begin to realize that just one of them in the right place can pull down the curtains once and for all. I've got to the point where I've become a fatalist. What is to be will be—being in the wrong place at the right time. The Old Man up above knows what he's doing and you, nor me, nor anybody else can anticipate Him."

"I didn't know you was religious, Yeo."

"I'm not. But I believe there's a God, and that's all I need to know in this life. How did we get on this subject?" Then to change the conversation, "We're all getting war-weary. We know there's a job to be done to end the war, and we just want it to end as quickly as possible."

Rennels said, "I'd better get on with the baking."

I finished my coffee and turned in.

Wahoo was submerged when I was awakened by Erickson for breakfast. While I was eating, I glanced hurriedly through the *Wahoo Daily Gazette*. It was dated 14 August 1943. There was a follow-up item on Mussolini's overthrow and escape to Germany. A naval battle at Kula Gulf. General Patton was rapidly taking over Sicily with his United States Seventh Army tanks, and General MacArthur was securing Salamaua and Finschhafen with mopping-up actions.

I relieved Krebs on sonar. At noon *Wahoo* was still cruising below the surface. The watch was routine.

The 1800–2000 watch went peaceably by without incident, with *Wahoo* prowling the surface and charging batteries.

Midnight found *Wahoo* submerged and making an approach on two medium-sized freighters and a smaller freighter. I was sitting on my stool in the conning tower with books, pads, and pencil ready. The scene had changed from previous ones. The Captain and I were the same, but now Lieutenant Commander Skijonsby was at the periscope. Simmonetti was efficiently handling Krause's previous job. Lieutenant Henderson, from Bethesda, Maryland, had moved up from the diving station below to handle the TDC in Lieutenant Paine's absence. Sisson was helping him. Carter was on the sound gear, and Gerlacher was on the helm. Below decks Lieutenant Jackson was the Diving Officer.

It was such a dark night that identification of the ships was difficult. *Wahoo* got into position and the torpedo gyros were set for proper depths. Outer doors were opened, the firing order made, and Terrell on the phones was kept busy relaying orders to the torpedo rooms.

With the order for firing, *Wahoo* went into a rage. Torpedoes began leaving her tubes and raced toward the targets. Something happened. A torpedo struck with a hollow sound against one of the hulls and failed to explode. A second torpedo exploded prematurely, throwing the gyros off setting in torpedoes that were following them. These torpedoes changed course, missing the targets by wide margins. More torpedoes were fired, and again prematures reacted on other torpedoes speeding behind them. More duds and once a torpedo struck another ship and only its air flask exploded. *Wahoo* was ten torpedoes lighter.

The Japanese ships turned away, notifying their own naval authorities by wireless that an enemy submarine was in the Sea of Japan. They in turn had torpedo boats out echo-ranging for us within the hour.

Wahoo turned toward Vladivostok, a Russian port. Captain Morton went over every move that *Wahoo* had made in the approach and attack and could find no error in calculations. The only possible thing that could have gone wrong was faulty torpedoes. He made a decision. "Hank, go down and relieve Jack on the dive. Tell him to come up here immediately."

"Yes sir, Captain."

Lieutenant Jackson was quick to come up the ladder.

"Jack, I want you to encode a dispatch to ComSubPac Pearl. Request permission to return Pearl for torpedo recheck duds and prematures."

"Yes sir, Captain." He went quickly below decks.

Wahoo kept moving away from the Japanese coast. Turning to the Executive Officer, Captain Morton ordered, "Prepare to surface."

Lieutenant Commander Skijonsby took over. "Lookouts to the conning tower. Control, prepare to surface." In a short time Lieutenant Jackson's voice came up from the radio room. "Captain, the message is ready for sending, sir."

"Very well. Surface."

Simmonetti cracked the hatch as the bridge rose above water, then throwing it open, went out on deck followed by Lieutenant Commander Skijonsby and helped along with a cyclonic rush of released air. Maulding and Morrison, the two lookouts, dug their toes into the ladder rungs and followed.

"Radio, get that message off as quickly as possible."

"Aye, aye, Captain." It was Buckley's voice.

In an incredibly short time Lieutenant Jackson was shouting through the voice tube. "Captain, Pearl Harbor got us right away. They receipted for the message."

"Very well. Helmsman come left ten degrees rudder."

"Ten degrees left rudder, sir."

"When we come around to zero-four-five degrees, steady on it."

"Come to zero-four-five and steady, Captain," Gerlacher answered.

I could feel the sharp slant of Wahoo's decks to port as she came about. A few moments later they leveled again.

"Steady on zero-four-five, Captain."

"Very well. Bridge, we're going to stay on this course for twenty minutes and then dive."

"Helmsman, all ahead emergency."

Gerlacher grabbed the annunciator handles, pushed them up and down, and then left the indicator on emergency. Bells tinkled. He swung back to the wheel, and the annunciator handles moved by themselves down and back to emergency accompanied by the bells again.

"Maneuvering has the word, Captain. All ahead emergency."

"Very well."

Twenty minutes later, Lieutenant Commander Skijonsby's voice came down the hatch. "Dive, dive." The ship's diving horn blasted, nearly deafening me. Wahoo's decks began to slope, and Morrison dropped through the bridge hatch being rushed by Maulding. Simmonetti came right on top of them, and then Lieutenant Commander Skijonsby dropped down the ladder, pulling the hatch closed after him. The latch clicked shut, and he came on down. Simmonetti was quick to climb back up the ladder and start twisting the steel wheel to make the hatch watertight. Morrison and Maulding had dropped out of view into the control room.

Capain Morton looked at me and grinned. "I hope the Japs go clear on into Vladivostok looking for us. We're going to be hugging the Japanese shore."

Wahoo stayed submerged. At noon the next day I relieved Renno on the sonar gear. He passed the information on to me that a Japanese torpedo boat was echo-ranging at some distance from us and went below. Lieutenant Junior Grade Fiedler was the Duty Officer. I dialed around until satisfied there was nothing else in the vicinity and made my report. Lieutenant Fiedler acknowledged the report. He was a small dark-complexioned officer with a pleasant even disposition. He never seemed to get excited.

Captain Morton came into the conning tower, and after being informed of the existing situation, he sat down heavily on a stool by the TDC. He assumed a head-in-chin position and sat staring across the small room at the bulkhead to the left of my shoulder.

I made a half-hourly report that the torpedo boat appeared to be remaining at the same distance. Captain Morton looked at me and grinned wanly.

"Think we'll get out of this one, Captain?"

"Sure we will, Yeo. We always have, haven't we?"

"I'm not worried, Captain. We been in worse fixes."

The Captain seemed to regain his natural composure. "How would you like to be interned in Vladivostok for the remainder of the war, Yeo?"

I stared at him. "It might not be so bad. Some of them Russian women are mighty pretty. You ain't thinking of going to Vladivostok are you, Captain?"

He said seriously, "If *Wahoo* got depth-charged pretty heavily and there was no other way out, we might have to."

The possibility had never entered my mind before. I wondered what being interned among the Russians would be like.

"Is it true that Russian ships carry women sailors, Captain?"

He said, "One of our submarines sank a Russian ship by mistake north of here. They picked up the survivors. There were three women sailors among them. One of the women had a breast nearly torn off."

I looked at the Captain skeptically. "They wouldn't have anything to worry about with the torpedoes we got on board."

Captain Morton's brow darkened, "Goddam it, I had my heart set on sinking a freight train."

"Freight train?"

He grinned. "The Japanese run ferries across the Inland Sea to Manchuria. They carry trains across. I sure would like to be the first submarine skipper to sink a freight train."

The afternoon passed and *Wahoo* had widened the distance considerably between herself and the patrol boat. I was relieved from watch by the oncoming duty section.

When it became dark, *Wahoo* surfaced. I was in the messroom when Buckley came in for a cup of coffee. "Hear the news, Yeo? We got permission to return to Pearl."

Wahoo transited the La Perouse Strait without difficulty. The next morning she was running along the Japanese mainland beach on the surface. I had the starboard lookout on the 0800–1200 watch. *Wahoo* was so close to land that I could make out trees on the sides of the hills, and once we passed a cluster of thatched fishing huts. Snow-capped mountains pointed to a hazy blue sky that was broken only by a few widely separated puffballs of white clouds. The scene was so peaceful that it made me wonder where the Japanese had acquired their warlike dispositions. In fact, it was hard for me to think of the scene in terms of war at all.

I was due to be rotated from lookout when a voice below coming from the bridge mike said, "Bridge, we have a ship contact on radar, bearing zero-one-zero, sir."

Swinging the binoculars in that direction I could see nothing.

"All clear on the starboard lookout," I volunteered.

"Very well," Lieutenant Junior Grade Misch answered.

Another ten minutes went by and I reported, "Sampan off the starboard bow, sir."

"Very well."

A commotion below announced the arrival of Captain Morton and the Executive Officer on the bridge.

Wahoo approached the unsuspecting fishing boat.

"Below decks, have the gun crews stand by for battle stations surface."

"Aye, aye, Captain."

Three minutes later the bridge speaker vibrated, "Gun crews standing by below decks, Captain."

"Very well, sound battle stations surface. On deck the gun crews."

I could hear the battle chimes going through the open hatch. The messroom hatch flew open and men poured out on deck. More men came pell-mell out of the bridge hatch. "Guns manned and ready for firing, Captain."

I focused my binoculars on the sampan. The fishermen were becoming curious about the black monster bearing down on them. They had stopped their activities and were staring toward us with hands shading their brows from the sun.

Wahoo slowed down and turned broadside to the boat. The fishermen became excited and began pointing at the Stars and Stripes.

Captain Morton hollered down to Carter, "Put a shot across their bow."

A shot rang out and a splash ahead and on the other side of the boat showed where the bullet struck the water. More splashes followed as the bullet ricocheted along the surface.

"Heave to and stand by to come aboard as our prisoners," Captain Morton shouted at them through a megaphone.

I counted six fishermen. Carr, O'Brien, and Carter were standing on the bow pointing guns at them. Lane threw a rope ladder over the side, and they all began waving their arms and pointing at the ladder.

"Fire over their heads."

Shots rang out and splashes arose on the far side of the fishing boat.

"Point the deck gun at them."

The huge barrel lowered in their direction. A young boy, perhaps not more than ten, dived into the water and swam toward *Wahoo*. He came up the rope ladder and stood dripping on deck. The other Japanese seeing that we did not harm the young one followed.

Captain Morton shouted down, "Make them strip off their clothes and send them up here."

When they arrived on the bridge they were stark-naked and shivering visibly from the chill morning air.

Going to the bridge speaker, Captain Morton shouted down, "Control, send Manalisay topside with that fifth of whisky in my stateroom."

He turned to Lieutenant Commander Skijonsby. "Commence firing."

It did not take the gun crews long to demolish the sampan and it sank quickly.

Manalisay reached the bridge with a bottle of Canadian Club whisky and a glass. Morton poured the glass full and offered it to the shivering Japanese fishermen. They shook their heads refusing the liquor.

Lieutenant Comander Skijonsby said, "Maybe they think it is poisoned."

Captain Morton turned to Simmonetti. "Drink some of it."

Simmonetti took a big gulp. Morton grinned.

"I didn't mean all of it."

Simmonetti filled the glass and offered it again. The young boy took the glass and drank from it. His face broke into a smile, and he spoke rapidly in Japanese to the others. Of a sudden they were all reaching for the glass.

Captain Morton said, "Carr, take them to the after torpedo room and see if you can find them some old dungarees."

Carr, Carter, and Kemp began herding them down the ladder. Captain Morton stepped to the opening and shouted, "Give them a salt-water shower when you go by the washroom and don't let them get near any butcher knives."

"Aye, aye, sir."

I looked the beach over carefully for any unusual activity on the shore. No one had come down to the beach to see what the gunfire was about.

"All clear on starboard lookout, sir."

"All clear on port lookout," House added.

"Very well."

Captain Morton walked back to the cigarette deck. I heard him say, "I'd sure like to have one of those glass fishing balls for a souvenir."

Splash, splash. Startled I looked toward the water. Whipp and Anders fully clothed were in the water swimming toward the debris of the fishing boat. Several glass balls were sending off scintillating flashes of reflected sunlight where they bobbled in the water.

"Get those men back on deck before they freeze to death in that water," Captain Morton roared.

There was a concerted rush to the side of the ship and a heaving line was thrown across to the men. Grabbing hold of the line they were dragged back aboard.

"Send those men to the bridge."

Anders and Whipp came dripping up the side of the superstructure.

Captain Morton said angrily, "What did you men think you were doing?"

Whipp said, "You wanted a glass ball didn't you, Captain? I jumped in to get one for you."

"Me, too," Anders echoed.

"Goddamit, who wants to lose good men over some damned old glass balls?" Captain Morton scolded as he poured the glass full of whisky. "Now you get your asses down below decks and get into some dry clothes."

Both men went below looking crestfallen.

Morton turned around. "Secure from battle stations surface." He went back on the cigarette deck and gripped the handrail with both hands. He was deeply moved. "All ahead, full."

Wahoo's screws dug in and she continued back toward Pearl, running on the surface.

I came off lookout into the control room. Captain Morton, Lieutenants Jackson and Henderson, Lieutenant Commander Skijonsby, and Simmonetti had the eldest of the Japanese surrounded, trying to get him to talk. Lieutenant Jackson had a pamphlet that appeared to be a dictionary of Japanese sentences. The fisherman was evidently illiterate and also having difficulty comprehending Lieutenant Jackson's pronunciation.

Captain Morton turned to me. "You been to China, Yeo. Do you speak Japanese?"

I grinned. "No sir, I didn't own a sleeping dictionary."

Lieutenant Commander Skijonsby said quietly, "Yeo, get that identification book on warships down here."

"Yessir." I quickly got the book and handed it to him. I hung around, curious to see what was happening.

The Executive Officer laid the book in front of the Japanese. He began turning the pages slowly, and a third way through the book, the fisherman started and bent over, pointing at a heavy cruiser and talking rapidly in his own tongue.

Captain Morton was quick to grasp the opportunity. "Simmonetti, get me a chart of these waters on the double."

In a few moments they had a navigational chart. Captain Morton pointed to the spot where we took the Japanese prisoners. "Boom, boom," he said and pointed at the old man. The fisherman nodded his head. Captain Morton pointed at the picture of the Japanese cruiser and ran his finger along the littoral boundaries of the Japanese mainland. The prisoner shook his head and pointed to a port on the Hokkaido Island shore.

Having got all the information possible for the moment, Captain Morton directed Carr to return the old man to the after torpedo room. I followed them as far as the messroom, where I turned off for noon chow.

Rennels was directing Miller and Mandjiak in cleaning up and setting the tables for another meal. I was given a hot plate with steak on it and seated in a corner. When the tables were set, Rennels went to the compartment phone. He twisted the dial to the after torpedo room and lifted the receiver. He waited a second and spoke into the receiver, "This is the messhall. You can send them prisoners up now. We're ready for them." He hung the phone up and looked around. "Make sure there ain't no butcher knives laying around handy," he ordered Mandjiak.

Smith came into the crew's messroom with a forty-five strapped to his waist and took a stand near the sink. He was followed by the six prisoners and Carr behind them. Carr was also armed.

The prisoners stopped. They looked at each of us in the messroom with Oriental calmness. Taking a cue from the old man, they turned to each of us and bowed stiffly from the waist, "Kumbawa."

Rennels pointed out seats to them and they sat down stiffly. The messcooks brought in steaks and French fries and poured cups of coffee.

I forgot my own food in watching them. They stared at the food and at their plates and then looked blankly at each other. The older fisherman picked up his spoon and tried to cut the steak with it. Rennels moved in and showed him how to use the table knife and fork. Soon they were happily chopping away at their food including the French fries. One of them tasted the coffee cautiously. He made a wry face and pushed it back. Rennels put a spoonful of sugar in the coffee and poured condensed milk in after it. The prisoner tried it again. He liked it. He put five or six spoonfuls of sugar in the coffee. Rennels had to butter bread for them before they learned that it went with the meal.

After the meal they sat staring around. Carr motioned for them to stand up. They stood up, bowed at everyone again, saying, "Ahrigato." Then they were marched aft.

Rennels came over and sat down while the messcooks cleaned up. "They're not such bad fellows. They're just like us, only different ways is all."

I said, "It's hard to believe those stories about the butchery of the soldiers after seeing these guys." Placing my plate in the sink, I said, "Let's go back to the after torpedo room and look at them, Jack."

We went through the engine rooms, past O'Brien at the big handled switchboard in the maneuvering room, and into the torpedo room. Rags had been spread on the deck, and the prisoners were sitting cross-legged looking at magazine pictures. Smith was sitting on a bunk guarding them.

He was pointing at the picture of a girl. "Floogie," he said. He pointed at several more girl pictures. "Floogie." The fishermen began pointing at pictures of women in the magazines and saying to each other, "Floo-gee."

The boy turned to me smiling. "Me Okomoto." He pointed at me and raised his eyebrows.

I said, "Jim."

He turned to the others. "Jeem." They all took up the word bowing and smiling. "Jeem."

I pointed at Rennels, "Bum cook."

They all said, "Bum cook," bowing and smiling.

Rennels said, "I'll murder you for this, Yeo."

Phillips came through the door. Rennels said, "Him bum cook too."

"Heem bum cook too." They bowed and smiled.

Phillips said, "What's going on here?"

"Heem bum cook too. Jeem. Bum cook. Floo-gee."

"They learn quick," I laughed.

Wahoo carried her own entertainment troupe with her the rest of the trip. We became so attached to our prisoners that we began to feel that they were a part of the crew. The guards became a formality. It was amazing how quickly our prisoners learned the English language—a lot of which could never be shown in the printed form.

Several days later Wahoo pulled into Submarine Base Pearl and tied up. Base crews were standing by to unload her torpedoes and rush them to the shops for inspection. Also standing by was a truckload of Marines with fixed bayonets.

The maneuvering watch was hardly secured before the Marines stationed themselves at the truck, the gangway, and along the decks. A few minutes later our Japanese friends were herded topside with sacks over their heads. A Marine sergeant prodded them from behind, and they ran stumbling along the decks. A Marine at the gangway rushed them across, while another at the truck tossed them into the body. They drove quickly away.

"Where they taking them to, Carr?"

"To a concentration camp somewhere on the island. They didn't have to be so rough. Them poor guys was harmless."

Lieutenant Commander Skijonsby on deck ordered, "Yeo, get the men off to the Royal Hawaiian Hotel."

"Aye, aye, sir."

Not long afterward we were comfortably settled. There were only two flies in the ointment: one, because of the short war patrol, we would only be there a week; two, the Royal Hawaiian Hotel was under quarantine. Someone had come down with the dengue fever and liberty away from the hotel grounds was restricted. Worse, there was very little liquor to be had.

I spent an afternoon on Waikiki Beach and the next six days in bed with daily visits from MacAlman who punctured sun blisters and rubbed soothing ointments on them. It was with a feeling of relief that the week-long rest period was over. I came back to the ship eager to work.

I changed the sailing list and turned my attention to the official mail. The relief yeoman had opened the mail, taken care of the most important business, and left the rest for me. Thumbing through the correspondence hurriedly I saw my name. I picked out the letter and scanned it hurriedly. Letting out a war whoop that could be heard the length of the ship, I rushed to the wardroom. Captain Morton and the Executive Officer were discussing a serious problem.

"Captain! ComServPac has approved my request for Steno School, sir." I showed the two officers the authorization for my transfer. I was trembling with excitement.

The Captain looked at the order uncomprehendingly. Then his eyes lighted up. "That's great news, Yeo." He studied the order a second longer and added, "Your class convenes 1 November, that right, Yeo?"

"Yes sir."

He turned and looked at me squarely. "Yeo, I'm going to ask a favor of you."

My heart sank within me. "Yes sir."

"Howsabout you making one more patrol with me? We'll be back in October. When we get in, I'll get you plane transportation back to the States. You might miss out on some leave, but you had thirty days in June. Howsabout it?"

I said, "Captain, your word is good enough for me. I'll get back to work."

He grinned at me. "Thanks, Yeo, I knew you wouldn't let me down."

Lieutenant Commander Skijonsby smiled, thought of something, and said, "Just a moment, Yeo. I've got a personal letter to a friend at BuOrd. I want you to type it up for me, and I know I can rely on you to keep it confidential."

"Yessir."

He handed me three pages written in longhand. I took it back to the office and began to type it up. After a few lines, I closed the door.

It was addressed to a Commander at the Bureau of Naval Ordnance. There was a paragraph of reminiscing and another inquiring into his friend's health and the welfare of his wife and children. Then the letter got down to the business in hand. In effect it went something like this: "When I was working in the Bureau, we thought we were doing a great job on the torpedoes but it wasn't enough. You have to go on war patrol and realize the fullness of the dangers in getting on station with a load of torpedoes to feel the heartfelt anguish and disappointment that goes with having them explode prematurely, or when striking a ship, turn out to be duds. The crews of these submarines are willing to go to any length to deliver them, but when they leave the tubes, they want them to sink the enemy. When ships turn away after an attack, the submarine's location is known and its greatest effective weapon, secrecy, is destroyed. Our lives are at stake in these gambles, and we depend upon you people at the Bureau to give us that protection. For God's sake, talk to your associates and see if something can't be done to cut the red tape and give us immediate results. Every moment counts out here."

I typed the letter, addressed an envelope, and took them to him. I said awkwardly, "Sir, I know that I'm stepping out of line to say this but I think that letter really is a masterpiece."

"Thanks, Yeo."

I caught a breather and went back to the messroom for coffee. O'Brien was there. "What's this I hear about you getting transferred?"

"Dammit, how do you guys find out these things?"

"Vidick was fixing the reading lamp in Mr. Skijonsby's stateroom. He overheard you in the wardroom."

"So that's how your spy system works. You grab a circuit tester and hang around the officers' country looking for shorts. Boy!"

"Is it true?"

"Yeah, only I'm going to make this trip, and 'Mush' is going to fly me back to the States when we get in."

"Yeo, I've made six runs. Do you think I can get new construction when we get in?"

"How do I know? There's one way to find out. Request it."

"Phillips and I both agreed we're going to put in for a transfer when you leave the ship."

"Aw, come off it, you guys."

Feeling uncomfortable, I took my coffee back to the office and began working. A strong odor of pipe tobacco nearly strangled me. I looked around and saw Bair smoking a weirdly carved pipe. He was calmly reading the official letter I had started which was still in the typewriter.

I said, "That's the first time I ever saw a smokestack in an outhouse."

"Like my pipe, Yeo?"

"You might call it a pipe. Where did you get it?"

"I collect 'em. I've got six on board and about ten at home. Would you like to see my pipes?"

"No."

"Aw, come on, Yeo. They're in the forward torpedo room."

I sighed, got up from the typewriter, and went with him. His bunk lay on top of a torpedo. He rummaged around in a green pouch attached to the frame of his bed and started pulling out smoking pipes. I got a lecture on the virtues of pipe collecting and smoking tobacco. When he finished, I hurt his feelings. "I don't go for pipes. Cigarettes are bad enough."

He followed me back to the office. "This pipe here is a real Meerschaum. My dad sent it to me from Montana."

"That's fine. Now can I go back to work?"

"Go right ahead." He stood behind me several silent moments and watched me typing. Finally he went away.

A yeoman from the Squadron came in. "I've got some tickets to a

U.S.O. show on the base for the *Wahoo*. If you don't want them just say so." He said the last sentence a little too quickly.

"I'll take 'em."

He made me sign a receipt and gave me ten tickets. "This all I get?"

"Only ten to a boat. If you don't want . . ."

"Never mind, I'll take them."

He went away and I looked at the printing on the tickets. Boris Karloff in "Arsenic and Old Lace." I kept five tickets. Then I went to the wardroom. Mr. Misch and Mr. Fiedler were having coffee. I tossed five tickets on the table and said, "Here's some tickets to the U.S.O. show tonight," and left before they could read the inscription.

At the chiefs' quarters, I pulled aside the curtains and saw Ware sitting on a bunk. I handed him two tickets. "U.S.O. show on the base tonight."

I secured the office. It was nearly time for evening chow. In the messroom, I pulled Rennels and O'Brien to one side. "Good show on the base tonight and I got tickets. Wanta go with me?"

O'Brien said, "If it's that U.S.O. show that's got Boris Karloff in it, hell yes."

"It is."

After chow, the three of us went to the Submarine Base theater and found good seats near the middle of the seating arrangement. When the curtain came up, the comedy caught our attention immediately. Boris Karloff came on, on cue, and the ovation was tremendous. But when the play reached the part where Boris turned on his doctor associate and said, "You made me look like that monster in the movies, Boris Karloff," the applause stopped the show. Boris waited a moment and then stepped to the footlights. He stood there making bow after bow. When the auditorium quieted down, he stepped back into his role with the ease of the professional actor.

This was our last night ashore before leaving on *Wahoo's* seventh war patrol.

Chapter 15

Using a rubber date stamp, I placed 5 September 1943 on the sailing list, put the list in a manila envelope, and went topside. The maneuvering watch had not been set yet. I stood by the gangway in case a last-minute change should be made. A jeep pulled up and the Captain got out. With him was a tall Commander with broad shoulders. Deaton had the deck watch. He shouted down the hatch, "Below decks watch, tell the Exec that the Captain is coming on board."

As the Captain and the Commander came aboard, Deaton saluted them. I walked over and said, "Commander, will you give me your name and . . ." I broke off, staring at him. "Why, you're Gene Tunney—*sir!*"

Captain Morton laughed. "Better give the Yeo your address, he collars everybody that comes on board."

Lieutenant Commander Skijonsby came out of the forward torpedo hatch and saluted Commander Tunney, who then turned to me. "Never mind placing my name on your sailing list. Admiral Lockwood knows I'm on board."

Captain Morton said to the Executive Officer, "Gene is going with us as far as Midway." They went below. Deaton said, awed, "Jeez, Gene Tunney, wait till I tell the guys about this."

I said, "Give this sailing list to Carr when he comes topside. He's our new Chief of the Boat," and I hurried down the messroom hatch.

"Hey, Rennels. Listen, guys! Guess who is on board?"

The men in the messroom turned their faces toward me and shouted in unison, "Gene Tunney."

Later on the maneuvering watch, I watched the same familiar send-off pattern and listened to "Aloha" as *Wahoo* backed away from the dock. Ten-ten dock swung into view and *Wahoo* headed out the fairway. Commander Tunney was on the bridge on the way out. Captain Morton was wearing a full Commander's hat and had the silver insignia that went with it. I thought, Gosh, I've been so dazzled by Gene Tunney that I never noticed Morton made Commander.

Captain Morton and Commander Tunney walked back to where I was standing with the phones.

"Well, what do you think of submarines, Gene?" Captain Morton asked.

"I have been giving the submarine personnel situation a good deal of thought, Captain, and I have developed a plan for their welfare."

"What is that?" 'Mush' asked, puzzled.

"Men aboard submarines don't get enough exercise. Now I am in favor of letting them have two or three days in which to do whatever they please when they come off war patrol. After that there will be daily exercises and hardening drills. Their liquor and cigarettes will be taken from them. By the time they are ready for sea again, they will be in excellent physical condition to withstand the rigors of undersea life."

I thought, Oh, brother, and this is the great Gene Tunney! No wonder he became a world's champion heavyweight boxer, but he sure don't know anything about submariners.

Captain Morton looked at me and grinned. "The Commander has a fine idea, don't you think so, Yeo?"

"The men will receive it with great enthusiasm, sir."

Commander Tunney looked pleased with himself.

I could hardly wait for the maneuvering watch to secure so I could tell the men below what Gene Tuney had said, but again the word had preceded me. I retorted to a grinning Rennels and O'Brien, "A big-shot newspaperman would have a hell of a time beating you guys to a scoop."

I had the lookout on the 1200–1600 watch. Captain Morton and Commander Tunney were on the bridge. I heard Captain Morton say, "Come on down into the control room and I'll show you how we dive ship . . ." As they passed LTJG Fiedler, the Captain said, "Take 'er down in five minutes."

"Yes, sir, Captain."

I edged over to the rail. When the OOD turned his face upward, I was on my way with Kirk right behind me. I came out with a clear margin on the control room deck.

"Conning tower hatch closed."

"All lights green, sir." It was Carr's voice.

"Pressure in the boat, sir."

"Five degrees down-angle, sir," and then frantically, "She's going to ten degrees, sir, I can't control it."

Wahoo took a sickening steep angle by the bow, and I braced my feet and grabbed onto a corner of the radio shack. I could hear pans and dishes crash to the deck in the crew's messroom.

"Blow bow buoyancy." Then, "What the hell's wrong? I said blow bow buoyancy."

"Bow buoyancy won't blow, sir."

"Tell the forward torpedo room to check the bow buoyancy valve."

Berg went running forward, not waiting for the phone.

"Blow negative. Blow all main ballast. Tell maneuvering to back 'er down."

"Bow buoyancy is beginning to blow, sir."

Wahoo's nose began to raise.

"Stop blowing negative. Stop blowing ballast. All stop, maneuvering."

Wahoo's decks became level. "All ahead one-third."

I stole a look at the diving gauge. Only once before had I been deeper, and that had been on the *Nautilus* in a controlled test of her hull strength.

Berg came back panting and reported to Lieutenant Henderson, the Diving Officer, "Sir, forward torpedo room reports that the bow buoyancy valve was closed shut. McSpadden was opening it when I got there."

Captain Morton turned to Lieutenant Commander Skijonsby. "Now how the hell do you suppose that happened?"

The Executive Officer said quietly, "I'll go forward and investigate it, Captain."

Lieutenant Henderson said, "You don't suppose some yard workman at Pearl closed it, do you, Captain?"

Captain Morton said, "Hells bells, everything was working all right on the trim dives and operational dives before we left Pearl. Bring her back up and stay at periscope depth."

"Aye, aye, Captain."

Wahoo pulled into Midway Island. Before leaving the bridge, Lieutenant Commander Skijonsby said, "The Captain and I are going over to the *Sperry*. We're only going to be here six hours, and then we will be pulling out. Have a sailing list ready to hand over when we leave."

"Yes sir."

I looked at my wrist watch. It was 1000. I went below and got a copy of the sailing list. Since Commander Tunney's name did not appear on it, I had no changes to make. I date-stamped it 13 September 1943, placed it in an envelope, and rolled it partway into the typewriter.

Going back to the messroom, I got a cup of coffee and asked Bailey where Rennels was.

"He's topside looking at the gooney birds."

I took my coffee topside and found Rennels looking toward Midway Island. I said, "Boy, you look as gloomy as I feel."

He said, "Yeo, I got a terrible feeling that something is going to happen to us this trip."

"Aw, snap out of it. I feel bad, too, but nothing's going to happen to *Wahoo* while I'm on here and don't you forget it."

He grinned, "Yeah, you been feeding that old boloney to all the crew, but this is Jack you're trying to kid."

His nose began to twitch and he looked around. He walked to the rail and blew his nose. Then he gave his fingers a flip, and I saw something yellow go spinning over the side. He threw his leg over the steel cable life line and I thought he was going to dive overboard.

"What is it, Jack?" I cried, alarmed and sprang to catch him. He pulled back and we stared at widening ripples in the water.

He said resignedly, "Now I know something bad is going to happen. I just lost the ruby ring that Lottie gave me when I was home."

We stared for a minute at the water. "It was large for my finger. I meant to get it cut down before we left Pearl and forgot to," he added.

There did not seem to be much to say after that, and we just stood on deck watching the birds. The sky was overcast and the weather misty but the sight of land, even Midway, was good.

Finally Rennels said, "Well, I gotta get noon chow ready," and he went below decks.

After chow I wandered topside again. I noticed a number of men topside. They were strangely subdued. Few words were spoken. I could feel restlessness in every attitude.

Two or three *Sperry* men and several *Wahoo* men were topping off fuel from a line that ran along the dock and was being valved into a metal-jointed tube that was attached to a connection on *Wahoo's* deck. Jacobs and Garman were overseeing the job.

Jacobs walked up to me, wiping oily hands on a rag he had taken from his hip pocket. He shook his head lugubriously. "I have a feeling that we're going to catch hell this trip out."

I said, "Forget it, Jake. The only thing that will catch hell will be the Japs. How's the wife and that prospective baby doing?"

He brightened, "Last letter I got, the wife told me not to worry none. They're just fine."

"That's fine. Another trip or two and you'll be back there bouncing him on your knees or whatever you do with newborn kids."

He shook his head. "I hope so."

Something got his attention and he hurried over to the fuel hose connection. There was a strong smell of diesel fuel in the air. They finished fueling and the hose was passed over and secured to the dock. I looked at my watch and it was 1430. I took another look around. The weather was getting drizzly, and I went below to the office. I sat down in the chair with my back to the door, cocked one foot up on a corner of the deck, and leaned back smoking. I wondered what Marie was doing. It would be about five or six hours later in Los Angeles. I heard someone coming through the door behind me, and the Captain's flat hand nearly slapped me off the seat. Turning, I said grouchily, "You nearly made me swallow my cigarette, Captain."

He was in a jovial good mood. "Got your orders made up, Yeo?" he asked, teasingly.

"No sir, Captain, but I could sure make them up in a damn quick hurry if you gave me the word."

He added, more seriously, "We've got an hour before we sail. Let's go up to the Squadron and get you a relief."

I could hardly believe what he was saying. "If you mean it, Captain, what we waiting for?"

He laughed heartily. "Come on."

We went topside and over the gangway together. I crawled into a jeep with him, and he drove along the dock recklessly. I still thought he was joking, and that when we got there, I would find a clerical job that needed attending to.

I went trailing behind him up the officers' gangway and into the Squadron Office. I followed him to the Squadron Commander's desk. Captain Morton said, "I'm giving up the best Goddam yeoman I ever had working for me. He's got orders to go back to Stenography School. I say there's nothing but the best for the best. Have you got a relief you can give me for him?"

Blushing, I turned around and saw that all hands were staring at me. Captain Morton's words were so loud I was sure they could be heard throughout the ship. At the same time I took on a swagger and threw out my chest with pride. I had been complimented by the best submarine Skipper in the Submarine Fleet.

The Squadron Commander looked up, laughing. "I think it can be arranged, 'Mush'." There was admiration in his voice. He called to three yeomen in white jumpers. They came quickly over and I noticed second-class chevrons on all of them.

Captain Morton said to me, "Which one is the best, Yeo?"

I answered, "Sir, I don't know which is the best, but this man here wants the Wahoo more than anybody else." I pointed at White. "He did a damn good job as relief yeoman on the Wahoo when we was at Goon—I mean Midway before, sir."

Morton said, "That's good enough for me." He turned to the Squadron Commander. "What do we do now? I'm sailing in forty-five minutes."

The Squadron Commander said, "We'll have White over there in half an hour. You tell your yeoman to make his orders out, 'Transferred by verbal orders, Squadron Commander.'"

Morton said, "Come on, Yeo, let's get moving."

Everything was happening so fast I could hardly keep up with the train of events.

Back on the *Wahoo* I quickly typed out my orders and record papers. Lieutenant Commander Skijonsby was very pleasant when he signed my papers. I ran through the ship to my locker and stuffed my sea bag with belongings. In the messroom the crew gathered about me enviously. "Yeo, when you get back to the States look up my wife and say hello for me." "Yeo, hows to drop in on my mother . . ." "Here's a note to my dad in . . ." I stuffed the addresses and notes in a shirt pocket.

I shook hands and said, "So long, be seeing you Stateside," to Phillips. He said, "I hope so, Yeo." He looked pale. I felt as though I had let him down.

O'Brien came in with, "Some guys sure do have a drag. Who did you bang ears with this time?"

I said, "I don't know, but if I get a chance I'll bang ears with 'em again."

"Howsabout a game of acey-deucey, Yeo, before you go? You got time and I'd like to beat you just once more," O'Brien said.

"To hell with you. You're trying to get me tied up so I'll be to sea before I realize it."

A change came into O'Brien's voice and he said quietly, "Yeo, here's my wife's address. When you get back, look her up and tell her I'll be home for Christmas."

I said, "Sure, O'B, sure thing."

Rennels went topside with me. The Executive Officer had asked me to take the sailing list over with me, and I had it, my orders, and records in hand. Rennels carried my sea bag topside in the old Navy custom. We shook hands, and he went below decks.

Maneuvering watch was stationed and I remained near the gangway. At precisely 1556, a jeep raced up to the gangway and White came on board. The officers were on the bridge, and I could see Gerlacher, with the earphones I had worn so often in the past year, looking down at me from the bridge.

I hastily scratched my name off the sailing list and scribbled White's name and address, someplace in the New England states, in my place. Then I saluted the Colors and Kemp the Deck Watch and crossed over to the pier.

The jeep driver was waiting to take me to the *Sperry*. I told him to go on back, that I would walk.

Standing on the dock with six or eight line handlers from the *Sperry*, I watched them single-up the lines, heard the diesels come to life, and helped push the gangway in toward *Wahoo's* deck. Then there was just the bowline left, and when the Captain ordered it thrown off, I pushed the line handlers away and pulled the bight clear of the bollard and heaved it into the water. *Wahoo's* fog horn sounded a loud parting blast and a whistle on the bridge sounded shrilly. I watched Wach take down the Union Jack. Out of the corner of my eyes I saw the Stars and Stripes on the cigarette deck as they furled out. *Wahoo* drifted away from the pier and began to move away slowly.

Captain Morton's voice came across the widening water. "Take care of yourself, Yeo."

"Good hunting," I shouted back. I waved at everyone I could see topside. All were waving and grinning as *Wahoo* pulled away.

When I looked around, the line handlers were near the other end of the pier walking back toward the *Sperry*. I threw my sea bag on the rough planks and sat down on it. I lighted several cigarettes and smoked them before *Wahoo*, a tiny submarine silhouette on the horizon, headed into a rain squall and disappeared from sight. Forever.

Epilogue

On 13 September 1943, *USS.Wahoo* (SS-238) departed Midway Island for er designated war patrol area the Japanese Sea; estimated time of arrival 20 eptember.

Referring to United States Submarine Losses World War II, by Naval listory Division, Office of the Chief Naval Operations, Washington: 1963, *Vahoo* made her presence known in the following manner:

"Although no transmission was received from *Wahoo* after her departure on atrol, the results of her attacks became known to the world via a Tokyo roadcast. Domei was quoted as reporting that on 5 October a 'steamer' was ınk by an American submarine off the west coast of Honshu near the Straits f Tsushima. It was said that the ship sank 'after several seconds' with 544 eople losing their lives. The submarine could have been none other than *Vahoo*: none other was operating in that area."

In reporting this broadcast, *Time* magazine of 18 October 1943 states: "In ıe rough Tsushima Straits where two-decker train-carrying ferries ply between apan and Korea, an Allied Submarine upped periscope, unleashed a torpedo. he missile stabbed the flank of a Jap steamer. Said the Tokyo radio: The teamer went down in 'seconds' with loss of 544 persons on board ... resumably the submarine knocking at the door last week was American. It had chieved one of World War II's most daring submarine penetrations of enemy vaters, a feat ranking with German Gunther Prien's entry at Scapa Flow, the ap invasion of Pearl Harbor, the U.S. raid in Tokyo Bay."

In the aftermath of World War Two, the "Report of the Japanese Imperial lavy" gives the sinking of five ships in *Wahoo's* patrol area in the Sea of apan as follows:

September 25,	*Taiko Maru,*	2,958 tons
October 2,	*Masaki Maru,*	1,238 tons
October 5,	*Konron Maru,*	7,908 tons
October 6,	*Kanko Maru,*	1,288 tons
October 9,	*#2 Kanko Maru,*	2,962 tons

Subsequently, the Japanese report states that on October 11, 1943, an army gun battery overlooking Soya Strait… "opened fire on a surfaced submarine as it passed through the strait, forcing it to dive." Further, the Japanese record states… "it was very likely that *Wahoo* struck a mine when submerged under gunfire. This damage caused the oil leak which in turn lead to her destruction."

A float plane was called in and at 0920 discovered an oil patch five meters wide and ten meters long. Circling overhead, the aircraft shortly afterwards spotted a black conning tower amidst the oil streak. Between 0920 and 1350 ten bombs and twenty-three depth charges were dropped on *Wahoo*. At 1350, search aircraft reported *neither the submarine nor her wake was visible.* An expanding oil slick 60 meters wide and three miles long covered the area. A sample taken showed the slick to be high grade diesel fuel.

In Richard O'Kane's excellent book *"Wahoo,"* copyright 1987, Presidio Press, Novato, California, the author used his close, thorough knowledge of Commander Dudley Morton and his own submarine expertise and experience to research and vividly reconstruct *Wahoo's* final (seventh) war patrol. The result is so close to reality, in imagination, the reader can feel that this is what actually happened.

Since World War Two ended, a dying organization of the officers and enlisted men who served on submarines from December 7, 1941 to December 31, 1946 formed The Submarine Veteran of World War Two. "To honor and perpetuate the memory of those submariners who lost their lives during World War Two." A spin-off from this national organization has led to four memorials dedicated to the *USS Wahoo* (SS-238) and her gallant crew.

The first *Wahoo* torpedo memorial, with bronze nameplate, was constructed and dedicated at Wahoo, Nebraska by the Nebraska "Corn Husker" SubVet chapter, Clint Orr president.

The second *Wahoo* torpedo memorial, with bronze nameplate, was constructed and dedicated in Williamsport, Pennsylvania by the Lehigh Valley SubVet chapter. Further information can be obtained from Martin F. Schaffer, 1710 Elm Street, Allentown, Pennsylvania, 18104-6765.

The third *Wahoo* torpedo memorial is dedicated to Commander Dudley W. Morton, U.S. Navy, and the *Wahoo* crew by the American Legion James L. Yates Post 9, 118 W. First Street, Owensboro, Kentucky. CDR Morton was born in Owensboro on July 17, 1907 and grew up among family and childhood friends there. The fourth

212

memorial is a joint Japanese / *Wahoo* Peace Memorial, with international implications, on Cape Soya, twelve miles distant from Wakkamai City, Hokkaido, Japan where *Wahoo* lies in 209 feet of water. "Old enemies met as brothers to dedicate that our countries shall have a lasting peace and war will never again destroy the friendship we now enjoy today."

For further details, contact Martin F. Schaffer or George E. Logue, who lost his brother, Robert Logue aboard the *Wahoo*, at *Wahoo* Memorial Foundation, 120 South Arch Street, Montoursville, Pennsylvania, 17754.

Five former *Wahoo* shipmates transferred to other submarines were lost when those submarines were sunk during the war.

10-17-43	Appel, Jessie L. (S1c)	*USS Pompano* (SS-181)
10-17-44	Clary, John W. (CMM)	*USS Escolar* (SS-294)
10-17-44	Krause, Fertig B., Jr. (Sig1c)	*USS Escolar* (SS-294)
04-07-44	Kohut, Stephan (CMM)	*USS Gudgeon* (SS-211)
02-26-44	Moore, John A. (Comdr)	*USS Grayback* (SS-208)
04-07-44	Zimmerman, Charles A. (GM1c)	*USS Gudgeon* (SS-211)

At the time of this printing [1997] there are fifteen known former *Wahoo* crew members, who made one or more patrols, who are still alive. Commander Richard O'Kane was detached from *Wahoo* at San Francisco prior to *Wahoo's* sixth war patrol to commission *USS Tang* and become her commanding officer. On *Tang's* fifth war patrol she was sunk by one of her own erratic torpedoes. O'Kane was among only nine survivors, all of whom were made Japanese prisoners-of-war. On this run, thirteen enemy ships were sunk and O'Kane was awarded the Medal of Honor. He retired as Rear Admiral and authored *"Clear the Bridge,"* the story of the *Tang,* and *"Wahoo."*

Lieutenant Roger Paine missed being on board *Wahoo* for the seventh war patrol when he developed appendicitis at Pearl Harbor. He later served aboard the *USS Pompano* and *USS Tinosa* and retired as Rear Admiral.

When *Wahoo* was at Pearl Harbor after her sixth run, the crew and I were at the Royal Hawaiian Hotel. While there, a relief Yeoman filled in for me aboard *Wahoo*. I left a list of men to be transferred. One of the names on the list was Oscar Finkelstein, TM3. On the sixth patrol it was discovered that Oscar suffered from chronic seasickness. Much to my surprise he was still on board, but John E. August, S1c, who was not on the list, was transferred. Finkelsteim was lost. August survived the war, married and had three daughters.

After finishing stenography school, I was transferred to *USS Comet* (AP-166), and was at the initial landings of Saipan, Tinian, Guam and Leyte before being returned to submarine duty at Pearl Harbor.

As of the writing of this epilogue, June 1997, I am a resident at the United States Naval Home in Gulfport, Mississippi. At midnight, January 1, 2000, in keeping with my predictions to my *Wahoo* shipmates, I expect to hoist a few beers and say to them: "Sorry, fellows. I should have been with you. I can never understand why Captain Morton changed his mind and transferred me at the last moment. My spirit has been with you all these years!"

Forest J. Sterling

Sailing list for USS Wahoo's final patrol

Anders, Floyd	F1c	Logue, Robert B.	FC1c
Andrews, Joseph S.	EM1c	Lynch, Walter L.	F2c
Bailey, Robert E.	SC3c	MacAlman, Stuart E.	PhM1c
Bair, Arthur L.	F1c	MacGowen, Thomas J.	MoMM1c
Berg, Jimmie C.	Ens.	McGill, Thomas J.	CMoMM
Browning, Chester E.	MoMM2c	McGilton, Howard E.	TM3c
Bruce, Clifford L.	MoMM2c	McSpadden, Donald J.	TM1c
Buckley, James P.	Lt.	Magyar, Albert J.	MM3c
Burgan, William W.	Lt.	Manalesay, Jesus C.	St3c
Campbell, John S.	Ens.	Mandjiak, Paul A.	MM3c
Carr, William J.	CGM	Massa, Edward E.	S1c
Carter, James E.	RM2c	Maulding, Ernest C.	SM3c
Davison, William E.	MoMM1c	Maulding, George E.	TM3c
Deaton, Lynwood N.	TM1c	Mills, Max L.	RT1c
Erdley, Joseph S.	EM3c	Misch, George A.	Lt. (jg.)
Fiedler, Eugene F.	Lt. (jg.)	Morton, Dudley W.	Comdr.
Finkelstein, Oscar	TM3c	Neel, Percy	TM2c
Galli, Walter O.	TM3c	Oneal, Roy L.	EM3c
Garman, Cecil E.	MoMM2c	O'Brian, Forest L.	EM1c
Garrett, George E.	MoMM2c	Ostrander, Edwin E.	F1c
Gerlacher, Wesley L.	S1c	Phillips, Paul D.	SC1c
Goss, Richard P.	MoMM2c	Rennels, Juano L.	SC2c
Greene, Hiram M.	Lt.	Renno, Henry	S1c
Hand, William R.	EM2c	Seal, Enoch H. Jr.	TM2c
Hartman, Leon M.	MM3c	Simonetti, Alford	SM2c
Hayes, Dean M.	EM2c	Skjonsby, Verne L.	Lt. Comdr.
Henderson, Richie N.	Lt.	Smith, Donald O.	BM1c
Holmes, William H.	EM1c	Stevens, George	MoMM2c
House, Van A.	S1c	Terrell, William C.	QM3c
Howe, Howard J.	EM2c	Thomas, William	S1c
Jacobs, Olin	MoMM1c	Tyler, Ralph O.	TM3c
Jasa, Robert L.	F1c	Vidik, Joe	EM2c
Jayson, Juan O.	CK3c	Wach, Ludwig J.	Cox
Johnson, Kindred B.	TM1c	Waldron, Wilbur E.	RM3c
Keeter, Dalton C.	CMoMM	Ware, Norman C.	CEM
Kemp, Wendell W.	QM1c	Whipp, Kenneth C.	F1c
Kessock, Paul H.	F1c	White, William T.	Y2c
Kirk, Eugene T.	S1c	Witting, Roy L.	F1c
Krebs, Paul H.	SM3c		
Lape, Paul H.	F2c		
Lindemann, Clarence A.	S1c		

Served on Wahoo prior to 7th war patrol

Allen, James H.	F3c	Jonson, Donald O.	TM2c
Appel, Jesse L.	S2c	Kennedy, Marvin G.	Lt. Comdr.
Ater, Richard W.	S2c	Kochis, John	MM1c
August, John F.	S2c	Kohl, Jerome T.	PhM1c
Baldes, Raymond O. J.	MM1c	Kohut, Stephan	MM1c
Ballman, Charles J.	MM2c	Krause, Fertig B.	SM1c
Beatty, Raymond G.	RM1c	Laftin, Sylvester J.	TM1c
Bland, Edward L. Jr.	SOM3c	LaMaye, Joseph R.	TM3c
Brockhauser, Carl A.	F1c	Lane, James E.	CBM
Burnam, Clyde A.	TM1c	Lavine, James E.	BM3c
Chick, Orville F.	F3c	Lemert, Richard H.	MM1c
Chisholm, Fred B.	MoMM1c	Lenox, Andrew K.	CMM
Clary, John W.	MoMM1c	Lindhe, Leslie J.	PhM1c
Clough, Jack E.	TM3c	Lokey, Stanley A.	BM3c
Collins, Harry	MoMM2c	MacMillan, Duncan C.	Comdr.
Cook, Kenneth R.	BM3c	Mayberry, Clyde C.	S1c
Coultas, William E.	F1c	Meditz, Henry J.	F3c
Dietrich, Helmit O.	SC1c	Miller, James H.	F2c
Dooley, David E.	S1c	Moore, John A.	Lt. Comdr.
Dye, Ira	Lt. (jg.)	Mooris, James	TM3c
Erickson, Dennis L.	EM2c	Muller, Edward F.	MM2c
Eyman, Dale E.	TM1c	Myers, Chester M.	TM3c
Flateau, Sidney F.	CMM	O'Kane, Richard H.	Lt. Comdr.
Frash, Oakley R.	MM2c	Osborn, Lester L.	S2c
Gilbert, Donald	MoMM2c	Paine, Roger W. Jr.	Lt.
Glinski, Henry P.	F2c	Parks, Joe D.	FC3c
Grider, George W.	Lt.	Patrick, Walter P.	TM2c
Griggs, John B.	Lt. (jg.)	Pruett, Ralph R.	CEM
Hall, James C.	S1c	Rau, Russel H.	CTM
Hanrahan, William J.	MM1c	Redford, Burnell A.	CMM
Hansen, Marius S.	MM1c	Robertson, Cecil C.	F1c
Hargrave, Daniel J.	F2c	Rowls, John C.	SC1c
Hartman, Theodore L.	EM3c	Schreier, Earl C.	F1c
Heiden, Walter C. E.	EM3c	Smith, C. J.	MA2c
Hodges, William H.	EM2c	Smith, Edward A.	SC3c
Holman, Earl T.	MM1c	Sterling, Forest J.	Y2c
Hood, Carl C.	FC2c	Thaxton, Kelly R.	MM2c
Hunter, Deville G.	SM1c	Valliancourt, Maurice J.	S2c
Jackson, Chandler C.	Lt.	Veder, David A.	S1c
James, Willie	MA1c	Vogler, Lonnie L.	S1c
Janicek, Clifford T.	S1c	Whaley, Harlan C.	S2c
Jesser, Edward	MM1c	Young, William F.	S1c
Johnson, Clarence E.	F1c	Zimmerman, Charles A.	S1c

Wahoo sinkings

DATE	Ship Name	Tonnage
December 10, 1942	*Kamoi Maru*	5,355 tons
January 26, 1943	Unknown	4,000 tons
January 26, 1943	*Boyu Maru*	5,447 tons
January 26, 1943	*Fukuei Maru #2*	1,901 tons
March 19, 1943	*Zogen Maru*	1,428 tons
March 19, 1943	*Kowa Maru*	3,217 tons
March 21, 1943	*Nittsu Maru*	2,183 tons
March 21, 1943	*Hozan Maru*	2,260 tons
March 23, 1943	*Katyosan Maru*	2,427 tons
March 24, 1943	*Kakaosan Maru*	2,076 tons
March 25, 1943	*Satsuki Maru*	827 tons
March 25, 1943	Unknown	2,556 tons
March 29, 1943	*Yamabato Maru*	2,556 tons
May 7, 1943	*Tamon Maru*	5,260 tons
May 9, 1943	*Takao Maru*	3,204 tons
May 9, 1943	*Jinmu Maru*	1,912 tons
September 25, 1943	*Taiko Maru*	2,958 tons
October 2, 1943	*Masaki Maru*	1,238 tons
October 5, 1943	*Konron Maru*	7,908 tons
October 6, 1943	*Kanko Maru,*	1,288 tons
October 9, 1943	*Kanko Maru #2*	2,962 tons

| TOTALS: | 21 ships | 62,963 tons |

USS *Wahoo* Presidential Unit Citation

The President of the United States takes pleasure in presenting the PRESIDENTIAL UNIT CITATION to the

UNITED STATES SHIP WAHOO

for service as set forth in the following

CITATION:

"For distinctive performance in combat in the New Guinea Area, January 16 to February 7, 1943. In bold defiance of an enemy destroyer attempting to run her down in a confined harbor, the WAHOO remained at periscope depth to counter with a daring attack, sinking the Japanese vessel by her torpedo fire. Pursuing similar tactics while under sustained fire, she fought a fourteen hour battle, attacking an unescorted armed enemy convoy and destroying the entire force, two freighters, one tanker and one transport and their personnel. The high combat efficiency of the WAHOO, her officers and men, is exemplified in the destruction of 31,890 tons of enemy shipping during a War Patrol from which she escaped intact."

For the President,

Frank Knox

Secretary of the Navy.

Glossary

AP	Transport ship.
AS	Submarine tender.
BuOrd	Bureau of Ordnance. Navy department responsible for weapons and ordnance.
CO	Commanding Officer.
Christmas Tree	A condition board located in the control room, indicating the status of all hull openings; tanks, valves, vents and hatches, etc.
CicPac	Commander-in-Chief Pacific Fleet.
ComSubPac	Commander Submarines Pacific.
Conning Tower	The small horizontal hull located directly above the control room and below the bridge. The compartment houses the TDC, torpedo firing panel, surface search radar, periscopes, sound equipment, fathometer and steering stand.
Control Room	This compartment is located midship directly beneath the conning tower. The control room houses all diving controls, auxiliary steering, gyrocompass, air-search radar, radio room and plot / chart table.
CPO	Chief Petty Officer.
DD	Destroyer.
DE	Destroyer Escort. Slightly small than a destroyer.
Depth Charge	Underwater explosive, shaped like a round metal trash barrel, set to detonate at a pre-determined depth.
Dogwatch	The 1600 to 1800 hour and 1800 to 2000 hour watches. In addition, any four-hour watch may be halved, or 'dogged.'
Escort	Anti-submarine vessel, such as a destroyer.
Exec.	Abbreviation for Executive Officer.
Fathometer	Depth gauge.
Fish	Navy slang term for a torpedo.

Glossary

GQ	General Quarters.
LT JG	Lieutenant (jg.) or Junior Grade.
Maru	Japanese name meaning freighter or merchantman.
OOD	Officer Of the Deck.
PBY	*Catalina*. American twin-engine flying boat / seaplane.
PCO	Prospective Commanding Officer.
Ping	Underwater echo noise caused by destroyer sonar, while searching for submerged submarines.
PO	Petty Officer.
Port	Left side of ship.
Q-ship	Enemy warship disguised as an unarmed vessel, used to lure submarines into gun range.
RAF	Royal Air Force.
R-boat	Old pre-war class American submarine.
Screws	Ship propellers.
SS	American submarine.
Starboard	Right side of ship.
SubPac	Submarines Pacific.
TBT	Target Bearing Transmitter. Located on the bridge outside the ship. Appears much like an ordinary set of 7-X-50 binoculars fixed to the bridge of the submarine. The T.B.T. is used to transmit target-bearing information into the conning tower.
TDC	Torpedo Data Computer. A large control panel located inside the conning tower. Used to keep the target's range, speed and bearing current and relative to that of the submarine.
USAAF	United States Army Air Force.
XO	Executive Officer.
Zero	Japanese Mitsubishi Type 0. Single-engine fighter (A6M). Sometimes referred to as a 'Zeke.'

About the Author

Born in Trenton, Missouri in 1911, Forest J. Sterling was just 3 years old when old when his family moved to Henryetta, Oklahoma. After graduating from high school in Ordway, Colorado, Sterling joined the United States Navy in 1930. Seven years later he left the Navy, and after traveling the country, settled in Los Angeles, California. When war broke out in December 1941, Sterling re-enlisted in the Navy and requested duty in submarines. Sterling said "They sent me to Pearl Harbor, where I went aboard the *USS Wahoo* in August 1942." He was assigned as *Wahoo's* new Yeoman. Home on leave in the summer of 1943, Sterling phoned his girlfriend Marie. Sterling said. "When I arrived in San Francisco aboard the *Wahoo* from Australia in June 1943, I called her in Los Angeles, where she was a telephone operator. I asked her, 'How would you like to get married?' She said, 'I'll be up on the next plane.'" A few months later, fate stepped in and Sterling was transferred off *Wahoo*. He left the boat only minutes before she sailed on her ill-fated war patrol. The boat was lost with all hands. After attending stenography school in San Diego, California, Sterling eventually returned to the Pacific before the end of World War II. In 1956, he retired from the United States Navy as a Chief Petty Officer.

Following his retirement, Sterling spent two years attending Ventura College earning an Associate of Arts degree. He then went to San Diego State for one more semester of college. Sterling wrote *Wake of the Wahoo* in 1960. When asked why he wrote the book, Sterling said, "I just wanted to tell about the fine officers and enlisted men who went to their deaths in that sub, so folks could learn what life in a sub is like, particularly during combat." *Wake of the Wahoo* was the first book on the submarine service written by an enlisted man. Three years later (in 1963), the United States Naval Institute chose Sterling's *Wake of the Wahoo* as one of the three best books written by an enlisted man from World War II. Since that time, *Wake of the Wahoo* has become a submarine classic.

Sterling, for years a resident of the U.S. Naval Home, in Gulfport, Mississippi, succumbed to congestive heart failure on May 23, 2002—just six days after celebrating his 91st birthday. He was laid to rest at the Biloxi National Cemetery in Biloxi, Mississippi.

USS *Wahoo* wreck site found

July 2006: A team of Russian divers have reported finding the American submarine *USS Wahoo*. Using information obtained from outside sources the men discovered the wreck in the La Perouse Strait at a shallow depth of just 185 feet. *Wahoo* was lost with all hands on October 11, 1943. At the time of her loss the sub was under the command of Commander Dudley "Mush" Morton. The boat is now resting up-right on the ocean floor. Periscopes fully extended, rudder and diving planes are in a straight and level position. It appears *Wahoo* was hit while at periscope depth. Post-war Japanese records state a submerged submarine was discovered in the La Perouse Strait on October 11. A plane dove on the target and dropped a bomb, which struck and sank the sub. Japanese destroyers then rushed in and began dropping depth charges. While no one is sure why Commander Morton exited the Sea of Japan in daylight hours, post-war photos have been uncovered, showing an oil slick trailing *Wahoo* as she attempts to rush through the strait while submerged. Based on the wreck-site photos, we now know *Wahoo* suffered a direct hit by the aerial bomb. The bomb penetrated the boat behind the bridge, passing through the conning tower into the control room where an immediate and catastrophic explosion took place. Flooding of the rest of the boat was surely immediate. It's safe to assume no one was alive by the time the Japanese destroyers dropped their depth charges.

Following the discovery of *Wahoo's* wreck, Admiral Gary Roughead, Commander, U.S. Pacific Fleet stated; "After reviewing the records and information, we are certain *USS Wahoo* has been located. We are grateful for the support of the *USS Bowfin* Submarine Museum and Park, and appreciate greatly the underwater video footage of the submarine provided by our Russian navy colleagues, which allowed us to make this determination. This brings closure to the families of the men of *Wahoo*—one of the greatest fighting submarines in the history of the U.S. Navy." Of *Wahoo's* loss, Navy Vice Admiral Charles A. Lockwood, Jr. wrote in his book "Sink 'Em All" "It didn't seem possible that Morton and his fighting crew could be lost. I'd never have believed the Japs could be smart enough to get him."

Book Order Form

Wake of the Wahoo

The Heroic Story of America's most daring WW II submarine,
USS Wahoo
by Forest J. Sterling

_____ Copies at $19.95 each
_____ Shipping total: $4.99 per order
_____ California residents please add $1.55 tax per book
_____ Total

Payment: Total enclosed: _____
Please include your mailing address and phone number

❑   Check or Money Order   (Please make payable to: R.A. Cline Publishing)
❑   Credit card: ❑ VISA, ❑ MasterCard

Card number: _____

Name on card: _____

Expiration date: _____ (month and year)

Credit card verification number _____ the last three digits
found on the back of your card

Mail orders: R.A. Cline Publishing
19971 Caraway Ln.
Riverside, CA. 92508

Website: **www.AllNavyBooks.com**